ANATOMY OF THE NOVELLA

*The European Tale Collection from Boccaccio
and Chaucer to Cervantes*

The publication of this work has been aided by a grant from
the Andrew W. Mellon Foundation

THE GOTHAM LIBRARY
OF THE NEW YORK UNIVERSITY PRESS

The Gotham Library is a series of original works and critical studies, published in paperback primarily for student use. The Gotham hardcover edition is primarily for use by libraries and the general reader. Devoted to significant works and major authors and to literary topics of enduring importance, Gotham Library texts offer the best in literature and criticism.

Comparative and Foreign Language Literature:
Robert J. Clements, Editor
Comparative and English Language Literature:
James W. Tuttleton, Editor

ANATOMY OF THE NOVELLA

*The European Tale Collection from
Boccaccio and Chaucer to Cervantes*

Robert J. Clements
and
Joseph Gibaldi

New York · New York University Press · 1977

Copyright © 1977 by New York University

Library of Congress Catalog Card Number: 76-52548

ISBN: 0-8147-1369-6 (cloth)
      0-8147-1370-X (paperback)
Library of Congress Cataloging in Publication Data

Clements, Robert John, 1912-
   Anatomy of the novella.

  (The Gotham library of the New York University Press)
  Includes bibliographical references and index.
  1. Literature, Medieval—History and criticism.
2. European literature—Renaissance, 1450-1600—History
and criticism.   I. Gibaldi, Joseph, 1942-   joint
author.   II. Title.   III. Title: Novella.
PN692.C55   809.3'2   76-52548
ISBN 0-8147-1369-6
ISBN 0-8147-1370-X pbk.

Manufactured in the United States of America

For
LORNA
and
ANITA

Contents

Foreword   x

Chapter One: The Renaissance Theory of the Novella

Introduction: The Problem of Definition   1
I.   The Nature of the Genre: Oral Medium vs. Literary Medium   4
II.   The Function of the Novella: Utility vs. Recreation   8
III.   Invention 13, Variety 15   12
IV.   Verisimilitude   16
V.   Unity and Harmony   19
VI.   Language and Style   22
VII.   *Brevitas*   25
Conclusion: A Note on Terminology   26
Notes   27

Chapter Two: The Structure of the Novella Collection

I.   The Cornice Tradition and the Justification of Fiction in the Renaissance   36
II.   Unity by Time 51, Theme 54, and Title 58   51
Notes   59

Chapter Three: Characters and Characterization

I.   Types and Stereotypes   62
II.   "Of Sondry Folk"   66
III.   Personages from Modern and Contemporary History   84
Notes   90

Chapter Four: Images of Society: Classes, Nations, Races, War

Introduction: The Novella and Society   92

I.   Monarchy 94, Court Life 97, Class Structure 98, Feudalism 103   93

II.   Nationalism 109, Patriotism, 110, Xenophobia 111, Racism, 114   109

III.   War   121

Notes   124

Chapter Five: Images of Society: Trades, Professions, Money, Medicine, Sciences and Pseudo-Sciences

I.   Trades and Professions 127, Money 129, Usury 132   127

II.   Scholars 134, Medical Men 135   134

III.   Astronomy 139, Sciences 140, Pseudo-Sciences 141   139

Notes   144

Chapter Six: Images of Society: Law, Justice, the Courts, Crime and Punishment

I.   Contemporary Law and Jurisprudence 145, Types of Law 146   145

II.   Law and Social Classes   150

III.   Judges 153, Lawyers 156, Law Officials 158, Crime and Punishment 160   153

Notes   163

Chapter Seven: Images of Society: Women and Marriage

I.   Status of Women 165 The *Querelle des Femmes* 169   165

II.   Marriage 173, Divorce 175, Abortion 176, Prostitution 177   173

III.   Special Plots Concerning Women   178

IV.   Growing Importance of Women in the Novella   180

Notes   182

Chapter Eight: Images of Society: Church and Churchmen, Sacraments, Reformation, Counter-Reformation

I.   Anticlericalism 184, Inquisition 185, Saints 187, Churchmen 188, Indulgences 189   183

II.   Clerical Misbehavior 190, Nuns 194, Abuses of Power 196   190

III.   Rites and Sacraments 197, Relics 198, Confession 204, Excommunication 206, Miracles 206, Pilgrimages 207   197

Conclusion: The Novella and Reform   209

Notes   214

Chapter Nine: The Fate of a Genre: From Novella to Modern Short Story

I.   *Brevitas* and the Claim of Historicity   216

II.   *Amplificatio* and the Novella   218

III.   Cervantes and the Modern Short Story   222

Notes   227

Appendix A   Principal Novella Collections   229

Appendix B   The Novella and the Elizabethan Drama   232

Index   242

Plates throughout are taken from the first illustrated incunabulum edition of the *Decameron* (De Gregori, 1492).

Foreword

Schooled in their Stagyrite, those few Renaissance critics who puzzled over the novella, finding it difficult to collocate, no less justify, could scarcely be aware that it would continue to be read in the twentieth century. If, as they picked and probed, they found it hard to establish the novella's "anatomy" (a favorite Renaissance word), they are more to be excused than those twentieth-century scholars who have appropriated the term only to stretch its length beyond reason and to disregard its historical unifying factors.

That this can lead only to confusion is evident from M. D. Springer's recent *Forms of the Modern Novella*, which complains that "one cannot draw any but the most tenuous connections—much too thin to help my problem of definition—between the original 'novelle' or short tales of Boccaccio and the modern works that begin around the 1900s on the Continent, in England, and in America." [1] The present authors have long felt that a clear anatomy of the mediaeval and Renaissance novella was called for—one that would protect its time-consecrated identity from later usurpations by students of novels, short novels, or novelettes, who are driven to seek inexistent "tenuous connections." Our anatomy endeavors to make clear how the novellas staked out a firm prior claim on their nomenclature through a structural, thematic, tonal, and historical homogeneity. This endeavor will chiefly occupy the first three chapters, while Chapter Nine will suggest the evolution of the seventeenth-century novella into the modern short story. No such generic identity can be found, we believe, for the short novel or the novelette, nor does it even seem historically necessary for one to keep defining these two protean terms. We believe that the chapters below will aid in the clarification of this lexical dilemma of literary history before it becomes too late for clarification.

Our second objective in preparing the present volume is to demonstrate that the mediaeval and Renaissance novellas, often disregarded by critics but devoured by all levels of the reading public, constituted a deluge of social comment and criticism which encouraged European man to rise from feudal, imperial, ecclesiastical, and other social repressions as the Middle Ages evolved into the Renaissance. Chapters Four through Seven consist of a repertory of criticisms and grievances concerning class inequality, monarchic and feudal privilege, despotism, warfare, race prejudice, legal injustice, corruption among law officers, bribery, unjust imprisonment, exemption of nobility from prosecution, use of torture, professional hypocrites, dishonest tradesmen and usurers, discrimination against women, and other types of social injustice. Chapter Eight will catalogue the grievances against the Church and churchmen which accelerated the arrival of the Reformation. Constantly understating their serious purpose, the novellists won a vast audience. The bolder ones encouraged the others. The initial tales of the first day of the *Decameron* or Chaucer's indictment of the Summoner were read by far more people than would later read, let us say, Luther's historic letter to Pope Leo X accusing Rome of becoming a Babylon. The novellists kept hitting away through fictions *jusqu'au feu exclusivement.* Since much of the social and religious criticism is couched in comedy and satire, we trust that the reader will find it both amusing and supportive of our thesis.

Sadly, modern critics, like their Renaissance counterparts, have tended to ignore this rich tradition of short fiction and to overlook both its esthetic achievement and its historical significance. It is the authors' fervent hope that this study will help generate in students, teachers, and scholars not only of mediaeval and Renaissance literature but of fiction in general a critical interest that will equal the centuries-old popular interest in the novella and that will ultimately result in further explorations into a literary genre that is perhaps more than any other at once *utiliter dulcis* and *dulciter utilis.*

Finally, we should like to acknowledge our gratitude to several generations of doctoral candidates in Comparative Literature at New York University whose class comments and term papers in the course G29.2841 contributed examples and insights that have no doubt filtered into the pages below. Some of these, like Yvonne Rodax, have become specialists in the field. We should also like to thank for their assistance in preparing this volume five young scholars: Anthony Boyle, Margaret Foley, Katharina Wilson, Karen Temple Lynch, and John Roger Palmour.

We express our thanks to the editors of four journals that have published excerpts of this work: *Comparative Literature Studies, Canadian Review of Comparative Literature, Studies in Short Fiction,* and *The Arizona English Bulletin.* The dedication of this book, however, makes clear to whom we owe our greatest debt.

R. J. C.
J. G.

Note

1. See Footnote I, 127 below.

CHAPTER 1

The Renaissance Theory
of the Novella

Introduction: The Problem of Definition

Novella, despite considerable protest, has in recent times been
drafted to serve as one of those ill-starred literary terms whose
misfortune it is to be so overused and abused that it comes to
signify anything and everything its employer of the moment has in
mind. Indeed, as Karl Konrad Polheim has shown, modern critical
opinion on the definition of the novella has become so divided that
anything approaching a consensus seems at this point a rather
remote possibility. In his valuable *Novellentheorie und Novellenforschung* Polheim undertook the unenviable task of trying to
explicate and evaluate the numerous modern-day theories of the
novella, including those celebrated, although vigorously challenged, attempts to define the form by the presence or absence in
shorter works of fiction of such characteristics as the *Falke,* the
Leitmotiv, the *Wendepunkt,* the *Mittelpunkt,* or the *Kristallisationspunkt.*
At the completion of his exhaustive study, however, after carefully
considering the views of scholars and critics like Ludwig Tieck,
Paul Heyse, Oskar Walzel, E. K. Bennett, Johannes Klein, Walter

1

Pabst, Benno von Wiese, and Nino Erné, Polheim can find in this mass of heroic but unconvincing efforts nothing but confusion, and, ultimately, failure to formulate a satisfactory definition of the elusive genre.[1] As Harry Steinhauer more colorfully (and perhaps hyperbolically) puts it, "The enormous mountain of German criticism has been labouring for two generations and has not even brought forth a mouse. The critical literature on the novella in Germany is immense, contradictory, obscure, and too often shallow and downright absurd."[2]

One hastens to add, moreover, that Germany has not at all been alone in its lack of success in attempting to grasp the essence of the novella form. Criticism in England and America has surely not fared any better. At present English and American scholars variously employ the term to designate three separate and distinct types of fiction. Still comfortably applied to signify the Renaissance tales of a Boccaccio or a Marguerite de Navarre,[3] *novella* has also been used of late as a synonym for the German *Novelle* (which flourished in the late eighteenth and nineteenth centuries and which attracted such writers as Goethe, E. T. A. Hoffmann, Storm, and Keller) [4] and as a label to describe modern works of fiction of "intermediate length," that is, between the short story and the novel.

This last usage, doubtless derived in part from Henry James's unfortunate use of the term *nouvelle* to describe his own short fiction,[5] is especially puzzling and problematic, for it employs the term *novella*—one of the original characteristics of which, as we shall see, was extreme brevity—to designate not the shortest but, ironically, the longest of today's short fiction. Yet this is unmistakably a usage that is fast gaining popularity. When Hemingway's *The Old Man and the Sea* with its 140 pages was first published in 1952, for instance, at least one reviewer casually referred to it as a novella.[6] More recently, two different contributors to an otherwise valuable collection of essays dealing with the theory of the novel labeled as novellas Thomas Mann's *Tod in Venedig* and André Gide's *Symphonie pastorale.*[7] To make matters worse still, an anthology given the promising title *The Art of the Novella* contains only modern works of prose fiction such as Tolstoy's *Ivan Ilych* (54 pp.),

Melville's *Benito Cereno* (76 pp.), Conrad's *Heart of Darkness* (81 pp.), and James's *The Turn of the Screw* (97 pp.); its editor, without any hesitation whatsoever, even goes so far as to inform us that "A novella is a short novel."[8]

Scientific precision in literary criticism is, of course, neither feasible nor perhaps even desirable. Nevertheless, one is compelled to argue at the very least for a certain rigor in the definition and use of literary terms that would preclude the kind of confusion and misinformation generated by this slapdash application of the term *novella*.

A principal reason for the inability of recent scholarship to come to terms with the novella is the proclivity of literary critics of our age to view the novella from a thoroughly modern perspective, through spectacles fashioned by a Goethe or a James, in an attempt to find common generic characteristics running from Boccaccio to the twentieth century—hence the current trend toward conferring the identical label upon both the tales of the *Decameron* and those collected in the woefully entitled *Art of the Novella*. What has not yet been assayed, however—and what seems most essential before one even begins to study whatever affinities may or may not exist between the brief narratives contained in the *Decameron* and the more modern forms of short fiction—is the exploration of Renaissance literary theory and practice to discover what exactly constituted a novella in its original manifestation.

The task of reconstructing as graphically and completely as possible the Renaissance conception of the novella is, as might be expected, more easily undertaken than accomplished. One's first objective in this endeavor, for example, must be to determine the precise generic nature of the novella, since, as we shall discover, the term was freely employed in the Renaissance to describe both written and spoken narratives. It must be decided, then, if a novella was an oral tale written down, or a literary tale intended for public recitation,[9] or some complex combination of the two. The resolution of this initial problem will yield not only a more sharply defined perception of the nature of the novella, but also a clue to the sources of information most relevant to the desired critical reconstruction.[10]

I. The Nature of the Genre: Oral Medium vs. Literary Medium

Its earliest users (e.g., Varro, Cicero, Vergil, Columella) applied the word *novella*—with its roots quite plainly in the Latin adjective *novellus* (the diminutive of *novus*), meaning "young or new"—primarily to matters dealing with husbandry (vines, goats, chickens, bulls, arbors, and so on). With Tibullus, Ovid, Livy, Pliny, and other later Latin writers, the word was more liberally used to mean anything new or young. We find, too, as early as Plautus an adverbial form of the word *(novelle)*, and subsequently during the sixth century A.D. two separate uses of the word as a noun: Corippus Johannis employs *novella* to signify a "newly planted tree," and the series of supplementary laws that were instituted by Justinian and his successors and which during the twelfth century became part of the *Corpus Juris Civilis* were called the *Novellae Constitutiones* or just the *Novellae* (known in English as the *New Laws* or the *Novels.*).[11]

The peregrinations of the term during the later Middle Ages are more difficult to chart. We do know, however, that by the fourteenth century there had already evolved in Italian three distinct meanings for the word. [12] In addition to its continued adjectival use as "young or new," *novella* had now also come to mean "news" (*notizie* in modern Italian). Thus in the Prologue to the *Decameron* Boccaccio notes how some people tried so completely to escape from the deadly plague afflicting Florence in the year 1348 that they not only shut themselves up but also tried to keep their ears and minds closed to any news ("alcuna novella").[13]

The late Middle Ages also extended the meaning of *novella* to yet a third possibility: an historical or imaginary story that could be new or recently acquired or just unusual in nature. In the *Inferno* (XVIII:57), for instance, Dante applied the word to the sordid story ("la sconcia novella") of how Venedico Caccianemico played the pander by yielding his sister Ghisolabella to the lust of Obizzo d'Este. Similarly, the pre-Boccaccesque collection of tales from the thirteenth century that is known to us as the *Novellino* or the *Cento novelle antiche* contains the famous story of the man of the court (number 89) who, fancying himself an excellent storyteller, for after-dinner entertainment is said to recite to an assembled group "una novella," which he thereupon relates at such great length that one of his listeners is moved to suggest that the person who taught him the story omitted one important item: the ending.[14]

By the time of Boccaccio, then, a novella was a story that could be true or fictional, new or simply unusual, written or recited. Hence, on the one hand, Boccaccio in the proem to the *Decameron* can speak of his published stories as "cento novelle," and then, on the other hand, in the ensuing frame-tale can also have Pampinea suggest to her companions that they pass the time in their Tuscan retreat "novellando," by spinning tales. Other interesting and enlightening uses of the term in the *Decameron* are to be found in the account of the lecherous Frate Alberto (IV:2) and in that of Madonna Oretta and the loquacious knight (VI:1). In the former, when the proud but incredibly naive Madonna Lisetta boasts to a local gossip that she shares her bed with no other lover than the angel Gabriel—actually Frate Alberto with an improvised set of wings—the gossip, we are told, can hardly wait to get away from the duped Lisetta in order to tell the other ladies of the town this juicy "novella." In the latter story, the knight offers Madonna Oretta a ride on his horse, and after she accepts, he commences to relate to her what he refers to as one of the world's lovely stories ("una delle belle novelle del mondo"). He then begins to tell the tale ("novellar"), but does it so badly that the lady, beginning to perspire, to feel ill and on the verge of death itself, remarks that she would prefer to walk the rest of the way because the knight's horse trots too roughly. Her companion, realizing that he is not much of a storyteller ("novellatore"), decides to leave the tale unfinished and turns his conversation to "altre novelle," apparently "other news" (rather than another fictional story), presumably of the court.[15]

If in the late Middle Ages and the Renaissance, therefore, a novella—*nouvelle* in French, *novela* in Spanish, and in English *novel* (pronounced "no-vel'")—could be either a written or a recited story, it is in the frame-tale or cornice that holds together the typical novella collection of the age that the two faces of the genre are fused, for the tales framed by the various novellistic cornices employed from Boccaccio down through Giraldi and Marguerite de Navarre to Basile and María de Zayas are simultaneously printed on paper for one to read as well as fictively recited by a storyteller to a usually most receptive audience.[16]

With the complex generic nature of the novella now somewhat clearer, our next task is to determine what source materials will best serve us in our reconstruction of the Renaissance theory of the novella. A perusal of the age's ample literary criticism for discussions of the novella proves to be a generally disappointing and frustrating experience. What E. C. Riley has written of the state of the novel in the Renaissance——"In the sixteenth and seventeenth centuries there was, strictly speaking, no theory of the novel"[17]—holds almost equally true for the novella. Indeed, many of the literary theorists of the age, such as Antonio Sebastiano Minturno, eliminated any kind of prose fiction from serious consideration simply because the ancients had ignored it. Such traditionalists, as Northrop Frye has suggested, tend to remind one of those Renaissance doctors who altogether refused to treat syphilis because Galen had said nothing about it.[18]

A most curious instance of silence regarding the novella concerns Giambattista Giraldi Cinzio, the author of one of the most celebrated of novella collections, the *Ecatommiti* (1565). Along with Tasso, Giraldi was one of the few Renaissance figures who excelled as both artist and critic. Although he joined Francesco Patrizi and other anti-Aristotelians in defending new genres such as the romance and the tragicomedy, there is in Giraldi's critical writings virtually no mention of the novella.[19]

Other Renaissance theorists, faced with the conspicuous popularity of the novella, did attempt to confront the new form, but it is obvious that many were completely baffled over what to do with it. Bernardo Segni, in the commentary to his translation of Aristotle's *Poetics,* remarks that Boccaccio's stories are nothing but poems written in prose.[20] Giason Denores, for his part, envisions some of the tales in the *Decameron* as perfect tragedies. The ninth tale of the fourth day, for example, contains for Denores the essential elements of tragedy: the change in fortune, reversal, the revolution of a single day, and morality.[21]

A few more adventurous critics, like Lionardo Salviati, another translator of the *Poetics,* seem to have sensed that the novella should probably be judged on its own terms. Thus Salviati, although he steadfastly holds poetry to be superior to prose, does concede that the *Decameron* is so excellent in prose that its author would have seriously erred had he employed verse.[22]

All in all, only one commentator of the age endeavored to treat the novella with any kind of seriousness or depth. In 1574 Francesco Bonciani read to the Accademia degli Alterati his *Lezione sopra il comporre delle novelle.* Even if Bonciani's work is a transparent attempt to fit a new genre into the critical system of the *Poetics,* it does reflect a sympathetic attitude toward the novella as well as an apparently intimate knowledge of its tradition, and, refreshingly, it more than once offers original interpretations of the sometimes all too familiar precepts of the orthodox Aristotelian theorists.[23]

Yet despite Bonciani's useful effort, it is certainly clear that a survey of Renaissance literary theory will give us only a very limited notion of contemporary thought regarding the novella. For further enlightenment on the form one must look elsewhere. Of course, the scattered but illuminating comments upon the genre made by the novellists in prologues, epilogues, and elsewhere will prove helpful from both a theoretical and a practical point of view. In addition, a rich source of information concerning the novella is, interestingly and perhaps surprisingly enough, to be discovered in the various discussions of the art of storytelling in public as recorded in the courtesy books and rhetorical treatises of the age.[24]

Just as Boccaccio and his disciples conceived of the novella as either a written or an oral story, so the writers of Renaissance courtesy books in their prescriptions for the artful use of storytelling in polite conversation also made little or no distinction between the literary and the recited novella. In his brilliant discourse on humor in Book II of Castiglione's *Cortegiano* (1528), Bernardo Bibbiena divides witticisms into three categories: extended stories, brief cutting remarks, and practical jokes. Extended stories ("le narrazioni lunghe"), Bibbiena explains, are related just as one tells "una novella." In fact, Bibbiena even cites Boccaccio's *Decameron* as an example of effective storytelling in public.[25] In the *Galateo ovvero de' costumi* (1552), the courtesy book second in influence only to Castiglione's, Giovanni Della Casa also uses *novella* as a synonym for the extended narrative in conversation, a usage thereupon carried over to Spain by Della Casa's famous adapter Lucas Gracián Dantisco, who in the *Galateo español* (1559) translates *novelle* as "las novelas y cuentos," faithfully rendered in turn by William Style, Gracián's English translator, as "Novellaes and Tales."[26]

Since a novella was considered both a rhetorical and a literary exercise, the Renaissance theory of the novella comprises primarily two distinct yet related elements: a literary tradition in the Aristotelian-Horatian mold and an oral tradition, springing ultimately from classical rhetoric but more immediately from Renaissance courtesy literature.[27] In subsequent sections, as we consider such questions as the function, language, style, unity, harmony, invention, variety, verisimilitude, and brevity of the novella, our observation of the continuous interaction of these two elements will help elucidate more fully the unique literary amalgam that is the novella.

II. The Function of the Novella: Utility vs. Recreation

Many novellists from the very beginning of the tradition readily fell into line and conformed to the Horatian dictum—duly sanctified by both the mediaeval church and later the Counter-Reformation—of the utility of art. It is the pre-Boccaccesque *El conde Lucanor* by Don Juan Manuel that sets the pattern for this branch of the novella tradition. Don Juan's Prologue begins with the premise that people learn most easily those things they find pleasing. In this the author believes he is emulating the physicians who, when they wish to make a medicine to treat the liver, sweeten it with honey or sugar because they know of the natural attraction the liver has for sweets. This method, he continues, incites the liver to draw to itself not just the sugar, but the medicine as well. Just so Don Juan hopes that his readers, attracted to his book by the sweetness of its style, will not be able to avoid its teaching, and hence (like the liver) they will receive benefits even if they do not wish any.[28]

Many later novellists, especially those writing during and after the Council of Trent, such as Giraldi, Parabosco, Lugo y Dávila, and Tirso de Molina followed the lead of the *Conde Lucanor* and dutifully paid tribute (albeit in many cases probably lip service only) to the Horatian doctrine.[29] However, it was not in a Catholic nation but in sixteenth-century England that the balance between the useful and the sweet in the novella was most frequently and most manifestly tipped over to the side of utility. William Painter hopes his *Palace of Pleasure* "maye render good examples, the best to be followed, and the worst to be auoyded."[30] Likewise, the puritanically stern moralist Geoffrey Fenton intends that his *Certain Tragical Discourses* give the reader excellent models "for imytaction of the good, destestynge the wycked, avoydynge a present mis- chiefe, and preventynge any evil afore yt fall."[31] For his part, George Pettie, inordinately concerned that his *Petite Palace of Pleasure* may lead people astray, exhorts the reader of his tales to eschew the practice of the spider and "suck not out the poison out of them, that by some light example you be not the sooner incited to lightness."[32] The most consistent of the novellists to stress the didacticism of his tales was John Rastell, who closed most of his tales with a variant of "By this tale you may learn" and attributed a moral truth to the most hilarious of tales.

If the wish of some novellists to instruct their readers corre- sponds to the dictum of the *Ars Poetica* of Horace, the often intense desire of a good many others solely to please seems to be derived from the more audience-conscious rhetorical tradition.[33] Orators as well as courtiers engaged in "civil conversation" were continually made keenly aware that nothing is more important for the public speaker than winning the favor of the audience, for as Thomas Wilson explains in *The Arte of Rhetorique* (1553), ". . . excepte menne finde delight, thei will not long abide: delight theim, and wynne theim: werie theim, and you lose theim for euer."[34]

The practice of conversing or telling tales primarily for the sheer entertainment of doing so is everywhere present in the novella tradition. Such diverse novellists as Grazzini, Straparola, Bandello, Lope de Vega, and La Fontaine, among others, all affirm that the artistic end they seek is to give pleasure and delight to their readers.[35]

This conception of the novella as strictly a medium of entertain- ment seems to be rooted in a belief in the recreational function of both hearing or reading stories. Following Cicero, who held

conversation to be a natural means of freeing our souls from the weariness of everyday care,[36] Giovanni Pontano in his *De Sermone* (c. 1550) argues that jokes and witty sayings are meant to give amusement and recreation after one's labors ("oblectationem tantum . . . ac recreationem post labores").[37] Likewise, Lodowick Bryskett advises the courtier in his *Discourse of Civill Life* (1606) to engage in conversation "for the reuiuing or recreating of his spirits."[38]

The Aristotelian theorist Bonciani also observed the recreational nature of the novella and interestingly attempted to connect it with the comments in the *Poetics* that are concerned with purgation and the delight found in imitation. Bonciani states that the kind of imitation that is in the *Decameron* helps to relieve the ills of human existence. In addition, literary types such as the novella for Bonciani have as their end the purgation of troubles and annoyances from man's life and the substitution of joy for these sorrows.[39]

Besides the practical applications of the restorative function of the novella to be found in numerous novellistic frame-narratives—the subject of our second chapter—there are several noteworthy pronouncements by various novellists on this question. In his *Genealogia deorum gentilium* Boccaccio includes among the many benefits derived from listening to fictitious narratives the attainment of some measure of comfort by those weary from oppressive labors and the restoration of strength and spirit to men worn out by the strain of serious crises. This is why, he continues, princes exhausted from the affairs of state frequently engage in conversation and storytelling to revive their spent forces. Similarly, recreation—from *recreare*, to restore, refresh, and create anew—is the principal purpose of the *Decameron* itself. In spite of the obligatory remark that his book contains "useful counsel," Boccaccio clearly intends that his readers receive from his tales delight, amusement, relief from boredom, and consolation for the pains of love.[40]

Over the next three centuries many of Boccaccio's followers were to make like claims for the restorative nature of their works. Sacchetti, himself a victim of the plague at San Miniato (1400), put it very well in the proem to his *Libro delle trecentonovelle:* "Considering the present times and the condition of mankind, subject to pestilence and mysterious deaths, and seeing how many disasters and wars, civil and foreign, the impoverishment of peoples and families, and with what bitter sweat they must bear their misery, ... and yet imagining how people must long to hear things of a happy mood, especially readings easy to understand and comforting, so that their sorrows will be mixed with some laughter, I have proposed—a rough man of modest culture—to write the present work."[41]

In the following century Sabadino degli Arienti writes in the dedicatory letter to Ercole I d'Este which is prefixed to the *Porrettane* that he is presenting lighthearted stories because the human spirit requires recreation in order to persevere in its daily labors.[42] Over in England Chaucer's Host promises those pilgrims en route to Canterbury that they will receive "disport" and "confort" if his suggestion "to talen and to pleye" is adopted.[43] In Spain Juan de Timoneda labels his sixteenth-century collection *El Patrañuelo* "pastime and human recreation" ("pasatiempo y recreo humano").[44] The Frenchman Bonaventure Des Périers pens a sonnet to the readers of his aptly entitled *Nouvelles récréations et joyeux devis* urging us to put aside our melancholy and anger in order to allow ourselves some laughter and folly and an hour of pleasure; some other time we will receive instruction.[45] Another French novellist, Jacques Yver, explains that it is only natural for the characters in the frame-tale of his *Printemps* to desire to relate entertaining stories after being buffeted about by the misfortunes of civil war: just as sailors rejoice at the passing of a tempestuous storm, and just as fledglings at the end of a long winter are cheerful among the new foliage, so after suffering, people seek pleasant and amusing rest.[46]

Finally, Cervantes, whose comments on the function of the novella coincide with his view of the function of the novel, proclaims in the Prologue to the *Novelas ejemplares* that in presenting his stories he is placing in the marketplace a billiards table that everyone can use to entertain himself without harm to either his body or soul because honest and pleasant exercise are profitable, not damaging. Since one cannot always be in church or engaged in business, there is time for recreation, by which the afflicted spirit rests. This is why, he concludes, there are such things as parks, fountains, and gardens.[47]

For E.C. Riley this forms Cervantes' "definitive statement" on the function of imaginative literature. With Cervantes, as perhaps with no other novellist, the two functions assigned to the novella—utility and recreation—conjoin: the recreational function of the novella provides its usefulness; its justification is its restorative power. More simply put, as Riley points out, this is to say that for Cervantes " 'delectare' *is* 'prodesse'."[48]

III. Invention and Variety

Variety seems always to have been an essential ingredient of the overall novellistic strategy to please one's listening or reading audience. Indeed, writers of novellas from Boccaccio and his predecessors to Cervantes and his successors almost without exception offered their readers a rich variety of fictive material.

A major factor in rendering the novellist's goal of variety somewhat easier to achieve was the age's rather liberal conception of what constituted a novella. We have already seen how Boccaccio could apply the term to a bawdy tale (IV:2) as well as to a courtly one (VI:1). In fact, in the Proem of the *Decameron* Boccaccio casually speaks of his stories as "one hundred novellas, or fables, or parables, or histories, whatever we wish to call them."[49] Walter Pabst has also shown that one of the very first literary applications of the term was to describe the sacred dialogue from the thirteenth century *De peccatore cum vergine* by the Milanese author Bonvesin da la Riva.[50] This flexibility of meaning and usage of the term *novella* persisted throughout Renaissance Europe, and hence we find as late as 1611 John Florio in his famous Italian-English dictionary entitled *Queen Anna's New World of Words* still defining novella as "a novel [i.e., "no-vel'"], a new discourse, a tale, a fable, a parable. Also a tiding or newes."[51]

A second important aid in the novellist's realization of diversity of narrative materials in his novella collection was the intriguing Renaissance conception of invention. In addition to the more "modern" notion—articulated in the Cinquecento by Sperone Speroni, Ludovico Castelvetro, Lionardo Salviati, and others—that invention means primarily originality of subject matter ("the creation of new things"),[52] the age also inherited and fostered the rhetorical view that *inventio* (from *invenire*, to come upon) entails the "discovery" and subsequent ingenious reworking of already existent materials.

Inventio, the first division of classical rhetoric (followed in order by *dispositio, elocutio, memoria,* and *pronuntio*) was defined by Cicero in *De Inventione* as the discovery of valid arguments to render one's cause plausible.[53] Subsequently, the French rhetorician Pierre Fabri writes that the first task of the orator is to find his proofs ("trouuer ses raisons").[54]

Torquato Tasso was among those in the Renaissance who applied this basically rhetorical concept to define literary invention. For him novelty does not reside in the fictitiousness of a subject unheard of before, but in the interweaving of complications and resolutions, in the skillful "working out" of a plot. Tasso therefore finds it irrelevant if the material is thoroughly known or has been previously treated by other authors because he believes quite simply that the novelty of a poem is in its form rather than in its subject matter.[55]

It was obviously this latter conception of invention to which the Renaissance novellist in general subscribed. In fact, Boccaccio in defense of his work insists without blush at the beginning of the fourth day of the *Decameron* that he is simply following other sources faithfully, and if his critics think otherwise, they should show him the originals and prove him false.[56]

Boccaccio and his disciples, then, in sharp contrast to the modern writer of short fiction, became for all intents and purposes not inventors but collectors of tales. The end of the novellist seems to have been principally to offer his avid reading public rare old wines in attractive new bottles; his prime concern was not with originality of subject matter but rather with the artful presentation of the familiar. It was, of course, Cervantes who radically broke with this tradition, boasting in the prologue to the *Novelas ejemplares* not only that he is the first to write novellas in Castilian, but also that his stories, unlike the others of his day, are neither imitated nor stolen but are rather the product of his own "genius."[57]

It remains nonetheless true, as students of sources and analogues continually discover,[58] that the typical pre-Cervantesque novella collection consisted predominantly, sometimes exclusively, of re-workings of previously used materials, resulting in a kind of "miscellany" incorporating an extraordinary variety of literary types. It is not at all surprising, for instance, to find within a single collection echoes of a *fabliau,* chivalric romance, *lai,* beast epic, fable, folk tale, fairy tale, miracle of the Virgin, and saint's life as well as assorted stories stemming from Biblical, Greco-Roman, Oriental, and historical sources.

The novellist's ideal of variety—like that of invention—may with some profit also be retraced to the acutely audience-conscious rhetorical tradition. In *De Oratore* Cicero encourages the speaker to make use of witticisms and jokes to relieve dullness and tone down austerity; in general, he insists that the treatment of a subject must be diversified so that one's listeners can neither perceive the art of it nor be worn out by monotony.[59] The Renaissance rhetorician Giovanni Pontano devotes an entire chapter to the importance of variety in speech.[60] In a similar vein, Stefano Guazzo advises the gentleman to sprinkle his conversation with "Sentences, pleasant Jestes, Fables, Allegories, Similitudes, Comptes, and other delight-full speache, varying from the common fourme of talke, which hathe no small force to content the hearers."[61]

Sixteenth-century literary critics likewise stressed the importance and value of variety in the novella. Written almost exclusively in prose, which in the Renaissance was generally considered to serve variety better than poetry,[62] the novella collection was doubtless deemed the paradigm of literary diversity in its day, as countless contemporary comments attest. Giovanni de' Bardi, for instance, praises Boccaccio because he like Ariosto followed modern taste and mixed high and low subjects together.[63] Francesco Caburacci, also linking Boccaccio with Ariosto, speaks of the *Decameron* as an example of a mixed genre which, like the *Orlando Furioso,* combines within a single work all possible literary materials—tragedy, comedy, and the epic.[64]

Bonciani, in his discourse on the novella, conceived the genre to be of the type composed in the mixed narrative manner ("il modo narrativo misto")—that is, the narrative may be interrupted by speeches and dialogues among the personages of the tales. For Bonciani the novella, as a generic hybrid, could also depict diverse actions ("diversi azioni")—the serious, the ridiculous, the heroic—and its plots could be both simple and complicated ("semplici e avviluppate").[65] We shall see in a subsequent chapter that in addition to the freedom allowed him to diversify both subject matter and literary style, the novellist also was not bound, as writers of tragedy, comedy, and the epic were, to portray characters of a certain rank only, since, as Girolamo Bargagli writes in the *Dialogo de' Giuochi,* a novella could be about persons of lower, middle, or even upper classes.[66]

The novellists themselves, apparently aware of both the literary freedom they possessed and the necessity to vary their material in order to entertain their audience, steadfastly strove to emulate the diversity exhibited by Boccaccio, whom Pietro Bembo regarded in the *Prose della volgar lingua* (1525) as the master of variety.[67] Consequently, Sacchetti with the *Decameron* obviously in mind claims in his preface to have gathered his tales from various sources both antique and modern and to have presented characters that include ladies great, humble, and in between; men both grand and small; and figures of every generation.[68] In the disclaimer prefixed to the "Miller's Tale" Chaucer thus states the wide offering available in his collection:

> And therfor, whoso list it nat yheere,
> Turn over the leef and chese another tale;
> For he shal fynde ynowe, grete and smale,
> Of storial thyng that toucheth gentilesse,
> And eek moralitee and hoolynesse.[69]

Then, too, some of the tale spinners of Grazzini's collection *Le cene* share the hope that everyone in their company knows matters Latin, Greek, and Tuscan so that each will offer stories containing novelty and no one's narrative will be lacking in invention,[70] and in seventeenth-century Spain the novellist Lugo y Dávila promises in his preface to present tales of both a happy and unhappy nature.[71]

Lastly, Cervantes, another master of variety like Boccaccio, presents in the *Novelas ejemplares* a dazzling diversity of subject matter, characterization, stylistic approaches, and narrative techniques—perhaps all the more remarkable since he is dealing with original, not borrowed materials. It is in Cervantes' response to Alonso Fernández de Avellaneda contained in the Prologue to the second part of the *Quijote* that the author acknowledges that it was his intention in the *Novelas ejemplares* to include a bit of everything—one of the more memorable examples of understatement in literature.[72]

IV. Verisimilitude

It has often been said that the novella tradition brought the literary depiction of reality to a new highwater mark. Erich Auerbach, for example, has written of Boccaccio, "It is in him that the world of sensory phenomena is first mastered, is organized in accordance with a conscious artistic plan, caught and held in words."[73] In their efforts to depict reality as it appears, the novellists, it may be argued, were merely putting into practice certain strictures already laid down by rhetoricians as well as by Aristotelian literary theorists.

Probabilitas, veritas, and *verisimilitudo* are the goals that Cicero and Quintilian repeatedly urge the orator to seek in order the more effectively to persuade his audience.[74] Through the influence of mediaeval and Renaissance rhetoricians like Guidotto da Bologna, Pontano, and Wilson, these ideals were kept very much alive right through the seventeenth century. It was during the sixteenth century that the authors of courtesy books adapted these concepts for use in oral narration. Della Casa argues that since we obtain the greatest pleasure from hearing things with which we can identify, the storyteller must keep his tale rooted in the everyday to keep the attention of his audience.[75]

The predilection of the novellist to depict the real as real follows too, of course, the Aristotelian doctrines of verisimilitude and imitation. At least two writers—both interestingly enough practicing novellists as well as literary theorists—applied these precepts to the novella. Girolamo Bargagli states that the novella must combine invention and verisimilitude, resulting in what he calls "verisimil raro," which is the presentation of something that can plausibly occur, but that rarely does.[76] Lugo y Dávila, who similarly stresses the need for a fusion of *admiratio* and *verisimilitudo,* advances the argument that the novellist, like the poet, must imitate nature. Of his own stories, Lugo writes that they are verisimilar and close to the truth, some of them actually being true.[77]

So pervading the entire novella tradition is the insistence on verisimilitude in the depiction of reality that Lugo's claim is, upon investigation, found to be anything but unique. Boccaccio, for one, maintains throughout the *Decameron* the notion that his frame-tale did in fact take place precisely as described. In his conclusion he concedes that the collection might have been better had some of the tales been omitted, but this he says would have rendered unfaithful his account of an actual event.[78]

The novellist's claim of being a reporter engaged in relating an actual congregation of people for the sharing of tales became a standard pose for the followers of Boccaccio. For some, it can be argued with good reason, this pretense was very likely just a literary expedient—a "protective screen"[79]to justify the inclusion of licentious or anticlerical stories. But whatever the motivation, novellists everywhere donned the mask of the faithful reporter. Chaucer, we recall, abjectly apologizes for his recitation of the "Miller's Tale," but excuses himself on the ground that he must tell the tales as he heard them or else issue a false report of what happened on the journey to Canterbury.[80] Sabadino degli Arienti claims he is merely presenting novellas recounted at the baths of Porretta by a gracious company of noble men and women.[81] Straparola asks us to disregard the low style of his work because he wrote the stories not as he wished to, but as he heard them told, neither adding to nor subtracting anything from them.[82] Jacques Yver also regards himself as "un fidèle secrétaire" simply transcribing the conversations and memorable tales of an illustrious company of ladies and gentlemen.[83]

Ultimately, it came to be expected that the novellist rigorously employ verisimilitude not just in his frame-tale, but in the individual novellas themselves. In fact, the celebrated Renaissance literary theorist Ludovico Castelvetro objected in the *Lettera del Dubioso Academico* (c. 1567) to the lack of verisimilitude in the *Decameron*. Boccaccio is criticized by the apparently rather sheltered Castelvetro for attributing to priests actions unbecoming to their office and also for allowing young women to meet clandestinely with young men when everyone knows that young ladies of good families are carefully guarded by their parents.[84]

The ideal of verisimilitude—coupled at times no doubt with the desire to avoid censure for offensive stories—led many writers of novella collections to claim that their tales record actual historical events. Masuccio Salernitano was among the first of Boccaccio's disciples to follow his master's lead and refer to his narratives as "novellas or histories" ("novelle o vero istorie").[85] A century later, Bandello can be found saying that his stories are not fables, but likewise true histories ("non sono favole ma vere istorie"). After the extravagant and seamy tale of Faustina and Cornelia (I,19) he insists again: "But be that as it may, I have told you this story no more or less than I heard it narrated."[86] Marguerite de Navarre maintains that her *Heptaméron* contains no novella that is not true ("nulle nouvelle qui ne soit veritable histoire").[87] Lastly, William

Painter brands his tales "these histories (which by another terme I call Nouelles). . . ."[88]

For Cervantes verisimilitude was a prime objective of the novella as well as of the novel. After reading aloud the *Novela del curioso impertinente*, the Curate in *Don Quijote* finds praise for the tale's invention, but unfortunately must fault it for its lack of verisimilitude.[89] On the other hand, Ginés de Pasamonte, one of Cervantes' most inspired creations, boasts that his picaresque autobiography *La vida de Ginés de Pasamonte* will surpass the famous novel *Lazarillo de Tormes* because his book contains truths so beautiful and so witty that no lies could every equal them ("verdades tan lindas y tan donosas, que no puede haber mentiras que se les igualen").[90]

Perhaps Cervantes' most comprehensive statement on imitation and verisimilitude is spoken in the *Quijote* by the Canon of Toledo, whose contention it is that the author must effect a marriage between his fictional plot and the reader's intelligence. This, he argues, can only be done by making the impossible seem possible so that, our souls being held in suspense, we can be amazed, surprised, delighted, and entertained all at the same time. But these accomplishments, the Canon concludes, will never be attained by the writer who flees from verisimilitude and imitation, in which consist the perfection of writing.[91] Almost identical advice, of course, had already been related to Cervantes himself by his *amigo* in the Prologue to Part I of the *Quijote*. Only utilize imitation in what you write, the friend is alleged to have told the author; the more perfect the imitation, so much the better will be your writing.[92]

This avid quest of Cervantes and his fellow novellists for the verisimilar in their art appears to mark the first concerted effort of any considerable size to shift the literary depiction of reality toward that mode of fictional representation that we have come to call realism.

V. Unity and Harmony

The novella was rarely conceived as of a self-contained unit to be published independently—two obvious exceptions being Machiavelli's *Belfagor* and Luigi Da Porto's *Romeo e Giulietta*. Instead, the typical novellist considered each of his tales as part of a vast tapestry of fiction that was often bound together by some kind of framing device. We shall later observe how in several collections (like those of Boccaccio, Giraldi, Marguerite de Navarre, and others) the stories within the individual days of the frame-narrative are further unified around a given theme. The unity and harmony that suffuse the book of novellas as a whole can be discerned within each and every tale as well. In this respect, the novella might well be considered a miniature oration.

The second division in classical rhetoric, after *inventio,* was *dispositio* (arrangement). According to Cicero, the ultimate goal of the orator is an harmonious composition. Matters must be marshalled in an orderly fashion with an eye for the weight of each argument; topics, facts, even the words one utilizes must be logically arranged. In short, Cicero's orator must never shift haphazardly from one topic to another, or go back to the beginning, or go too far, or omit anything pertinent. Quintilian adds that one's materials will remain a confused heap until *dispositio* orders and interrelates it.[93]

In the Middle Ages and the Renaissance one discovers similar thoughts not only in rhetorical treatises, like the *Fiore di rettorica* from the thirteenth century by Guidotto da Bologna,[94] but in courtesy books as well. Della Casa urges the speaker to put his words in order ("mettendole in filza"), not heap them together ("non ammassandole"). Moreover, one must discreetly apportion what one wishes to say ("compartire discretamente le cose che tu a dire arai"), and not join diverse things together ("guardera' ti congiugnere le cose difformi").[95] Castiglione characteristically insists that the principle of orderly composition applies equally to speech as well as to writing.[96]

In the seventeenth century, the Spanish novelist Lugo y Dávila brings Aristotle into the discussion. The novella, Lugo suggests, must like tragedy possess unity of action. He observed, too, that the elements of the novella are again those of tragedy: recognition, reversal, and perturbation.[97] The novellist's task, then, was to combine these elements into a unified, harmonious whole. The theorist Bonciani likened the result not so much to tragedy as to comedy, for with an apparent glance at the ancient commentators of Terence, like Evanthius and Donatus, Bonciani states the quantitative parts of the novella to be three: first, the prologue, which introduces the characters and circumstances of the story; next, the "scompiglio," or knotting of the action; and finally, the "sviluppo," the unknotting or unfolding of the action which brings on the conclusion.[98] Such a narrative structure could readily merge with Aristotle's "beginning, middle, and end" as well as with three parts of the classical oration: the *exordium* or *prooemium* (the introduction that renders the auditor well disposed, attentive, and receptive); the *narratio* (the full exposition of the events that have occurred); and the *conclusio* or *peroratio* (the summing up and conclusion).[99]

One of the more illuminating illustrations of Boccaccio's attitude regarding the importance of the orderly presentation of the novella is contained in the aforementioned tale of Madonna Oretta and the tongue-tied knight (VI:1). Here are vividly shown to the reader the ingredients of a miserably told story. The knight breaks all the rules: he repeats the same things over and over again; he reverses the order of events; and in his befuddlement he keeps going back to the beginning to start all over again. In short, order, unity, and harmony are woefully absent, making Oretta (and no doubt Boccaccio himself) thoroughly ill.

At the other end of the novella tradition one finds Cervantes still retaining the storyteller's concern for the well-balanced, orderly recitation of his tale. In the Prologue to Part I of the *Quijote* the author's *amigo* reminds him to make sure, above all, that his words are well placed ("bien colocadas").[100] Then within the *Quijote* itself the Canon of Toledo passionately pleads for logically arranged narrative structures. He laments that he has never seen a book of chivalry that held the body of the story complete with all its members in a manner that the middle corresponded to the beginning and the end to the beginning and the middle; rather they are composed with so many members that the author's intention seems to be more that of forming a chimera or a monster than shaping a well-proportioned figure.[101] Finally, in the novella "Coloquio de los perros" the dog Berganza, echoing the Canon, scolds his over-anxious canine listener Cipión for seeking to know the middle of Berganza's story before hearing its beginning. Cipión is told to have patience and listen to the orderly recital of his friend's adventures; it is in this way, coaxes Berganza, that one obtains the greatest pleasure.[102]

VI. Language and Style

The principle of decorum in language and style was apparently held among the chief qualities of the Renaissance novella, along with variety, verisimilitude, unity, and harmony. The theorist Bonciani, following the strictly Horatian doctrine of decorum and citing Boccaccio's practice in the *Decameron*, argues that the appropriate manner of speech for the novella is "humble and minute" ("umilissimo e rimesso"), not grand. Since the novella is in prose and generally deals not with epic or tragic figures but with ordinary men, Bonciani believes it improper for the novellist to utilize that greatness of speech ("quella grandezza del favellare") found in tragedy and the epic.[103]

Others in the Renaissance, including the authors of courtesy literature, interpreted decorum to mean not only appropriateness of representation, but also conformity to what is decent, proper, moral, and even Christian. Hence, Castiglione says the storyteller must relate his tale without foul words ("senza dir parole sporche").[104] Della Casa also advises the speaker to avoid any obscenities in his narrative.[105] Periphrasis and circumlocution were of necessity highly considered stylistic devices. In point of fact, novellists generally did adhere to this latter doctrine. Although Chaucer's Miller and Host, for example, sprinkle their conversation with assorted crudities (*queynte, ers, coillons,* and so on), in the process actually being quite faithful to Horace's notion of decorum, Boccaccio is more representative of the typical novellist. Throughout the *Decameron* are strewn witty and occasionally elegant euphemisms for the sexual act: Boccaccio's young lovers are variously said to put the devil in hell (III:10), place the tail on the mare (IX:10), and make the nightingale sing the night through (V:4).

In classical rhetoric *elocutio* came after *inventio* and *dispositio*. In the oral tradition one thus finds very practical and very detailed advice concerning the selection of style and language. Cicero suggests that the orator choose a style appropriate to the occasion and calculated to hold the attention of the listeners as well as to persuade them.[106] More specifically, both Cicero and Quintilian counsel the use of a style that is clear, plain, and direct. Of course, Latin is to be used, and, most important, the speaker must employ words that are in current use.[107]

Guidotto da Bologna's *Fiore di rettorica* of the thirteenth century adapts these principles of classical rhetoric to its own times. According to Guidotto, the speaker must still utilize words currently in use ("parole usate"), but the language now should not be Latin, but the vernacular ("il volgare"). Moreover, one must avoid foreign words ("parole straniere") as well as a Latin syntax.[108]

For Thomas Wilson in the sixteenth century, the ends of rhetoric are to teach, to delight, and to persuade. Yet to achieve these he thinks it necessary, in addition to presenting one's ideas in an orderly fashion, to make use of plain language:

> First, therefore an Orator muste labour to tell his tale, that the hearers maie well knowe what he meaneth, and vnderstande him wholy, the whiche he shall with ease do, if he vtter his mind in plain wordes, suche as are vsually receiued, and tell it orderly, without goyng aboute the bushe."[109]

Wilson goes on to consider a speech useless if no one can understand the speaker. Therefore, "ouer olde, and ouer straunge woordes" are not to be employed; this again holds true for Latin too: "... speake thy minde now, as menne do at this daie."[110]

Such rhetorical principles were applied readily enough by the courtesy books of the age to conversation and to the telling of stories in polite company. For Castiglione the eloquent courtier also must use current language ("parole ... usate ancor dal populo") and must try at all times to clarify any ambiguity.[111] Della Casa restates the familiar arguments that one must eschew words that are foreign, or have fallen into desuetude, or have more than one meaning; in brief, the words used to tell a story should be clear enough to allow each of one's listeners to understand them easily.[112]

The employment of the language of one's audience was equally held of great importance by the novellists themselves. Although Boccaccio's *Decameron*, the very fountainhead of the novella tradition, was composed in Tuscan, Bandello and Straparola made use of northern dialects, and Basile wrote his *Pentamerone* in Neapolitan. In addition, clarity and directness of both language and style were highly esteemed by Boccaccio and his followers. Sacchetti, for instance, insists that his tales are easy to understand ("agevoli a intendere").[113] Parlemente, Marguerite de Navarre's *porte-parole* in the frame-tale of the *Heptaméron*, has such a deep concern for the authenticity of the stories to be exchanged and for the plain style required to relate them that she goes so far as to suggest to the other *devisants* that in narrating the tales the beauty of rhetoric ("la beaulté de la rhetorique") must not be used so as to spoil the truth of the story ("la verité de l'histoire").[114]

Once again, as we move to the seventeenth century, we find Cervantes reiterating many of these same concepts in both the *Novelas ejemplares* and the *Don Quijote*. In the "Coloquio de los perros" Cipión judges as lewd and evil the labeling of certain things by their proper names. Modest words, Cipión declares, are an indication of the modesty of whoever speaks or writes them.[115] Cipión's companion Berganza, for his part, strongly advocates that the speaker utilize the language of his audience. This voluble quadruped roundly criticizes those who sprinkle their speech with bits of Latin ("listas de latín") and is even more severe towards those who use Latin when addressing an audience totally ignorant of the language.[116]

This train of thought can be traced back to the Prologue to Part I of the *Quijote*. Here Cervantes' *amigo* advises the author to employ a style that is clear and and smoothly flowing and that works rather to render one's thoughts easier to comprehend than to obscure them ("intricarlos y oscurecerlos").[117] Decorum, simplicity, and general accessibility remained the novellist's concerns throughout the three-hundred-year efflorescence of this tradition.

VII. *Brevitas*

Although it is true that Horace bluntly advised the young writer, "Esto brevis" (v. 335), the question of brevity is another of those major issues ever present in discussions of rhetoric and public speaking, whether classical or modern. For Cicero accessibility alone is not enough: to retain the attention of his audience the orator should be brief.[118] Quintilian believes that before all else it is *narratio* of the oration that must be kept brief.[119] The Renaissance rhetorician Pontano devotes an entire chapter each to the problems of verbosity and loquacity in public speaking.[120]

Those contemporaries of Pontano who composed guides for proper courtly conduct similarly perceived the virtues of brevity in civil conversation. Stefano Guazzo maintains that a speaker must not use "superfluous wordes, nor bee tedious to his hearers with long Prefaces, and other impertinent circumstances besides the matter."[121] In the *Galateo* Della Casa severely berates those who begin a story but do not know when to stop.[122]

Della Casa's observation immediately prompts recollection of the previously cited story from the *Cento novelle antiche* of the verbose man of the court who is mocked for knowing all of his story so well except for its ending. Even the laconic Boccaccio, in the conclusion to the *Decameron*, displays concern that some of his tales may perhaps be too long ("troppe lunghe").[123] Of course, one of the Host's objections to the "Tale of Sir Thopas" is that its teller, Chaucer the pilgrim, is simply wasting time: "Thou doost noght elles but despendest tyme."[124]

Generally speaking, Italian books of novellas all the way from the *Cento novelle antiche* through Boccaccio, Sacchetti, and Bandello down to Basile as well as those earlier collections from Spain and France, like the *Conde Lucanor* or the *Cent Nouvelles nouvelles,* did strictly adhere to the principle of brevity. Yet, as one moves geographically and chronologically from Italy of the thirteenth and fourteenth centuries, one notes the steady gravitation of the novella, as it gradually lost is connection with the oral tradition, toward the expansion of the form. This is especially evident in

England and Spain in the works of, among others, Fenton and
Cervantes. The kinds of amplification discernible in the later
novella and the possible relationship between this Renaissance
genre and subsequent forms of fiction are matters best reserved for
fuller discussion in a final chapter.

Conclusion: A Note on Terminology

A loose end yet remains: the question, suggested in the
introduction to this chapter, of the proper usage of the term *novella*
in modern literary scholarship in English. One may, on the one
hand, choose to follow those students of the novella who favor the
continued use of the term to apply to each of the three forms of
fiction it is currently used to designate: the Renaissance genre; the
literary type that flourished in Germany during the late eighteenth
and nineteenth centuries; and the modern work of fiction that is of
intermediate length. Employing what Polheim has labeled the
"historical approach" to the study of the novella,[125] critics such as
Fritz Martini—to mention but one—view whatever differences that
exist between the three forms as merely mutations within the same
genre.[126] Though convenient, this approach must be rejected
because it tends to render the term meaningless. Such a practice
would be tantamount to banishing the terms epic, romance, and
lyric, remaining content to label *The Odyssey, Sir Gawain and the
Green Knight,* and Leopardi's "L'Infinito" simply as "poems."
   Surely, our study, if anything, has indicated that the Renaissance novella constituted a tradition very much *sui generis.* Indeed
scholars like Lutz Mackensen and Heinrich Henel have stren-
uously argued that the German *Novelle*—with its greater scope, its
complexity of plot, and its proclivity toward symbolism—has
scarcely anything to do with the novellas composed in the
Renaissance. As for the modern works of intermediate length, even
the uninitiated will readily discern along with M. D. Springer that
works like Mann's *Tod in Venedig* have only the "most tenuous
connections" with those narratives contained in the *Decameron* and
its literary descendants.[127]
   Yet, on the other hand, setting up impenetrable terminological

barriers between these three forms seems equally undesirable. This course—which conforms to what Polheim calls the "normative approach" toward defining the novella: the establishment of an *Urform* with which all other potential examples of the genre must be compared—would deny that any affinities whatsoever exist between the three types of short fiction.

Although finding difficulties with both the historical and the normative approaches, Polheim does suggest that any successful resolution of the problem of defining and employing the term *novella* must entail a synthesis of the two approaches. A possible way out of the critical dilemma—and one that combines the historical approach with the normative approach—is to adopt (at least for criticism in English) the following set of terms: novella for the Renaissance form, "Novelle" for the Romantic and post-Romantic tradition of German short fiction, and "novelette or "short novel" for modern works of intermediate length (retaining "novel," of course, for the full-length work of fiction).[128] Such a scheme seems both conceptually and etymologically satisfying, for it implies a certain kinship yet retains the basic literary distinctions that exist between these related yet diverse forms of fiction.

Notes

1. Karl Konrad Polheim, *Novellentheorie und Novellenforschung* (Stuttgart: J. B. Metzlersche Verlagbuchhandlung, 1965), pp. 101-09. An excellent companion book is the anthology of criticism, *Novelle,* ed. Josef Kunz (Darmstadt: Wissenschaftliche Buchgesellschaft, 1968).

2. Harry Steinhauer, "Towards a Definition of the Novella," *Seminar,* 6 (1970), 154. Steinhauer, however, as we shall see, despite his evident facility with words, is hardly any more successful in defining the novella than his predecessors have been.

3. E.g., Yvonne Rodax, *The Real and the Ideal in the Novella of Italy, France and England* (Chapel Hill: Univ. of North Carolina Press, 1968); and *The Early French Novella: An Anthology of Fifteenth- and Sixteenth-Century French Tales,* ed. Patricia and Rouben Cholakian (Albany: State Univ. of New York Press, 1972).

4. E.g., *Ten German Novellas,* ed. Harry Steinhauer (New York: Doubleday, 1969). But also note the more cautiously entitled *Great German Short Novels and Stories,* ed. Bennett A. Cerf (New York: Modern Library, 1933).

5. See Henry James, *The Art of the Novel,* ed. Richard Blackmur (New York: Scribner's, 1934), esp. pp. 217-31 and 267-87.

6. Robert Gorham Davis, *New York Times Book Review,* 7 Sept. 1952, p. 1. See,

too, the subsequent letter of protest by Robert J. Clements against this use of the term, *New York Times Book Review*, 28 Sept. 1952, p. 45.

7. Respectively, W. J. Harvey and Philip Stevick, *The Theory of the Novel*, ed. Philip Stevick (New York: Free Press, 1967), pp. 251 and 334.

8. *The Art of the Novella*, ed. Arnold Sklare (New York; Macmillan, 1965), p. 1. Note also Steinhauer, "Towards a Definition of the Novella," and Gerald Gillespie, "Novella, Nouvelle, Novelle, Short Novel?—A Review of Terms," *Neophilologus*, 51 (1967), 117-27 and 225-30, both of whom take the similar position that a novella is a work of "intermediate length," with the usually reliable Gillespie making the rather surprising suggestion (p. 126) that we "lop off" from the novella category nothing less than the *Cento novelle antiche* itself.

9. Maurice Valency, among others, has significantly described the *Cento novelle antiche* as a "manual for raconteurs," *Palace of Pleasure*, ed. Valency and Harry Levtow (New York: Capricorn, 1960), p. 2.

10. It is perhaps worthwhile to note that several of the characteristics of the novella to be discussed below (such as its tripartite narrative structure, brevity, and variety) have similarly been observed in two recent studies: Roger Dubuis, *Les Cent Nouvelles nouvelles et la tradition de la nouvelle en France* (Grenoble: Presses Universitaires, 1973), and Marga Cottino-Jones, "Observations on the Structure of the *Decameron* Novella," *Romance Notes*, 15 (1973), 378-87. However, each of these critics has essentially extrapolated his or her conclusions from the observation of tales within a *single* novella collection. The discussion offered in this chapter will consider the novella tradition as a whole—its efflorescence throughout Europe over some three centuries—in an effort to define the genre by placing it within the context of Renaissance literary and rhetorical theory. Incidentally, a helpful critique of Mr. Dubuis's "interior" approach has been provided by Alexandre Lorian, "Deux Cent Nouvelles nouvelles," *Hebrew University Studies in Literature*, 2 (1974), 151-70.

11. See C. T. Lewis and Charles Short, *A Latin Dictionary* (1879; rpt. Oxford: Clarendon, 1966), p. 1219.

12. See Carlo Battisti and Giovanni Alessio, *Dizionario etimologico* (Florence: G. Barbera, 1950-57), IV, 2605.

13. *Decameron*, ed. Vittore Branca (Florence: Le Monnier, 1965), p. 17. The employment of the term to denote "news" continued right through the Renaissance and beyond; e.g., Alessandro Striggio, the librettist for Monteverdi's *Orfeo* (1607), refers to the report of Euridice's death as "l'amara novella" ("bitter news"); see Claudio Monteverdi, *L'Orfeo*, ed. Giacomo Benvenuti (Milan: Classici musici italiani, 1942), p. 63.

14. *Novellino e Conti del Duecento*, ed. Sebastiano Lo Nigro (Turin: UTET, 1968), pp. 197-98. For the reader's convenience an appendix listing the principal novella collections chronologically by nation has been provided.

15. *Decameron*, respectively, pp. 6, 44, 489, and 703-05. We have adopted the following procedure for referring to tales within collections: with the *Decameron*, *Pentamerone*, and other works that present tales as belonging to a specific day of the frame-story, we have indicated the day number in Roman numeral followed by a *colon* and the tale number in Arabic numeral (e.g., I:1); with works that have no cornices but that were published in more than one volume, particularly Bandello's *Novelle* and Painter's *Palace of Pleasure*, we have indicated the volume or part number in Roman numeral followed by a *comma* and the tale number in

Arabic numeral (e.g., I,1); and, needless to say, with those collections which number their tales consecutively, like the *Cent Nouvelles nouvelles* and Marguerite de Navarre's *Heptaméron* (even though it does have a frame-tale), we have simply given the Arabic numeral of the story.

16. A different kind of fusion of the dialogue form with the anthology of tales—with the balance decidedly tipped toward the former—is Pietro Aretino's *Ragionamenti,* which has in fact been discussed as a *Novellensammlung* by Johannes Hösle, *Pietro Aretinos Werk* (Berlin: De Gruyter, 1969), pp. 89-114.

17. *Cervantes's Theory of the Novel* (Oxford: Clarendon, 1962), p. 1.

18. *Anatomy of Criticism* (1957; rpt. Princeton: Princeton Univ. Press, 1971), p. 13.

19. See, for example, Giraldi's famous *Discorsi intorno al comporre de i Romanzi, delle Comedie, e delle Tragedie* (Ferrara: G. Giolito, 1554).

20. *Rettorica et poetica d'Aristotile* (Florence: L. Torrentino, 1549), p. 281. See too Bernard Weinberg, *A History of Literary Criticism in the Italian Renaissance* (Chicago: Univ. of Chicago Press, 1961), I, 405.

21. *Discorso intorno a que' principii, cause, et accrescimenti, che la comedia, la tragedia, et il poema heroico ricevono dalla philosophia morale, & civile, & da' governatori delle republiche* (Padua: G. Riario, 1586), p. 29v. (See Weinberg, I, 623.)

22. "... niun componimento ne da' moderni, ne da gli antichi si grazioso, e si bello fu fatto per auuentura: e guai all'Autore, se l'hauesse fatto in versj," *Poetica d'Aristotile parafrasata e comentata* (Florence, 1586), MS. II. II. 11., Biblioteca Nazionale Centrale, Florence, fol. 140v. (See Weinberg, I, 616-17.)

23. *Lezione sopra il comporre delle novelle* (1574); rpt. *Prose fiorentine,* Pt. II, Vol. I (Florence: Tartini and Franchini, 1727), pp. 161-212.

24. For some glimpses into the long and noble tradition which lay behind this Renaissance conjunction of matters written and matters spoken, see Cicero, *De Oratore,* ed. E. W. Sutton and H. Rackham (1942; rpt. Cambridge, Mass.: Harvard Univ. Press, 1967), I, xvi, 70; Ernst Robert Curtius, *European Literature and the Latin Middle Ages,* trans. Willard R. Trask (1948; trans. New York: Pantheon, 1953), esp. pp. 62-78 and 145-66; C. S. Lewis, *The Discarded Image* (1964; rpt. Cambridge: Cambridge Univ. Press, 1967), pp. 190-91; the *Genealogia deorum gentilium* in Giovanni Boccaccio, *Opere in versi, Corbaccio, Trattatello in laude di Dante, Prose latine, Epistole,* ed. Pier Giorgio Ricci (Milan: R. Ricciardi, 1965), p. 958; Castiglione's *Cortegiano* in *Opere di Baldassare Castiglione, Giovanni Della Casa, Benvenuto Cellini,* ed. Carlo Cordié (Milan: R. Ricciardi, 1960), p. 52. hereafter cited as *Opere* for both Castiglione and Della Casa; and Marvin T. Herrick, *Comic Theory in the Sixteenth Century* (1950; rpt. Urbana: Univ. of Illinois Press, 1964), pp. 6-11.

25. *Opere,* pp. 148-49.

26. Ibid., p. 410. See too Lucas Gracián Dantisco, *Galateo español* (Valencia: n.p., 1601), p. 151; and William Style, *Galateo Espagnol, or the Spanish Gallant* (London: W. Lee, 1640), p. 125.

27. The novellist most keenly aware of the relationship of the novella to the rhetorical tradition was perhaps Lugo y Dávila, author of the *Teatro popular* (1622), who admits in the Proem to his collection that the novella "abraza la Rétorica y Oratoria, los Tropos, las Figuras, así de las sentencias como de las palabras, con la variedad de estilos que enseñan Cicerón, Quintiliano y demás autores," *Teatro popular,* ed. Emilio Cotarelo y Mori (Madrid: Librería de la Viuda

de Rico, 1906), p. 15. Several decades earlier, Bonciani in his *Lezione sopra il comporre delle novelle* related the novella to what the ancients called the "fictitious oration" ("orazione falsa"), *Prose fiorentine*, Pt. II, Vol. I, p. 167.

28. Don Juan Manuel, *El conde Lucanor*, ed. José Manuel Blecua, 2nd ed. (Madrid: Clásicos Castalia, 1971), pp. 47-49.

29. Giraldi (1565) seeks to mix the useful with the sweet ("in ogni parte d' essa è in guisa accoppiato l'vtile col diletto"), *Hecatommithi* (Venice: Enea de Alaris, 1574), in preliminary letter, "A gentili spiriti"; Girolamo Parabosco offers in the *Diporti* (c. 1550) "utilità e diletto," *Novellieri minori del Cinquecento: G. Parabosco—S. Erizzo*, ed. G. Gigli and F. Nicolini (Bari: G. Laterza, 1912), p. 15; Lugo y Dávila (1622) promises his readers "útil y apacible entretenimiento," *Teatro popular*, p. 27; the title of Tirso de Molina's *Deleitar aprovechando* (1635) is self-explanatory.

30. *Palace of Pleasure*, ed. Joseph Jacobs (1890; rpt. New York: Dover, 1966), I, 5, hereafter cited by the editor's name to avoid confusion with the similarly entitled volume by Valency and Levtow.

31. *Certain Tragical Discourses*, ed. Robert L. Douglass (1898; rpt. New York: AMS, 1967), I, 4.

32. *A Petite Palace of Pettie his Pleasure*, ed. I. Gollancz (London: Chatto and Windus, 1908), I, 6.

33. Cicero and his followers strongly urge the orator to be ever-mindful of the time, the place, the occasion, the nature of the audience, and the expectations of the listeners; see Cicero, *De Oratore*, I, xxvi, 120 and II, xlii, 178; Quintilian, *Institutiones Oratoriae*, ed. M. Winterbottom (Oxford: Clarendon, 1970), II, xli, 178; and Giovanni Pontano, *De Sermone*, ed. S. Lupi and A. Risicato (Lucania: Thesaurus Mundi, 1954), p. 18. The authors of courtesy books adapted this advice for their own purposes. Della Casa insists that when telling a story one should always keep in mind "gli uditori," *Opere*, p. 384. In the 1581 translation of Stefano Guazzo's *La Civil conversatione* (1574) by the novellist George Pettie we read that the speaker must choose his conversation "according to the diversitie of places, times, matters, and persons to whom hee shall speake," *Civile Conversation*, ed. Edward Sullivan (London: Constable, 1925), I, 135. Similarly, Lodowick Bryskett's *A Discourse of Civil Life* (1606), a rather free adaptation of Giraldi's *Tre dialoghi della vita civile* (1565), requires that the perfect courtier must "continually have great regard to the time, place, persons, and other circumstances, according to which he is to order his pleasant conceits and merry iests. . . , " *Literary Works of Lodowick Bryskett*, ed. J. H. P. Pafford (London: Gregg International, 1972), p. 246.

34. *The Arte of Rhetorique*, ed. Robert Hood Bowers (Gainesville, Fla.: Scholar's Facsimiles and Reprints, 1962), p. 16.

35. The confabulators within the frame-tale of Grazzini's *Cene* agree to tell stories that are "festevoli e gioconde," *Novelle del Cinquecento*, ed. Giambattista Salinari (Turin: UTET, 1964), I, 254. Similarly, the gathered company in the cornice of the *Piacevoli notti* by Straparola are said to exchange tales designed to yield "piacere e diletto," *Le piacevoli notti*, ed. Giuseppe Rua (Bari: G. Laterza, 1927), I, 3. Bandello in his letter to the reader in the first volume of his *Novelle* writes of his stories, ". . , affermo bene che per giovar altrui e dilettare le ho scritte," *Tutte le opere di Matteo Bandello*, ed. Francesco Flora (Milan: Mondadori, 1952), I, 3, hereafter cited by the editor's name to avoid confusion between tale numbers and the volumes and pages of this edition. In the dedicatory epistle to

the novella "El desdichado por la honra" Lope de Vega confesses, "... yo he pensado que tienen las novelas los mismos preceptos que las comedias, cuyo fin es haber dado su autor contento y gusto al pueblo...," *Novelas a Marcia Leonarda,* ed. Francisco Rico (Madrid: Alianza Editorial, 1968), p. 74. Lastly, at the end of the novella tradition, La Fontaine, citing his beloved Terence, declares in the preface to the first part of his *Contes et nouvelles,* "En cela, comme en d'autres choses, Térence lui doit servir de modèle. Ce poète n'écrivoit pas pour se satisfaire seulement, ou pour satisfaire un petit nombre de gens choisis; il avoit pour but: *Populo ut placerent quas fecisset fabulas,"* *Oeuvres,* ed. Henri Regnier (Paris: Hachette, 1883-97), IV, 6.

36. See *De Oratore,* II, vi, 22-23 and II, ix, 35. For the Middle Ages, see Glending Olsen, "The Medieval Theory of Literature for Refreshment and Its Use in the Fabliau Tradition," *Studies in Philology,* 71 (1974), 291-313.

37. *De Sermone,* p. 17.

38. *Literary Works,* p. 246. Similarly, Della Casa writes, "Vera cosa è che noi possiamo in alcun modo menare questa faticosa vita mortale del tutto senza sollazzo né senza riposo; e, perché le beffe ci sono cagione di festa e di riso e, per conseguente, di ricreazione, amiamo coloro che sono piacevoli e beffardi e sollazzevoli," *Opere,* p. 406.

39. *Prose fiorentine,* Pt. II, Vol. I, pp. 162 and 182-84.

40. See respectively, *Opere in versi ... Prose latine,* p. 962; and *Decameron,* pp. 25-27 and 673.

41. Franco Sacchetti, *Il libro delle trecentonovelle,* ed. Ettore Li Gotti (Milan: Bompiani, 1946), p. 3.

42. In *Prosatori volgari del Quattrocento,* ed. Claudio Varese (Milan: R. Ricciardi, 1955), p. 885.

43. Chaucer, *Works,* ed. F. N. Robinson (Cambridge, Mass.: Houghton Mifflin, 1961), p. 24.

44. Juan de Timoneda, *El Patrañuelo,* ed. Federico Ruiz Morcuende (Madrid: Ediciones de "La Lectura," 1930), p. 7.

45. In *Conteurs français du XVIᶜ siècle,* ed. Pierre Jourda (Paris: Gallimard, 1965), p. 365.

46. Jacques Yver, *Le Printemps* (1841; rpt. Geneva: Slatkine Reprints, 1970), p. 521.

47. "Mi intento ha sido poner en la plaza de nuestra república una mesa de trucos, donde cada uno pueda llegar a entretenerse sin daño de barras; digo sin daño del alma ni del cuerpo, porque los ejercicios honestos y agradables antes aprovechan que dañan.

"Sí; que no siempre se está en los templos, no siempre se ocupan los oratorios, no siempre se asiste a los negocios, por calificados que sean; horas hay de recreación, donde el afligido espíritu descanse.

"Para este objecto se plantan las alamedas, se buscan las fuentes, se allanan las cuestas y se cultivan con curiosidad los jardines," *Obras completas,* ed. Angel Valbuena Prat (Madrid: Aguilar, 1956), p. 770. This statement was anticipated to a large extent by the comments made by the Curate in Chapter 32 of the first part of the *Quijote* that the purpose of fiction is "entretener vuestros ociosos pensamientos; y así como se consiente en las repúblicas bien concertadas que haya juegos de ajedrez, de pelota y de trucos...," ibid. p. 1172.

48. *Cervantes's Theory of the Novel*, pp. 86-87.

49. "... cento novelle, o favole of parabole o istorie che dire le vogliamo. ..." *Decameron*, p. 6.

50. *Novellentheorie und Novellendichtung* (Berlin: Cram, De Gruyter, 1953), p. 23.

51. John Florio, *Queen Anna's New World of Words*, 2nd ed. (1611; rpt. Menston, Eng.: Scholar's Press, 1968), p. 335.

52. See Weinberg, I. 79-81, 169-70, 240, and 286; and II, 1005, 10017, and 1049.

53. Cicero, *De Inventione*, ed. H. M. Hubbell (Cambridge, Mass.: Harvard Univ. Press, 1949), I, vii, 9.

54. Pierre Fabri, *Le grand et vray art de pleine Rhétorique*, ed. A. Héron (Geneva: Slatkine Reprints, 1969), p. 4.

55. See the relevant comments contained in the *Discorsi dell'arte poetica* (c. 1567), *Apologia in difesa della Gerusalemme Liberata* (1585), and *Discorsi del poema eroico* (1594) in Torquato Tasso, *Prose*, ed. Ettore Mazzali (Milan: R. Ricciardi, 1959), pp. 352, 428, 523, and 532.

56. *Decameron*, pp. 458-59.

57. *Obras completas*, p. 770.

58. See, for example, A. C. Lee, *Decameron: Its Sources and Analogues* (London: Nutt, 1909); William F. Bryan, *Sources and Analogues of Chaucer's "Canterbury Tales"* (Chicago: Univ. of Chicago Press, 1941); and James W. Hassell, Jr., *Sources and Analogues of the "Nouvelles récréations et joyeux devis" of Bonaventure Des Périers*, 2 vols. (Vol. I: Chapel Hill: Univ. of North Carolina Press, 1957; Vol. II: Athens: Univ. of Georgia Press, 1969).

59. See *De Oratore*, I, v, 17; II, lviii; and II, xli, 177.

60. Chapter 4 of Book I: "Maximam esse in hominibus orationis varietatem ac diversitatem," *De Sermone*, p. 5.

61. *Civile Conversation*, I, 136-37. For obvious reasons the English translation of *La Civil conversatione* by the novellist George Pettie is being utilized in our discussion rather than Guazzo's original version.

62. See, for example, Agostino Michele, *Discorso in cui si dimostra come si possono scrivere le comedie e le tragedie in prosa* (Venice: G. B. Ciotti, 1592). (See Weinberg, II, 679.)

63. *In difesa dell'Ariosto* (Florence, 1583), MS. Magl. VI, 168, Biblioteca Nazionale Centrale, Florence, fol. 66v. (See Weinberg, II, 986.)

64. *Breve discorso in difesa dell'Orlando Furioso di M. Lodovico Ariosto* (Bologna: G. Rossi, 1580), p. 81. (See Weinberg, II, 982.)

65. *Prose fiorentine*, Pt. II, Vol. I. pp. 163-76 and 194.

66. *Dialogo de'giuochi* (Siena: L. Bonetti, 1572), p. 209. Bonciani subsequently concurred that the personages of the novella include the "potenti, infimi, e mezzane," *Prose fiorentine*, Pt. II, Vol. I. p. 205.

67. Pietro Bembo, *Opere in volgare*, ed. Mario Marti (Florence: Sansoni, 1961), pp. 339-40.

68. *Il libro delle trecentonovelle*, p. 3.

69. Chaucer, *Works*, p. 48.

70. *Novelle del Cinquecento*, I, 252.

71. *Teatro popular*, p. 24.

72. "Pero, en efecto, le agradezco a este señor autor el decir que mis novelas son más satíricas que ejemplares, pero que son buenas; y no lo pudieran ser si no tuvieran de todo," *Obras completas*, p. 1272.

73. *Mimesis,* trans. Willard R. Trask (1946; trans. 1953; rpt. Princeton: Princeton Univ. Press., 1971), p. 216.

74. See Cicero, *De Inventione,* I, xxi, 29, and *De Oratore,* III, lvii, 215; and Quintilian, *Institutiones Oratoriae,* IV, ii, 31 and 44.

75. *Opere,* p. 412.

76. *Dialogo de' giuochi,* p. 210. Bonciani was later to find in the novella "l'imitazione delle umane opere," *Prose fiorentine,* Pt. II, Vol. I, p. 163.

77. *Teatro popular,* pp. 15, 23, and 24.

78. *Decameron,* p. 1241.

79. On this point see the informative study of William Nelson, *Fact or Fiction: The Dilemma of the Renaissance Storyteller* (Cambridge, Mass.: Harvard Univ. Press, 1973).

80. Chaucer, *Works,* p. 48.

81. *Prosatori volgari del Quattrocento,* p. 885.

82. Straparola, *Le piacevoli notti,* pp. 3-4.

83. Yver, *Le Printemps,* p. 521.

84. Ludovico Castelvetro, *Opere varie critiche* (Milan: P. Foppens, 1727), pp. 108ff. (See Weinberg, I, 183.)

85. Masuccio Salernitano, *Novellino,* ed. Giorgio Petrocchi (Florence: Sansoni, 1957), p. 11. Cf. Boccaccio, *Decameron,* p. 26.

86. See Flora, respectively, II, 422, and I, 235.

87. In *Conteurs français du XVIe siècle,* ed. Jourda, p. 709.

88. Jacobs, I, 5.

89. *Obras completas,* p. 1195.

90. Ibid., p. 1115.

91. "Hanse de casar las fábulas mentirosas con el entendimiento de los que las leyeren, escribiéndose de suerte que facilitando los imposibles, allanando las grandezas, suspendiendo los ánimos, admiren, suspendan, alborecen y entretengan de modo que anden a un mismo paso la admiración y la alegría juntas; y todas estas cosas no podrà hacer el que huyere de la verosimilitud y de la imitación, en quien consiste la perfección de lo que se escribe," ibid., p. 1251.

92. "Sólo tiene que aprovecharse de la imitación en lo que fuere escribiendo; que cuanto ella fuere más perfecta, tanto mejor será lo que se escribiere," ibid., p. 1034.

93. See Cicero, *De Oratore,* I, v, 17; I, xii, 50; I, xxxi, 142; and II, lxxvi, 307; and *De Inventione,* I, xx, 29; and Quintilian, *Institutiones Oratoriae,* VII, Proem.

94. E.g., "... tutte le parole della diceria s'acordino insieme. ..," *Prosa del Duecento,* ed. Cesare Segre and Mario Marti (Milan: R. Ricciardi, 1959), p. 109.

95. *Opere,* p. 421.

96. Ibid., p. 58.

97. *Teatro popular,* pp. 22-23.

98. *Prose fiorentine,* Pt. II, Vol. I, p. 210. Evanthius divided comedy into four parts: *prologue, protasis, epitasis,* and *catastrophe.* For a full discussion of mediaeval and Renaissance theories of the dramatic structure of comedy, see Herrick, *Comic Theory in the Sixteenth Century,* pp. 106-29.

99. Cicero divides the oration into six parts: *exordium, narratio, partitio, confirmatio, refutatio,* and *concluso,* in *De Inventione,* I, xiv-lvi. Quintilian reduces these to five: *prooemium, narratio, probatio, refutatio,* and *peroratio,* in *Institutiones Oratoriae,* III, ix, 1.

100. *Obras completas,* p. 1034.

101. Ibid., p. 1251.
102. Ibid., p. 1002.
103. *Prose fiorentine*, Pt. II, Vol. I, p. 210.
104. *Opere*, p. 151.
105. Ibid, p. 385.
106. See *De Oratore*, I, xxxi, 138; III, xxiv, 97; and III, lv, 210.
107. See Cicero, *De Inventione*, I, xvi, 23; and I, xx, 29; and *De Oratore*, I, xxxii, 44; III, x, 37-39; and II, xliii, 167; and Quintilian, *Institutiones Oratoriae*, IV, ii, 31-44; VIII, Proem; and VIII, ii, 24.
108. *Prosa del Duecento*, pp. 109-10.
109. *The Arte of Rhetorique*, p. 14.
110. Ibid., p. 15.
111. *Opere*, pp. 58-59.
112. Ibid., p. 412.
113. *Il libro delle trecentonovelle*, p. 3.
114. Jourda, p. 709.
115. *Obras completas*, p. 1006.
116. "De eso podemos inferir que tanto peca el que dice latines delante de quien los ignora como el que dice ignorándolos," ibid.
117. Ibid., p. 1034.
118. See *De Inventione*, I, xvi, 23; and *De Oratore*, I, v. 17.
119. "Breuis erit narratio ante omnia. . . ," *Institutiones Oratoriae*, IV, ii, 40. See also IV, ii, 31 and 43 and IV, iii, 2.
120. *De Sermone*, Book I, Chaps. 19 ("De verbosis") and 20 ("De loquacibus").
121. *Civile Conversation*, I, 133.
122. *Opere*, p. 422.
123. *Decameron*, p. 1242.
124. *Works*, p. 167.
125. *Novellentheorie und Novellenforschung*, pp. 7-8.
126. See, e.g., Fritz Martini, "Die deutsche Novelle im 'bürgerlichen Realismus,' " *Überlegungen zur geschichtlichen Bestimmung des Formtypus, Wirkendes Wort*, 10, (1960), 257-78.
127. See, e.g., Lutz Mackensen, "Die Novelle," *Studium Generale*, 11 (1958), 751-59; Heinrich Henel, "Conrad Ferdinand Meyers' 'Nach einem Niederländer,' " *Wächter und Hüter, Festschrift für Hermann J. Weigand* (New Haven: Yale Univ. Press, 1957), pp. 108-20; and M. D. Springer, *Forms of the Modern Novella*, (Chicago: Univ. of Chicago Press, 1976), p. 17. In a lecture delivered as part of the panel "Told in Brief: Tradition and Form in the Short Prose Narrative" at the New York Comparative Literature Conference, New York University, 27 April 1974, James V. Mirollo spoke of the greater debt of modern short fiction to the novel rather than to the novella, preferring to view the modern short story as a "mini-novel," but the novella as an "expanded anecdote."
128. For others who have previously hinted at this solution, see E. K. Bennett and H. M. Waidson, *A Short History of the German "Novelle"* (Cambridge: Cambridge Univ. Press, 1961); and *The Novelette before 1900*, ed. Ronald Paulson (Englewood Cliffs, N.J.: Prentice-Hall, 1965). Some, incidentally, seem to prefer the label "short novel" to designate the work of intermediate length: e.g., *Ten Modern Short Novels* (New York: Putnam, 1958) and *Seven Short Novel Masterpieces*

(New York: Popular Library, 1964), both ed. Leo Hamalian and Edmond L. Volpe; *Eight Short Novels*, ed. Dean S. Flower (New York: Fawcett World, 1967); and *Classics of Modern Fiction: Eight Short Novels*, ed. Irving Howe (New York: Harcourt, Brace and World, 1968).

CHAPTER 2

The Structure of
the Novella Collection

I. The Cornice Tradition and the Justification of Fiction in the Renaissance

The use of a cornice or frame-tale—a narrative situation that plausibly motivates the relation of and lends structural unity to a series of otherwise diverse and unrelated stories—is probably the artistic characteristic that at first glance most blatantly distinguishes the novella collection from its modern counterpart, the book of short stories. Indeed, there is little even in earlier Western literature to prepare one for the widespread creative employment of the framing device by novellists from Boccaccio to Basile.

Upon investigation one uncovers only a bare handful of examples from classical antiquity of narrative structures that recommend themselves as possible candidates for consideration as distant literary ancestors of the novella cornice tradition. The Phaikian banquet in the *Odyssey*, for instance, serves as the backdrop for the minstrel Demodokos' song of the illicit love of Ares and Aphrodite as well as for Odysseus' relation of his fantastic adventures. The awesome autobiographical account of the latter was, of course, to be emulated by Vergil's Aeneas at Carthage.

Discussions devoted to the nature of Eros are heard at a banquet of a very different kind in Plato's *Symposium*. One recalls too that Herodotus interwove several fictional stories into his *History of the Persian Wars* and that the authors of the Roman novels *The Satyricon* and *The Golden Ass* similarly included short narratives within their works, most notably Petronius' "Matron of Ephesus" (recited by Eumolpus during the shipboard voyage sequence)—discussed below in Chapter Seven—and Apuleius' "Cupid and Psyche" (overheard by Lucius after he has been metamorphosed into an ass). Yet within the literature of classical antiquity perhaps the closest analogue to the novella frame-tale is that extended passage in Book IV of Ovid's *Metamorphoses* in which the daughters of Minyas decide to lighten their household tasks by each in turn telling a short tale—the result being the exchange of such famous mythological stories as "Pyramus and Thisbe," "Mars and Venus," and "Salamacis and Hermaphroditus,"[1] the first two of which were still being spun by Pettie in the Renaissance.

By the time of Ovid, however, the practice of binding together a series of short narratives by a frame-tale had already developed into a rich tradition in Oriental literature.[2] An early work in this idiom is the *Panchatantra,* the famous and influential collection dating back to around the fifth century B.C., which concerns King Amara Sakti of Mahilaropya in Deccan, who in despair of teaching his two dull sons engages the wise Brahmin Vishnu Sarman. After pledging to impart wisdom to the princes within six months, the Brahmin proceeds to teach his pupils lessons on human nature through fables with appropriate morals.

In subsequent centuries, the East produced many other works of this type. In the *Brihat Katha* cycle, for example, Gunadhya to obtain release from a curse must spread around the earth stories told to him by the goblin Paisacha. The *Vetala Panchavimsati,* known in English as the *Twenty-Five Tales of the Vampire,* is about a king who hears stories with riddles from a corpse that is haunted by a goblin or vampire. In the *Suka Saptati,* or *Seventy Tales of a Parrot,* a pet bird successfully keeps his wayward mistress Prabhavati from straying into infidelity by distracting her with tales that mock women, dull husbands, and Brahmin monks— stories in fact, as Lin Yutang has noted, that strongly suggest

Boccaccio.[3] The most famous of these books is the Persian *Hazar Afsana,* the work more commonly called in the West the *Thousand and One Nights,* with its suspenseful frame of the ingenious Scheherazade and her attempts to stave off death at the hands of the cruel, sadistic Shariar by beguiling him with stories night after night.

Two other Oriental collections of importance, which, like the *Panchatantra,* eventually found their way into Europe, were the *Bakhtiyar-nama* and the *Sindibad-nama,* both of which, it is believed, are Pehlevi versions of a lost Sanskrit work (perhaps entitled the *Sindhapati).* In the *Bakhtiyar-nama* a prince, separated since birth from his royal parents and raised by robbers, returns to his homeland and strongly impresses the king, who like his son is unaware of the boy's true identity. Having been given the name Bakhtiyar, the young man is made a servant to his majesty, thus invoking the jealousy of the king's ten viziers. When the queen (actually his stepmother), like Potiphar's wife, accuses Bakhtiyar of an attempted seduction, the king must condemn his favorite, but cannot bring himself to have the sentence carried out. On each of ten consecutive days, one of the viziers urges action on the part of the king, who always manages to have the execution postponed by telling a story related to his own predicament. On the eleventh day, just as the execution is about to take place, the robber captain appears and proves the young man is really the prince. The viziers are themselves thereupon executed, and in short time Bakhtiyar becomes king. In the *Sindibad-nama,* it is the viziers (seven in number here) who wish to delay the execution and thus relate tales until the truth is ascertained.

The diffusion of many of these Oriental works into Europe has produced some of the more fascinating pages in literary history. There were, generally speaking, several stages in the transmission of these collections from the Orient to the Occident: usually originating in India, such works more often than not were received in Persia, where they were translated into Pehlevi (the literary language of Persia), thereafter passing into Syriac and Arabic, then Greek and Hebrew, and finally Latin and the vernacular languages of Western Europe.

The *Sindibad-nama,* for instance, was translated into many

different tongues between the tenth and thirteenth centuries, including Syriac *(Sindban),* Greek *(Syntipas),* and Hebrew *(Mishle Sendebar).* From an unidentified Arabic source in the thirteenth century came the Spanish rendering the *Libro de los engannos et los assayamientos de las mugeres.* Even earlier two Latin versions of the work had surfaced: in the twelfth century the *De rege et septem sapientibus* (also and probably better known under the title *Dolopathos,* after one of its principal characters) and the very different and more famous *Historia septem sapientium* from the twelfth or thirteenth century. The latter of these was quickly translated into French, Italian, German, Dutch, Danish, Swedish, Icelandic, and several Slavic languages.

The *Panchatantra* was ultimately rendered into Arabic in the eighth century as *Kalila wa-Dimnah* and was widely known throughout mediaeval Europe in both its Latin version (the *Directorium humanae vitae)* and its Spanish version *(Calila y Dimna).* The Arabic adaptation and its descendants offer a frame-tale that is also a fable. Dimnah, a lynx, becomes envious of the favor that the ox Senecba has gained with the lion (the king) and plots to destroy his rival. But the treacherous lynx is himself brought to trial, found guilty, and starved to death. It is in the course of the debate that anecdotes are introduced to illustrate and reinforce the arguments of the opposing sides.

Lastly, a most curious literary odyssey was charted for the *Jatakas.* Written in the Pali language of Buddhist scripture, this well-known collection from perhaps the fourth century B.C. contains over five hundred stories (fables, fairy tales, legends, and moral tales) concerning the Buddha's earlier incarnations. A Sanskrit derivate of the *Jatakas* is the *Lalita Vistara,* which, dating from before the second century, is likewise a legendary account of the youth of the Buddha. The *Lalita Vistara* was translated into Greek as *Barlaam and Josaphat* in the seventh century by a monk (traditionally St. John Damascene), who gave it a Christian adaptation: Buddha becomes Josaphat, Barlaam the mentor who guides his pupil (with the aid of short instructive stories) to the religious life. A Latin version of *Barlaam and Josaphat* from perhaps the tenth or eleventh century led to the enormous popularity of the story throughout Europe and to its subsequent translation into

French, Italian, English, Spanish, and other languages. Ironically, Barlaam and Josaphat were each to be canonized in both the Greek and the Roman churches and their story included in many mediaeval books of saints' lives, most notably Voragine's *Legenda aurea.*

The Christian exemplum and the Oriental tradition of framed collections of short narratives merged again in the early twelfth century in the very influential *Disciplina clericalis* by the converted Jew Petrus Alphonsi. With a retrospective glance at the Oriental collections and their European counterparts,[4] the author of the *Disciplina clericalis* sets some thirty-four tales within a frame-tale which concerns an old man approaching death who gives advice in the form of short narratives to his son. The father admonishes his offspring to shun vice and to love and obey God.

In the early fourteenth century a noble successor to the *Disciplina clericalis* emerged: the *Libro de los enxiemplos del Conde Lucanor et de Patronio,* more familiarly known as simply the *Conde Lucanor,* by Don Juan Manuel, a nephew of Alfonso El Sabio. The frame-tale of the work, which reflects its author's stated didactic intention, tells of young Count Lucanor and his frequent consultations with the old counselor Patronio on questions of morality and public policy. For every inquiry, Lucanor receives not only often austere instruction, but tales and fables as well, each of which ends with a rhymed couplet supplying the moral of the story.

Such was the cornice tradition inherited by Boccaccio, who to some extent himself experimented with the framing device in both the *Filocolo* and the *Ninfale d'Ameto.* It was, of course, with the *Decameron* that the Italian author created a frame-narrative that virtually dwarfed all previous efforts in that idiom and that simultaneously set a standard of artistic achievement his numerous imitators rarely even approached.

The *Decameron* cornice, which recounts in most graphic detail the deadly plague that attacked Florence in 1348, taking within five months the lives of some 100,000 persons, and the consequent withdrawal of ten young people—seven women and three men— from this human inferno to the beautiful Tuscan highland, has not unexpectedly attracted considerable critical attention. Some scholars have preferred to see the importance of the frame-narrative in relation to the tales which it so masterfully embraces. Maurice Valency, for example, has written, "The plague is the point of the *Decameron:* the human comedy, feverish, multi-colored and gay, is played against a backdrop of death. It is this contrast which gives the *Decameron* its scale and its richness."[5] For his part, Vittore Branca has convincingly argued that Boccaccio's cornice serves to introduce the reader to the three major themes that are to dominate the work's one hundred tales: fortune, love, and wit. More specifically, for Branca those two worlds in opposition—the horrific world of tormented Florence and the idyllic world established and temporarily inhabited by the *lieta brigata*—present us with many of the motifs subsequently developed within the individual stories of the *Decameron,* such as hypocrisy, greed, immoderation, and egoism on the one hand, and honesty, civility, and generosity on the other.[6]

A second tendency among students of Boccaccio has been to consider the frame of the *Decameron* independently, as a work of art in its own right which not only holds the reader's attention but even rivals in narrative interest the novellas themselves. Among its merits that have been mentioned, for instance, are its importance as a social document illustrating the nature and form of polite entertainment in its time; its considerable historical value— namely, the depiction of one of the terrible calamities common to mediaeval life; the varied literary effects that it permits, including the introduction of lyrics and *ballate* by the novellistic participants or descriptions of nature by the author himself; and the presenta- tion and analysis therein of elements of conflicting ideal societal states (Arcadia and Utopia).[7] No one, however, seems yet to have approached the *Decameron* cornice in terms of the light it may throw upon Renaissance attitudes toward imaginative literature and the corresponding defenses adopted by writers and defenders of fiction in the age.

"The first problem of Renaissance criticism," as Joel E. Spin- garn once noted, "was the justification of imaginative literature."[8] Confronted on one side by the inherited mediaeval distrust of any piece of literature that failed to serve as either the "handmaid of philosophy" or the "vassal of theology," and on the other side by the growing body of neo-Platonic attacks on poetry,[9] a sizable number of Renaissance literary theorists in countless discourses and dissertations staunchly and tirelessly defended their appreciation of both ancient and modern works of fiction, enlisting in their efforts a veritable arsenal of arguments. One of the chief of these, as William Nelson has pointed out, rested upon the hypothesis that the pursuit of recreation by "appropriate people" at "appropriate times" is a worthwhile activity for the body, the mind, and perhaps even the soul.[10] It was, accordingly, the firm belief of many of the apologists that imaginative literature is essentially "recreative" in nature and therefore can and indeed often does fulfill a most beneficial psychological function.

An early advocate of this recreational justification of fiction, as we have already seen from his remarks in the *Genealogia deorum gentilium*, was none other than Giovanni Boccaccio himself. But by the time of the *Genealogia* Boccaccio had already expressed his conviction that fiction was useful for certain people at certain times; he illustrates his belief directly, through the complex narrative structure he fashioned for the *Decameron*. Indeed, the use of the plague as the frame for the mostly lighthearted stories contained in the work lends to the entire collection a kind of *chiaroscuro* effect, the *oscuro* of the cornice serving at once as a backdrop and as the motivating force and hence the justification for the *chiaro* of the tales. The author's narrative strategy is further enhanced by his selection of storytellers who are all of good families, well educated, and well bred, and who, wishing to maintain their sanity as well as their lives, seek not just physical withdrawal but also psychological relief from the recent horror. Thus during their temporary retreat they understandably live most gaily, dining on delicately cooked foods, drinking exquisite wines, playing musical instruments, singing, dancing, and inevitably, entertaining each other with tales.

Since he utilizes what Wayne C. Booth would call "dramatized narrators,"[11] Boccaccio so structures his novella collection that the "reality" of his frame-situation necessarily colors and helps determine the reader's perception of and attitude toward the narrated tales. Consequently, by enframing his novellas with a "disaster cornice," Boccaccio conveniently furnishes his *Decameron* with a built-in defense against the censure of any reader or critic who may find some of the stories trivial if not licentious or outright blasphemous. This ingenious structural device also permits Boccaccio to assert, as indeed he does in the famous conclusion, that no reasonable reader can possibly judge any of his one hundred tales to be offensive since they were all related in a proper setting (not in church or in a school of philosophers but in beautiful gardens) by the right kind of people (admittedly young but mature and not easily led astray by stories) during a time in which it was only natural for any Florentine to seek some sort of diversion—in short, the tales constitute appropriate recreation for appropriate people at an appropriate time.[12]

Boccaccio's use of his frame-narrative both as a structural device and—like his claim of the historicity of the events which transpire in his cornice—as yet another "protective screen" to justify the possibly questionable nature of some of his novellas was widely imitated by the bulk of his many European followers. In fact, one readily discovers throughout the three-century efflorescence of the novella tradition a seeming myriad of cornices involving a company of usually refined and sophisticated men and women who experience some form of discomfort which impels them to pursue for a brief period of time, through storytelling and other like entertainments, sorely needed and justly deserved reaction. The various discomforts devised by Renaissance novellists to achieve the desired *chiaroscuro* effect, as we shall see, customarily combined physical hardship or danger with psychological affliction and were often, as in the *Decameron* itself, rather extreme in both nature and dimension.

Giovanni Sercambi was one of the very first of Boccaccio's disciples to continue the tradition of the disaster cornice. In his *Novelle* Sercambi presents a group of refugees in flight from the ravages of another historical plague, that of Lucca. As they pass through one Italian city after another, waiting for the pestilence to subside before they attempt the return home, the travelers decide to spend part of this anxious period of time listening to entertaining stories narrated by a single member of the group, who (as it turns out) proves to be Sercambi himself.

The frame-scheme of Marguerite de Navarre's *Heptaméron* in the sixteenth century revolves around a party of five men and five women—aristocrats all—who are marooned by floods in a Pyrenean abbey in southern France. Before they reach the monastery, each of the ten also passes through some rather harrowing personal experience: the matron Oisille travels a long distance on foot through untold dangers, losing most of her servants and horses; Parlemente, her husband Hircan, and Longarine are attacked by bandits and saved through the aid of Dagoucin and Saffredent, but not without Longarine first witnessing the murder of her husband; Gerburon, barely clothed, literally runs for his life from another pack of thieves; Simontault attempts to cross a river but gets caught in the swift current, and, like Oisille, loses his servants and goods; and Nomerfide and Ennasuite are set upon by a huge bear and flee with such speed that their horses drop lifeless as they enter the abbey gates. Safe within the Notre-Dame de Serrance at last, Marguerite's *devisants* seek to pass the time before the floods recede and a bridge can be built with some pleasant and virtuous occupation ("quelque occupation plaisante et vertueuse"). Parlemente, Marguerite's *porte-parole,* makes the suggestion—which is, of course, adopted— that the exchange of tales could well be the pleasurable pastime best suited to mitigate the present annoyance ("adoulcir l'ennuy").[13]

Although the disaster cornice persisted in popularity for a full century or so after the publication of the *Heptaméron,* it is intriguing to note that the calamities depicted in the frame-narratives of novella collections from the late sixteenth and seventeenth centuries were by and large no longer of the "natural" variety (plagues, floods, and so on), but (perhaps an index of the times) were nearly all—no matter the country—connected in some way with the ultimate man-made catastrophe: war.

The well-known dramatist and literary theorist Giraldi, for example, begins his *Ecatommiti* with a mercilessly detailed description of the Sack of Rome in 1527. With Counter-Reformational indignation and righteousness, Giraldi tells how the foreign army, stained with that "pestifera eresia di Lutero," attacked the holy city, and, filled with "barbarico furore," had no respect whatsoever for sex, age, station, the sacraments, or even God Himself. After killing as many men as they could or imprisoning them and subjecting them to every kind of torment and cruelty imaginable, the sadistic soldiers commence to rape untold women (sometimes on church altars) and even slaughter innocent children. A pestilence follows the sack of the city and takes the lives of still more multitudes of Romans. But in the midst of this horrendous historical moment, a *brigata* of gentlemen and gentlewomen, ensconced in the palace of the nobleman Fabio, resolves to escape the city by sea and seek refuge in France. Once on board ship twenty of these fugitives (ten men and ten women), again with well-motivated and understandable abandon, indulge in entertainments, including songs, dances, and storytelling, as their ship moors at various points between Civitavecchia and Marseilles.[14]

Similarly, the religious wars in France serve to introduce Jacques Yver's *Printemps*. The English author Robert Greene sets the frame-events of his *Farewell to Folly* in Italy during the time of the skirmishes between the Guelphs and the Ghibellines. The opening scene of *La quinta de Laura* by popular Spanish writer of the seventeenth century Alonso del Castillo Solórzano is also placed in Italy—this time during a local war near the Po.

Some novella collections shunned the disaster cornice but still managed to retain the *chiaroscuro* effect by presenting the exchange of tales as a logical response to some milder form of discomfort rather than to a single catastrophic event. Chaucer's pilgrims, one recalls, decide to lighten their arduous journey to Canterbury by engaging in a storytelling contest suggested by the Host. The entertainments of Matias de los Reyes' *Para algunos* likewise take place during a pilgrimage to Our Lady of Guadalupe. In Castillo Solórzano's *Jornadas alegres* the stories are related during a December trip—slowed down because of the pregnancy of one of the travelers—from Talavera to Madrid.

Other discomforts which motivate an exchange of stories are frequently related to the weather. In Parabosco's *Diporti* we find a company of many illustrious men, including among them Pietro Aretino, who have gone to fish and hunt along the Venetian lagoon, but who find themselves passing the time away reciting anecdotes when kept indoors for three days by storms. The frame-characters of Antonio Eslava's *Noches de invierno,* as the work's title indicates, tell stories to amuse themselves during the long winter nights, whereas those in Sebastiano Erizzo's *Sei giornate* and Tirso de Molina's *Cigarrales de Toledo* engage in similar diversions to stave off the summer doldrums.

Some novellists maintained the *chiaroscuro* effect by relating the frame merely to the physical or psychological distress of one or more of its personages. Ser Giovanni Fiorentino's *Pecorone* presents two lovers in holy orders, Frate Auretto and Suor Saturnina, who meet daily in the parlor of a convent at Forli and solace each other by relating very proper stories. The fairy tales of Basile's *Pentamerone* are told during the last few days of the pregnancy of the scheming Lucia. The group in Part I of María de Zayas' *Novelas amorosas y exemplares* gathers to entertain their friend Lisis during her convalescence from a recent illness. In Castillo Solórzano's *Alivios de Casandra* several ladies attempt to assuage the melancholy of the young Casandra. Finally, some solicitous neighbors seek to mitigate the sorrows of a recent widow in Mariana de Caravajal's *Navidades de Madrid*.

One of the more ingenious uses of the *chiaroscuro* effect occurs in Scipione Bargagli's *Trattenimenti*. Bargagli lays the frame of his sixteenth-century work in Siena during the siege of that city by Cosimo de' Medici in the years 1554 and 1555. In spite of the woes that beset them, the Sienese citizens refuse to lose courage and indeed attempt to amuse themselves with games and other pastimes. Bargagli zeroes in on one group in particular which, like a true descendant of Boccaccio's *lieta brigata*, decides to organize its entertainments for three full days, which in this case happen to be the last three days of carnival. Bargagli's setting of his frame simultaneously during a period of war and the pre-Lenten season gives double justification for whatever merriment one finds in the *Trattenimenti*, for any lightheartedness at such a point in time and place is manifestly defensible as urgently required balm both for past suffering and for future privation.

Although never reinforcing it with calamitous circumstances, several novellists had made use of a carnival frame before Bargagli had, some even decades so. Grazzini utilized it to bind together his lively but unfortunately incomplete *Cene*. The *brigata* in this work gathers on the last three Thursdays of carnival at the house of a rich Florentine widow for supper and the relation of tales. Once again the occasion provides the ready-made justification for the gaiety and levity of the entertainments: since during carnivaltime, as one of Grazzini's interlocutors argues in defense of the group's activities, it is permitted even for members of religious orders to enjoy themselves by participating in sports, singing, dancing, putting on plays, and so on, then surely the derivation of pleasure from telling and listening to stories can in no way be either improper or immoral.[15]

The carnival cornice, with all the justificatory powers invested in it by Grazzini, found particular favor in Italy and subsequently in Spain. Straparola's *Piacevoli notti* offers a plausible historical situation reminiscent of Parabosco's *Diporti* and even Castiglione's *Cortegiano.* For political reasons Ottaviano Maria Sforza, heir to the duchy of Milan, has sought temporary sanctuary in a luxurious palace on the island of Murano, where his daughter Lucrezia Gonzaga entertains certain illustrious guests (one of whom is Pietro Bembo) duing the last thirteen days of carnival. In Ascanio de' Mori's *Giuoco piacevole* a company of men and women, disappointed at the postponement of a new tragicomedy, create their own diversions at the home of Beatrice Gambara on the very last day of the festive season.

Among the number of Spanish novellists who took up the
carnival cornice during the seventeenth century, most distributed
their tales over several days, like Grazzini, Straparola, and
Bargagli, instead of following Mori's concentration on a single day
toward the very end of the season. Tirso de Molina's *Deleitar
aprovechando* takes place during the last three days of the joyful
period, the second part of the *Novelas amorosas y exemplares* by María
de Zayas during the final ten days before Lent. Castillo Solórzano
scattered the entertainments of his *Tiempo de regocijo y Carnestolendas,
de Madrid* and his *Sala de recreación* respectively over three and six
consecutive days. Finally, the three days just prior to Ash
Wednesday provide the setting in time for both Gaspar Lucas
Hidalgo's *Diálogos de apacible entretenimiento* and the *Carnestolendas de
Cádiz* by Alonso Chirino Bermúdez.

Yet another large group of novellists, discarding the *chiaroscuro*
effect altogether, apparently thought it justification enough to
utilize any kind of festive or happy occasion—not just the carnival
season—to frame their collections of tales. For example, several
works, such as George Whetstone's *An Heptameron of Civil Discourses,*
Castillo Solórzano's *Noches de placer,* Part I of María de Zayas'
Novelas amorosas y exemplares, and Mariana de Caravajal's *Navidades
de Madrid,* take place during Christmas celebrations. Sabadino
degli Arienti, for his part, presents in his fifteenth-century collection the *Porrettane* a gracious company of men and women gathered
around Count Andrea Bentivoglio during a holiday at the baths of
Porretta in the year 1475, while a century and a half later a triple
wedding serves as the plot material for the cornice of Castillo
Solórzano's *Fiestas del jardín.*

The proclivity of later novellists especially to eschew the
employment of the *chiaroscuro* frame-narrative appears to be
indicative of a changing literary climate throughout Europe
during the late Renaissance and the seventeenth century. Instead
of repeating the familiar defenses of fiction, which their predecessors had gleaned primarily from Aristotle and Horace, certain
critics from the last decades of the sixteenth century onward began
to emphasize the sheer entertainment value of imaginative literature, which they insistently deemed to be good in and of itself and
not in need of any kind of justification. A case in point is the

Cinquecento theorist Ludovico Castelvetro, who wrote in his *Poetica d'Aristotele* (1570) that poetry was invented solely to delight.[16] A century later John Dryden in the *Defence of "An Essay of Dramatic Poesy"* (1668) fully agreed that "delight is the chief if not the only end of poesie."[17] About midway in time between these two declarations, Lope de Vega in the dedicatory letter to *El desdichado por la honra* stated his belief that the novella along with comedy specifically has as its end the granting of pleasure to its audience.[18]

The effects of this increasingly liberal artistic atmosphere were, of course, fully reflected within the novella tradition. Partly because of a desire to experiment with new forms, but also no doubt partly because of the decreasing necessity to justify their fictitious narratives, many of the later novellists—Cervantes in particular—altogether abandoned the use of a cornice, choosing instead to present their tales as discrete narratives with no connective frame-plot to bind them together. Those novellists, on the other hand, who retained the framing device—whether for reasons of structure, esthetics, or tradition—by their growing preference for setting tales within cornices which did not represent disasters, arduous journeys, carnivals, holidays, or other extraordinary events, but depicted instead scenes of a more normative and everyday nature, accordingly tended more and more to emphasize the pure delight rather than the recreational benefits to be derived from their respective collections.

Once again Italy and Spain provide the most vivid illustrations. Firenzuola's incomplete *Ragionamenti* from the sixteenth century, for example, is set in a villa near Florence, where a group of three young men and as many women, admittedly very much like the company of the *Decameron* assembles in the spring of 1523 around their "queen," the beautiful Costanza Amaretta, and decides to spend a few idyllic days exchanging stories and discoursing on love. Pietro Fortini's *Novelle*, divided into two parts—the *Giornate delle novelle de' novizi* and the *Piacevoli et amorose notti de' novizi*—presents a band of virtuous and witty ladies who together with several elegant youths meet over a number of days in a garden, a meadow, and elsewhere and engage in entertainments, including storytelling, for no apparent reason other than their desire for some amusement.

In these and other such cornices cold winters and uncomfortable summers naturally give way to the mildest times of the year. Hence it is that the three friends Celio, Fabio, and Montano of Lugo y Dávila's *Teatro popular* spend several springtime afternoons in a garden relating *novelas*. The prolific Castillo Solórzano contributed two frames of this type. In his *Tardes entretenidas* two families decide to pass the month of May on the banks of the Manzanares near Madrid. The later *Huerta de Valencia* presents five gentlemen who retire to their villas along the seashore and for several pleasant days entertain each other with stories, verse, and music. Finally, Pérez de Montalbán offers in his *Para todos* a frame in which various friends meet in a city dwelling as well as in country settings to relate tales, perform plays, recite verse, and so on, again apparently just for the sheer joy of doing so.

As the late Rosalie L. Colie remarked, a thorough understanding and appreciation of Renaissance literary theory is impossible if one neglects to take into account the "real" literature of the age, for it is here that one discovers—or "recovers"—the "unwritten poetics by which writers worked and which they themselves created."[19] The novella cornice tradition clearly offers the modern reader a rich vein or documentary material concerning the very nature and substance of the "unwritten poetics" of the Renaissance. Our survey of the frame-narratives which bound together innumerable collections of tales throughout the three centuries during which this genre flourished has taken us from a time in which imaginative literature had to be defended and justified as a source if not of historical truth or moral teaching at least of recreation for "appropriate people" at "appropriate times," to the very threshold of the time in which fiction could be accepted and studied simply as the complexly seductive, enigmatically protean thing it is.

Finally, it should be noted that the practice of binding together a series of short narratives with a frame-tale did not altogether end with the Renaissance. Indeed, writers of German *Novellen* revived the long dormant tradition in the Romantic Age, as indicated by such works as Goethe's *Unterhaltungen deutscher Ausgewanderten* (1795), Wieland's *Das Hexameron von Rosenhain* (1805), E. T. A. Hoffmann's *Die Serapionsbrüder* (1819-21), and Jeremias Gotthelf's *Die schwarze Spinne* (1842). In the latter half of the nineteenth century the *Rahmen* tradition was continued by writers like Theodor Storm, Gottfried Keller, and C. F. Meyer, and, as evidenced by Longfellow's *Tales of a Wayside Inn* (1863) and William Morris' *The Earthly Paradise* (1868-70), even seems to have worked its way into England and America. Still, one is compelled to conclude that the employment of the frame-narrative to illustrate and reinforce the author's claim of the recreational function of his tale collection seems unique to the Renaissance novella tradition.

II. Unity by Time, Theme, and Title

The novellist's quest for the ideals of order, unity, and harmony in his work did not stop with the use of a cornice. In fact, along with a unity of place often supplied by the frame-story, one frequently finds in many a novella anthology a conscious unity by time. Like the author or compiler of, for example, the Eastern *Thousand and One Nights* (Sir Richard Burton's title *The Arabian Nights* abandons a tradition), the novellists tended to incorporate such a time span within their very titles. Typical titles of collections include the *Decameron,* the *Heptaméron,* and the *Pentamerone.*

Boccaccio's ten-day limitation, moreover, at least as old as the *Bakhtiyar-nama,* generally inspired his followers to imitate not only his egregious total of stories (e.g., the *Cent Nouvelles nouvelles* and Rastell's *One Hundred Merry Tales),* but his use of the decimal time limit as well. Marguerite de Navarre's incomplete *Heptaméron,* originally entitled *Le Decaméron,* was apparently intended likewise to cover a span of ten days. Furthermore, like Boccaccio's collection, it too presents ten storytellers, each of whom recites one tale a day. The more complex frame-tale of Giraldi's *Ecatommiti* includes some twenty personages, ten young ladies and as many gentlemen, only ten of whom, however, are allowed to recite during any given day. One hundred novellas are told during ten days of the trip to Marseilles, not including a previous ten exchanged by only the men on the first day of the shipboard voyage.

Some of Boccaccio's disciples, with a respect reminiscent of Vergil, reduced their master's time limit precisely in half. Yver divided his *Printemps* into five "journées." Basile relates in the *Pentamerone* the events of the last five days of Lucia's pregnancy. In Tirso de Molina's *Cigarrales de Toledo* a group of wealthy gentry agrees to pass an equal number of days—each one in the villa of a different member—playing games, acting in plays, reciting verse, and relating tales. Doubtless in imitation, Castillo Solórzano's *Huerta de Valencia,* Part I of María de Zayas's *Novelas exemplares y amorosas,* and Mariana de Caravajal's *Navidades de Madrid* all similarly take place over a course of five days.

A convenient way for some novellists to give their collections unity by time was to connect their stories to the seven days of the week. George Whetstone's *An Heptameron of Civil Discourses* begins on Christmas and ends on New Year's Day. Although the Spanish novellist Pérez de Montalbán also set the frame-narrative of his *Para todos* over seven days, his fellow countryman Castillo Solórzano, more properly omitting a sabbath day, composed more than half dozen collections which transpire over six consecutive days, four of which incidentally—the *Tardes entretenidas,* the *Jornadas alegres,* the *Alivios de Casandra,* and the *Quinta de Laura*—retain and even extend the Boccaccesque sense of symmetry by presenting not only six storytellers, but a total of six stories as well.

Finally, the number three, always popular in Western literature as a structural device, was conspicuously employed by another prominent group of novellists. Three carnival days, we recall, provide the setting in time for Grazzini's *Cene,* Bargagli's *Trattenimenti,* Hidalgo's *Diálogos de apacible entretenimiento,* Castillo Solórzano's *Tiempo de regocijo,* Tirso's *Deleitar aprovechando,* and Bermúdez's *Carnestolendas de Cádiz.* A most original contribution to this widespread practice was *Penelope's Web* by Robert Greene. The frame of Greene's work tells of the patient Penelope during the absence of Ulysses. Following Homer, Greene has the faithful wife promise to wed a wooer only after she completes the web which she is weaving. This goes on (at least in this version) for three nights, during each of which Penelope relates many tales to her maids as she dutifully unravels what she has woven during the day. At the end of the third night, Ulysses returns, bringing the cornice, of course, to an abrupt end.

One important factor that probably helped dictate the number of days chosen was the requirement of verisimilitude, for the total had to correspond logically with the lapse of time required for the situation which prompted the relation of tales to run its natural course. Hence a fortnight–ten days for telling stories, the others for observing the holy days—is an adequate time span for the plague substantially to subside in Boccaccio's Florence and also for the young people of the *Decameron* cornice to absent themselves from the stricken city without provoking a scandal. The eight days needed to journey from Southwark to Canterbury and back again, as estimated by Robert Dudley French,[20] who does not take into account any number of stops along the way, is surely adequate enough time for each of Chaucer's pilgrims to tell his or her four tales.

Later novelists appear also to have sought such a logical correspondence between the number of tales and the time inevitably elapsing during the cornice situation. Apparently familiar with the swift-coursing rivers of the Pyrenees, Marguerite de Navarre knew that eight or ten days at the Notre-Dame de Serrance would be adequate for the swollen rivers from that watershed to return to normal levels. Even the local workmen, unconsciously focusing on the time limit of the *Decameron*, assure the abbé that they could not bridge the local river in fewer than ten or twelve days. Likewise, it is altogether fitting for the sportsmen in Parabosco's *Diporti* to wait three days for a storm to blow over before they resume their venatical and piscatorial pleasures, or for Erizzo's students to take a six-day summer break in their studies.

This unique blend of verisimilitude and unity by time is no less obvious in larger collections which require a cornice of greater flexibility. Giraldi's fugitives in the *Ecatommiti* allow themselves considerable time to share their more than one hundred stories on their long sea voyage to Marseilles, and the peregrines of Sercambi's *Novelle* have ample time to hear 155 tales as they make a circular flight from the plague in Lucca to Naples, Brindisi, Venice, Genoa, and back to Luni, northwest of Lucca.

Another commonly encountered example of the novellist's passion for organization and unity is the conscious division of tales according to theme. Once again Oriental precedents exist. The tales of the *Panchatantra* (or *Book of Five Headings*) are classified under the following rubrics: discord among friends; the winning of friends; war and peace; loss of property; and the consequences of ill-considered action. The four topics that motivate the stories of the *Lalita Vistara* and its European adaptation *Barlaam and Josaphat* are old age, sickness, poverty, and death.

Although almost every one of the stories and anecdotes of the pre-Boccaccesque *Cento novelle antiche* falls into one or more of the general categories announced in the Proem of that collection (e.g., worthy deeds, acts of courtesy, love),[21] it is once again Boccaccio who, perhaps recalling this earlier Italian work or the Eastern collections, was the first novellist to structure his book of novellas according to theme. Each day of the *Decameron* frame-narrative finds a new king or queen who decides the topic for that day. Filomena and Neifile declare that the stories of the second and third days should deal, respectively, with those who reach an unhoped-for end after passing through various adventures and with those who through ingenuity acquire something greatly desired or recover something lost. Days Four and Five, thanks to Filostrato and Fiammetta, offer contrasting themes: loves that have an unhappy ending and those that after unfortunate experiences have a happy outcome. After Elisa's day of tales in which shrewdness, witticisms, or quick retorts enable people to escape loss, danger, or contempt, there is another pair of days with complementary themes suggested this time by Dioneo and Lauretta: tricks played by wives on their husbands (Day Seven) and tricks played by men upon women, women upon men, and men upon men (Day Eight). On the final day, presided over by Pamfilo, the theme of liberality in human behavior is treated. It is interesting to note that under the separate rules of Pampinea and Emilia on the first and ninth days, respectively, the party is allowed to recount stories on any subject. The inclusion of such *ad libitum* days might well indicate that Boccaccio and subsequent novellists as collectors of tales often could not apportion the hoard of stories in hand into a balanced disposition.

Masuccio Salernitano in the late fifteenth century distributed the fifty novellas of his *Novellino* according to the following topics: ecclesiastic or monastic misconduct; jealous men; females treated cruelly; miscellaneous subjects; and magnanimity. Another writer of novellas of the following century who is also most precise about the themes of his tales is Giambattista Giraldi. After an introductory group of ten tales dealing with the shameful loves of certain young men toward unchaste women, Giraldi assigns a theme to each *deca* of the *Ecatommiti:*

    I   On any subject that is most pleasing to everyone.
    II On those who loved secretly or against the wishes of their elders and ended either happily or unhappily.
    III On the infidelity of husbands and wives.
    IV On those who perpetrate treacherous acts but in the end are duly punished.
    V On the fidelity of husbands and wives.
    VI On acts of courtesy
    VII On witty sayings and quick retorts.
  VIII On ingratitude.
    IX On the fickleness of fortune.
    X On acts of chivalry.

The classification of witty and quick retorts initiated by Boccaccio spills over into Bandello's work, where they occupy Novella III, 32, 41, and 48. In the last of these Bandello even furnishes a cornice for them, a dinner shared by "a few gentlemen" in Milan's Convento delle Grazie. Like Boccaccio, the company agrees that "a witty saying can save one from great danger."

In France Marguerite de Navarre, as conscious an imitator of Boccaccio as Giraldi, explicitly explains the subject of each of the eight days of her *Heptaméron:*

    I   On evil tricks played by women on men and by men on women.
    II On whatever comes into the imagination of each teller.
    III On women who only seek honesty in love, and the hypocrisy and wickedness of those in religious orders.

   IV   On the virtuous patience and long waiting of women for
        their husbands and the prudence of men toward women.
    V   On the virtue of girls and women who have preferred
        honor to pleasure, and those who have done the opposite.
   VI   On deceits performed by man to woman, woman to man,
        or woman to woman.
  VII   On those who have done the opposite of what they should
        have or wanted to do.
 VIII   On the greatest and truest follies against which everyone
        may be on guard.

The three stories enframed in another sixteenth-century collection,
Greene's *Farewell to Folly,* are devoted to three of the Seven Deadly
Sins: pride, lust, and gluttony.

   English novellists, with the exception of Greene, as a rule rarely
grouped their tales under assigned headings; one does detect,
nonetheless, in the work of Chaucer and Fenton, for example, a
more subtly arranged unannounced grouping of stories. In the
Canterbury Tales, as George Lyman Kittredge has shown, Chaucer
seems consciously to have fashioned from the "Wife of Bath's
Tale" through the "Clerk's Tale" and the "Merchant's Tale" to
the "Franklin's Tale" a series of related tales on the subject of
marriage.[22] The moralistic Fenton, perhaps encouraged by Boccaccio's practice, appears to divide his *Tragical Discourses* into pairs.
The first two stories deal with the subject of love and marriage:
Anselmo and Angelica marry and share a happy future (Discourse
I), whereas Lyvyo and Camilla, forbidden to marry, attempt an
illicit sexual relationship but die as they are about to consummate
their desires—one of inordinate joy, the other of excessive grief
(Discourse II). The next two stories present us with two figures, one
male and one female, who let passion rule their reason and
consequently commit acts of extreme violence. Discourse V,
basically a fabliau, can be interpreted only as comic relief, as an
interlude which is indeed a welcome breeze after the two previous
accounts of Senecan horror. The next four tales offer two pairs of
contrasting women. Parolina of the sixth story is a model of virtue;
the Countess of Celant, on the other hand, submits to the demands
of the flesh, then dabbles in adultery and murder, and is finally

executed (Discourse VII). The next contrasting pair consists of the chaste Julya, who upon being sexually violated throws herself into the sea rather than live a life of shame (Discourse VIII); and the Lady of Cabrio, another adulteress and accessory to murder, who concludes her life in disgrace (Discourse IX). The tenth and eleventh tales are concerned with two young men confronted with fleshly temptation: Luchino, who virtuously resists when his beloved is at his mercy; and Philiberto, who thoroughly succumbs when given the same opportunity. Coming full circle, the two final stories treat the themes of love and marriage just as did the first pair. In Discourse XII the married Perillo and Carmosyna by a quirk of fate die, as did Lyvyo and Camilla, in bed as they are on the very brink of tasting the first fruits of their love. In the last of Fenton's stories, as in his first, a maiden's lack of love is metamorphosed into true affection, and all ends in marriage with happiness ever after.

Of the two books of the *Novelas amorosas y ejemplares,* María de Zayas gives only the second thematic unity. These novellas must be true stories ("casos verdaderos") dealing with disillusionments ("desengaños").[23] Seventeenth-century Spain produced also Montalbán's *Para todos,* which offers an elaborate grouping of tales related to the days of the week. Hence, the seven gentlemen involved in its cornice on succeeding days present stories concerning Apollo (Sunday), the moon (Monday), Mars (Tuesday), Mercury (Wednesday), Jupiter (Thursday), Venus (Friday), and Saturn (Saturday).

Such was the strength of the novellistic impulse to organize and unify that even among those collections eschewing the use of a frame-tale one finds many that implied a cornice or some other kind of literary device to bind the tales together. For the *Cent Nouvelles nouvelles,* Pierre Champion has created a realistic Burgundian cornice for the tale spinning at the court of Duke Philippe le Bon:

> Evenings were long and tedious for people of those days, whether in court or cottage. A few friends, to please their master, a man troubled by the *démon du midi,* told a few racy and pleasant tales. The Duke wanted more "nouvelles his-

toires." To enjoy the candlelight and the warmth of the coals in the hearth, others joined his audience. . . . Who couldn't remember some story from that adventurous life led by the people of Holland, England, Italy, Flanders, or Burgundy? They talked of churchmen and women, some seeking in their book of memory or the book of Poggio—no matter which. Each has his little "rakeful" to tell, as discreetly as possible, without mentioning names or places. The chivalrous spirit of the Duke would not permit that.[24]

Perhaps in imitation of Masuccio Salernitano, who ostensibly sent off his novellas one by one as they were written, to friends and patrons, Bandello attached to each of his stories a dedicatory letter to a person of position or influence, usually containing a description of the occasion on which the story was told and the circumstances connected with its narration—a concession to the cornice principle. (One of these dedications was to his fellow novellist Marguerite de Navarre.) Walter Pabst has significantly referred to these prefatory epistles as "individual frame-letters." [25]

William Painter imagines his collection to be a "Palace of Pleasure" that "is bedecked and garnished with sumptuous hanginges and costlye arras of splendent shewe" which record "princely partes and glorious gestes of renowned wights." [26] In some cases, such as Rastell's *Hundred Merry Tales* and Des Périers' *Nouvelles récréations,* a title serves to lend unity and cohesion to the assorted novellas within.

From the eighteenth century to the present scholars have tried to isolate the most meaningful motifs in the *Novelas ejemplares.* Agustín Amezúa y Mayo's study, *Cervantes creador de la novela corta española* (1956) lists the major classifications since 1797. Typical are those categories which vary from generic and tonal to thematic or topical.

1797: Heroic, comic, popular, and humorous (Pellicer)
1890: Ideal of perfection, social vices and prejudices, sheer satire (Orellana y Rincón)
1917: Lived experience, invented tales, mixture of each (Rodríguez Marín)

1933: Everyday life, customs, sententious wisdom (Pfandl)
1946: Love, marriage, miscellaneous (Casalduero)

More recently Chandler and Schwartz in their history of Spanish literature separate the tales between idealistic/romantic and realistic/satirical *costumbrismo*.[27] Finally, E. C. Riley has declared that Cervantes "looks on exemplariness as a common attribute of the stories, binding them into a sort of unity, which in the collections of Boccaccio and most later *novellieri* had been provided by the background or the frame of the story-telling." [28]

The pursuit of such artistic ideals as unity, harmony, order, balance, and equilibrium, so intense and so prevalent in the novella tradition, may well indicate that many novellists, complementing the efforts of theorists like Bonciani, strove to transform the popular new literary type into an art form consistent with the aims of Renaissance classicism, attempting perhaps in doing so to rival in artistic legitimacy and achievement those of their contemporaries who worked in the more accepted literary genres.[29]

Notes

1. See Richard L. Hoffmann, *Ovid and the "Canterbury Tales"* (Philadelphia: Univ. of Pennsylvania Press, 1966), pp. 3-20, who also suggests that other Ovidian "tales within tales," such as Phoebus and the Raven (Book II) and the contests between the Muses and the Pierides (Book II) and between Pallas and Arachne (Book VI), may have lent additional inspiration to the development of the novella *cornice* tradition. Gilbert Highet mentions the possible Plato and Petronius analogues in *The Classical Tradition* (1949: rpt. New York: Oxford Univ. Press, 1970), p. 89.

2. The following discussion has greatly benefited from the solid scholarship of such basic books as Krishna Chaitanya, *A New History of Sanskrit Literature* (London: Asia Publishing House, 1962), esp. pp. 360-401; A. J. Arberry, *Classical Persian Literature* (London: Allen and Unwin, 1958), esp. 164-85; John Dunlop, *The History of Fiction*, 3 vols. (Edinburgh: Longman, 1816); Marcelino Menéndez y Pelayo, *Orígenes de la novela*, ed. Enrique Sánchez Reyes, 4 vols. (Madrid: Consejo Superior de Investigaciones Científicas, 1961); Letterio Di Francia, *Novellistica*, Vol. I (Milan: F. Vallardi, 1924-25); and George Tyler Northup, *An Introduction to Spanish Literature*, ed. Nicholson B. Adams (Chicago: Univ. of Chicago Press, 1960).

3. Lin Yutang, *The Wisdom of China and India* (New York: Random House, 1942), p. 297.

4. On this point see Gaston Paris, *La littérature française au moyen âge* (Paris:

Hachette, 1890), p. 112; and Joseph Bédier, *Les fabliaux* (Paris: Champion, 1925), pp. 83-84 and 133-35.

5. Valency and Levtow, p. 10.

6. Vittore Branca, "Coerenza dell'introduzione al *Decameron,*" *Romance Philology,* 13 (1960), 351-60.

7. For a broad sampling of critical writings on the novella cornice see John Addington Symonds, *Renaissance in Italy: Italian Literature* (1881; rpt. New York: Capricorn, 1964), esp. II, 44-92; Thomas F. Crane, *Italian Social Customs of the Sixteenth Century* (New Haven: Yale Univ. Press. 1920); Letterio Di Francia, *Novellistica,* Vols. I and II; Caroline B. Bourland, *The Short Story in Spain in the Seventeenth Century* (Northampton, Mass.: Smith College Publications, 1927); Edith Kern, "The Gardens in the *Decameron* Cornice," *PMLA,* 66 (1951), 505-23; Walter Pabst, *Novellentheorie und Novellendichtung;* Janet M. Ferrier, *Forerunners of the French Novel* (Manchester: Manchester Univ. Press, 1954); Vittore Branca, "Coerenza dell'introduzione al *Decameron"* (see n. 6 above): Maurice Valency, *Palace of Pleasure,* esp. pp. 2-8; Yvonne Rodax, *The Real and the Ideal in the Novella of Italy, France and England;* Helaine Newstead, ed., *Chaucer and His Contemporaries* (New York: Fawcett, 1968), pp. 9-27; Erich Auerbach, *Zur Technik der Frührenaissancenovelle in Italien und Frankreich* (Heidelberg: C. Winter, 1971), pp. 4-19; Robert J. Clements, "Anatomy of the Novella," *Comparative Literature Studies,* 9 (1972). 3-16; and Joseph Gibaldi, "The *Decameron* Cornice and the Responses to the Disintegration of Civilization," *Kentucky Romance Quarterly,* 24 (1977), in press.

8. Joel E. Spingarn, *Literary Criticism in the Renaissance* (1899; rpt. New York: Harbinger, 1963), p. 3.

9. See Spingarn's first chapter, "The Fundamental Problem of Renaissance Criticism," especially the section entitled "Mediaeval Conception of Poetry," pp. 3-15; and the chapter "Platonism: I. The Defence of Poetry" in Bernard Weinberg, *A History of Literary Criticism in the Italian Renaissance,* I, 250-96.

10. William Nelson, *Fact or Fiction,* p. 56.

11. Wayne C. Booth, *The Rhetoric of Fiction* (Chicago: Univ. of Chicago Press, 1961), esp. pp. 151-53.

12. "Appresso assai ben si può cognoscere queste cose non nella chiesa . . . né ancora nelle scuole de' filosofanti . . . ma ne' giardini, in luogo di sollazzo, tra persone giovani, benché mature e non pieghevoli per novelle, in tempo nel quale andar con le brache in capo per iscampo di sé era alli più onesti non disdicevole, dette sono," *Decameron,* p. 674.

13. Jourda, p. 706.

14. See Giraldi, pp. 1-7.

15. "E, per dirne la verità, noi semo ora per carnevale, nel qual tempo è lecito ai Religiosi di rallegrarsi; e i frati tra loro fanno pallone, recitano comedie, e travestiti suonano, ballano e cantano; e alle monache ancora non disdice, nel rappresentare le feste, questi giorni vestirsi da uomini, colle berrette di velluto in testa, colle calze chiuse in gamba, colla spada al fianco. Perchè dunque a noi sarà sconvenevole o disonesto il darci piacere novellando?," *Novelle del Cinquecento,* I, 252-53.

16. ". . . la poesia sia stata trouata solamente per dilettare . . ." *Poetica d'Aristotile Vulgarizzata,* 2nd ed. (Basel: P. de Sedabonis, 1576), p. 29. (See Weinberg, I, 504.)

17. John Dryden, *Of Dramatic Poesy and Other Critical Works,* ed. George Watson (London; Dent, 1962), I, 113.

18. *Novelas a Marcia Leonarda,* p. 74.

19. Rosalie L. Colie, *The Resources of Kind: Genre-Theory in the Renaissance,* ed. Barbara K. Lewalski (Berkeley: Univ. of California Press, 1973), p. 4.

20. Robert Dudley French, *A Chaucer Handbook* (New York: Appleton-Century-Crofts, 1947), pp. 196-98.

21. " . . . facciamo qui memoria d'alquanti fiori di parlare, di belle cortesie e di belli risponsi e di belle valentie, di belli donari e belli amori . . ." *Novellino e Conti del Duecento,* p. 1.

22. George Lyman Kittredge, "Chaucer's Discussion of Marriage," *Chaucer Criticism,* ed. Richard Schoeck and Jerome Taylor (Notre Dame: Univ. of Notre Dame Press, 1960), pp. 130-59.

23. María de Zayas y Sotomayor, *Novelas amorosas y exemplares,* ed. María Martínez del Portal (Barcelona: Bruguera, 1973), p. 333.

24. Pierre Champion, *Les Cent Nouvelles nouvelles* (Paris: Droz, 1928), Preface.

25. Pabst, *Novellentheorie und Novellendichtung,* p. 55.

26. Jacobs, I, 14.

27. All the preceding sets of motifs are listed in R. J. Clements, "Anatomy of the Novella," *Comparative Literature Studies,* 9 (1972), 1.

28. See Riley, *Cervantes's Theory of the Novel,* p. 103.

29. Salinari adds his belief that the cornice gives "unità e compattezza alle diverse composizioni e ai diversi argomenti, secondo le simpatie rinascimentali verso opere ampie, decorative e composte e che corrispondono poi a un ideale di equilibrio, di ordine e di serenità . . ." *Novelle del Cinquecento,* I, 22.

CHAPTER 3

Characters and
Characterization

I. Types and Stereotypes

Within the brief discussion accorded the *Decameron* in *The Rhetoric of Fiction,* Wayne Booth makes the common observation that Boccaccio's characters are essentially "two-dimensional, with no revealed depths of any kind."[1] There can, indeed, be little question that the personages who populate the fictive landscape of the novella tradition, beginning even with Boccacio's precursors, belong with few exceptions to the type of literary characterization variously described as "flat" (E. M. Forster)[2] or "static" (Wellek and Warren).[3] Of course, in an artistic medium for which brevity was demanded, it is no wonder that the novella was in the main a strictly plot-centered genre. Maurice Valency rightly notes:

As a rule, the chief interest of the *novella* is in the narrative sequence, the story line or plot. Few of these stories, if any, were intended to create a mood, and very few go beyond the most elementary sort of characterization.[4]

Nor were the Italians the only novellists to employ "flat" and "static" characters. Professors Patricia and Rouben Cholakian, excepting Marguerite de Navarre, write of the typical figure in the French *nouvelle*, "He was a stock character, a stereotype, who behaved like a puppet in a preordained manner." [5] With Cervantes aside this time, Caroline B. Bourland in her study of the Spanish *novela* in the seventeenth century adds, "Generally speaking, there is little to distinguish one hero or one heroine from another, and the Claras, Leonardas, Elviras of Montalbán, Castillo Solórzano, Zayas, Lozano and the rest, seem cut from the same piece of cloth." [6]

The personalities of such recurrent novellistic types as the jealous older husband, the lively young wife, the persistent paramour, the magnanimous knight, the faithful but falsely accused lady of the court, the star-crossed lovers, the quick-thinking rogue, and the lecherous priest are, to use Booth's terminology,[7] usually *told* rather than *shown*—or, more properly, *told* and then *shown*—to the listener-reader. The customary practice was to inform the audience of a character's stock personality at the outset or "prologue" of the tale and then to present striking illustrations of that personality in action. Thus at the beginning of his very first novella Boccaccio says of Ser Ciappelletto, "He was perhaps the worst man ever born." [8] Needless to say, nothing in the miscreant's subsequent behavior works in the least to alter that judgment. Likewise is Monna Giovanna's complete character summed up in Boccaccio's introduction of her in V:9 as not only among the most beautiful women in our time, but one who was "no less virtuous than beautiful."[9]

Chaucer, as is often pointed out, was in both his frame-narrative and his tales perhaps without equal in this kind of character depiction. Here in quick, broad, masterful strokes are some justly celebrated examples of novellistic portraiture as practiced in the General Prologue of *The Canterbury Tales:*

The Knight:

> A Knyght ther was, and that a worthy man,
> That fro the tyme that he first bigan

> To riden out, he loved chivalrie,
> Trouthe and honour, fredom and curteisie.[10]

The Wife of Bath:

> In felaweship wel koude she laughe and carpe.
> Of remedies of love she knew per chaunce,
> For she koude of that art the old daunce.[11]

The Parson:

> . . . rich he was of hooly thoght and werk.
> He was also a lerned man, a clerk,
> That Cristes gospel trewely wolde preche;
> His parishens devoutly wolde he teche.[12]

The Miller:

> His mouth as greet was as a greet forneys.
> He was a janglere and a goliardeys,
> And that was moost of synne and harlotries,
> Wel koude he stelen corn and tollen thries.[13]

In the tale recited by the last of these pilgrims we have a familiar cast of characters: the husband John ("Jalous he was . . . and he was old"), his eighteen-year-old wife Alisoun ("She was wylde and yonge"), and their lodger Nicholas ("Of deerne love he koude and of solas;/And therto he was sleigh and ful privee").[14] The Pardoner's exemplum of the three "riotoures" begins thus:

> In Flaundres whilom was a compaignye
> Of yonge folk that haunteden folye,
> As riot, hasard, stywes, and tavernes,
> Where as with harpes, lutes, and gyternes,
> They daunce and pleyen at dees both day and nyght,
> And eten also and drynken over hir myght,
> Thurgh which they doon the devil sacrifise

Withinne that develes temple, in cursed wise,
By superfluytee abhomynable.[15]

There is in the novella, furthermore, little of what teachers of
literature like to refer to as "character development." If a moral or
spiritual or psychological transformation does occur within a
personage, it is usually on the sudden, and the metamorphosis is
completed almost instantaneously—more a revolution than an
evolution in character. In older collections of tales, religious
conversion is common. The eightieth story in the late mediaeval
Gesta Romanorum concerns a hermit who is traveling with an angel
and who witnesses his celestial companion successively strangle a
sleeping infant, purloin a golden cup, and drown an innocent
wayfarer. When the horrified hermit refuses to accompany the
seemingly treacherous angel any farther, the latter explains that
the death of the infant enabled the child's father to become a more
devout Christian, that the theft of the cup returned its of late often
intoxicated owner to his former sobriety, and the drowning of the
pilgrim prevented this holy man from falling into the mortal sin
for which he was headed. Hearing this explanation, the hermit, we
are told, falls at the feet of the angel and entreats pardon,
returning at last to his hermitage no longer a doubter but a good
and pious Christian.

Other sudden though not necessarily spiritual metamorphoses
abound in the *Gesta*. In Tale 39 it is fear that brings about the
transformation. When a man maliciously lays waste the lands of
his own brother, the emperor determines to punish the offender
with death. The hunted criminal immediately goes to his brother
to ask for forgiveness and for protection against the emperor's
decree. The injured sibling thereupon sues and receives from his
sovereign a pardon for his now reformed brother, and all ends in
peace and harmony. Sometimes such metamorphoses in the *Gesta*
come about after some tragic event. The queen in the thirteenth
story turns to the religous life after she has committed incest and
infanticide, Julian in Tale 18 after he has ignorantly killed both his
parents.

In the *Decameron* and later collections witty comments or love or exhibitions of generosity are more likely to effect a radical change of character. The insinuating anecdote related by Bergamino in the seventh story of the *Decameron* succeeds in driving out the avarice which had begun to appear in Can Grande della Scala (I:7). Just one look at the sleeping Efigenia changes the formerly brutish Cimone of V:1 into a refined, civilized, and virtuous young man, "passing in very short time [we are informed] from one way of thinking to another." [16] In the fifth tale of the last day Messer Ansaldo, the ardent suitor of Madonna Dianora, marvels at the liberality of the husband Gilberto, and at once, even though his beloved is sexually at his mercy, "his fervor began to change into compassion,"[17] resulting in his own generous refusal of the lady's favors.

II. "Of Sondry Folk"

If the demand for brevity in the novella precluded on the part of most novellists any significant psychological probing or any individuation of character, the end product being instead flat, static, two-dimensional characterization, the novellistic quest for variety insured that the novella collection could at least offer a rich and glorious gallery of character-types. Among the diverse characters of the *Conde Lucanor,* for instance, Enrique Moreno Baez numbers "rich and poor, Moors and Christians, nobles and peasants, beggars and merchants, priests and picaros, wise men and madmen, bourgeois and prelates, philosophers and courtesans, as well as many animals that speak in its fables and historical personages that are Spanish, not to mention Richard the Lion-Hearted, Emperor Frederick the Great, and Saladin." [18] In the General Prologue of the *Canterbury Tales* Chaucer presents as interlocutors members of the feudal system, the town, and the church, included among whom are the indigent and the prosperous, the obtuse and the clever, the corrupt and the virtuous, the worldly and the spiritual. Although atypical among novellistic frame-narratives, most of which detail the experiences and entertainments of more aristocratic groups, the cornice of the *Canterbury Tales,* along with the stories in the *Conde Lucanor,* nevertheless

provides a useful and enlightening introduction to the varied
dramatis personae to most Renaissance novella collections, a
motley cast of characters which indeed often ranges up and down
the fictive chain of being from God Himself all the way to the
lowliest of beasts.

Religious figures are few in the tradition, and, when discovered,
are likely to be in those collections antecedent to Boccaccio.
Derived from biblical as well as extra-biblical sources, such
characters often fell victim to legend and consequently to confusion and distortion. In the eighty-third story of the *Cento novelle
antiche* we encounter Christ in an apocryphum warning his
disciples against the thirst for gold. Like the Christ of the miracle
plays, the Savior reveals himself twice in *Gesta Romanorum* 110. The
knight Placidus is hunting a stag when Christ appears as an image
on the brow of the beast, ordering the knight to hasten to the city
of Rome and be baptized. Placidus' wife meanwhile sees Christ in
a vision, and the whole family is baptized by the bishop of Rome.
In Tale 13 of the *Gesta Romanorum* the Virgin Mary herself appears
to the confessor of the incestuous, infanticidal queen to help effect
the salvation of the sinful woman. The *Gesta* also contains several
Old Testament figures. Noah, for example, is shown as the
discoverer of the wine which will cause his downfall (159), Queen
Esther in her more traditional role as the savior of her people (177).
Ultimately drawn from II Samuel and I Kings are the handful of
stories in the *Cento novelle antiche* which tell of David and Solomon.

Books of the lives of the saints, such as those of Iacopo da
Voragine and Domenico Cavalca, provided the sources for a
number of early novellas. Significant episodes from the biographies
of Saints Alexius, Julian, Eustachius, Peter, Bernard, and Gregory
are in the *Gesta Romanorum*. Gregory also figures in the *Cento novelle
antiche,* as does Paulinus. St. Dominick performing a miracle is the
subject matter for Cuento 14 of the *Conde Lucanor*. But saints, like
God the Father, Christ, and the Virgin Mary, are more often cited
than actually present in the novellas. The *Decameron,* for instance,
refers to Saints Arrigo, Benedict, Bernard, Brancazio, Dominick,
Francis, Galeone, George, Gregory, John, and Julian, just to start
down the alphabet.

After Boccaccio, who himself introduced Solomon in a story

recited on the penultimate day of the *Decameron*, the only novellist to make substantial use of religious material was Chaucer. The anti-Semitic tale narrated by the Prioress is an example of the literary type known as the Miracle of the Virgin. The "Second Nun's Tale," derived from the *Legenda aurea*, recounts the life of St. Cecilia. Among the "tragedies" related by the Monk are those of Adam, Samson, Nebuchadnezzar, Belshazzar, and Holofernes.

Included in the *Gesta Romanorum* are several angels (e.g., Tales 80, 127, 165) as well as, to give the other side its due, several devils. Two of its stories (160 and 162) concern females possessed by demons; another (163) tells of the Faust-like Celestinus, a young man who, unable to write some verses assigned to him by his tutor, exhorts the devil to do the homework for him, in the process very nearly ceding his soul to eternal damnation. Chaucer's Monk narrates the fall of Lucifer, once the "brightest of angels alle," but now "Sathanas," a creature of misery forever.[19] In the lighter "Friar's Tale" the devil disguised as a yeoman carries to hell a wicked summoner. By far the most humorous of novellas dealing with diabolical figures is Machiavelli's much imitated account of Belfagor, the demon who is chosen by his infernal colleagues to ascend to earth in order to see if women are as evil as scores of condemned souls claim they are, but who after not too many experiences with the "gentler sex" elects to return to hell rather than bear any further the innumerable sufferings which he finds attendant to the state of matrimony.

Characters drawn from mythology are likewise more apt to crop up in the earlier collections. Myths pertaining to Atalanta, Ariadne, Argus, Arion, Ulysses, Achilles, Pallas (the son of Evander in the *Aeneid*), and even Isis and Serapis are in the *Gesta Romanorum*. Stories devoted to Narcissus, Hercules, and the sons of Priam can be found in the *Cento novelle antiche*. Although Boccaccio paid scant attention to myth for the plots of his novellas, Chaucer included several mythological figures in the *Canterbury Tales*. Derived, interestingly enough, from Boccaccio's own epic poem the *Teseida*, the "Knight's Tale" anachronistically concerns "a duc that highte Theseus," the "lord and governour" of Athens who "conquered all the regne of Femenye" and then "weddede the queene Ypolita." [20] The Monk places within the personal *De casibus virorum* which he

relates the downfall of Hercules. Book II of Ovid's *Metamorphoses* is
the apparent source of the Manciple's tale of Apollo and the
telltale crow. The two narratives of the sixteenth day in Ser
Giovanni Fiorentino's *Pecorone* tell of the passing of Aeneas from
Troy into Italy. Sercambi treats in his Novella 131 the myth of
Pyramus and Thisbe.

There seems to have been something of a revival of interest in
mythological subjects among the novellists of the late Renaissance.
The sixth day of the *Giornate de' novizi* portion of Fortini's *Novelle*
contains the stories of Cupid and Psyche, Diana and Actaeon, the
Judgment of Paris, Venus and Mars, and Laocoön. Annibale
Romei made sophisticated use of myth for his *Discorsi,* in one of
which the relationship between the brothers Eros and Anteros is
employed to explain the nature of true love. Some of the
experiences undergone by Ulysses' long-faithful wife as she awaited
the return of her wandering spouse provides, as previously
mentioned, the frame of Greene's *Penelope's Web.* All but the last of
the stories in Pettie's *Petite Palace* are well-known classical tales,
including "Tereus and Progne," "Admetus and Alcestis," "Minos
and Pasiphae," and "Pygmalion." In seventeenth-century Spain
several writers of *novelas* turned to classical myths for subject
matter. Recited during the second *cigarral* of Tirso de Molina's
Cigarrales de Toledo is the "Fábula de Siringa"; the same author's
later *Deleitar de aprovechando* includes a *fábula* on Pyramus and
Thisbe. There is a romance devoted to the separation of Aeneas
and Creusa in Castillo Solórzano's *Tardes entretenidas,* and in the
Navidades de Madrid Mariana de Caravajal offers *fábulas* based on
the myths of Orpheus and Eurydice and the ever-popular Judgment of Paris.

More abundant in the novella tradition than either religious or
mythological figures are personages from ancient history. The
presence of such historical individuals alongside fictional counterparts lends a sense of historicity and authenticity to the whole.
This was apparently felt to be true even when the dropping of a
regal name served merely to set the historical period in which
events occurred. Thus Painter, for one, announces, "In the time
that Scipio Affricanus had besieged the City of Carthage ..."
(II,11), and Rastell, "In the reign of the most mighty and

victorious Prince, King Henry VIII . . ." (61). The compiler of the *Gesta Romanorum* was especially addicted to mentioning Roman emperors' names at the outset of his tales, to the discomfiture of modern scholars, who are called upon to clarify that "Pompey the Great" was not a prince of Rome (84), that Domitian was not wise and just (103), and so on.

Within many a tale figures from ancient history were themselves the central characters. As promised by its title, the *Gesta Romanorum* contains more than a score of stories dealing with Roman generals, politicians, and emperors, among whom are Pompey, Julius Caesar, Tiberius, Vespasian, Titus, Domitian, Trajan, Jovianus, and Theodosius. From even earlier times the compiler of the *Gesta* has chosen as subjects of his tales celebrated personages like Codrus, the last king of Athens; the famous tyrants of Sicily, Phalaris and Dionysius; King Demaratus of Laecedemon; the philosopher Aristotle; Philip of Macedon; Alexander the Great; and Darius III of Persia.

Aristotle and Alexander also appear in the *Cento novelle antiche* alongside Antigonus, Diogenes, Thales of Miletus, Socrates, Seneca, and Cato. Chaucer's Monk presents brief accounts of the lives and deaths of Croesus, Alexander, Zenobia, Julius Caesar, and Nero. Stories about Crassus, Boethius, Attila, and Constantine are in Ser Giovanni's *Pecorone.* Sercambi, another enthusiast of ancient history, relates novellas about Aristotle, Lucretia, Scipio, Hannibal, Julius Caesar, and Pompey.

That the sources of information about Greco-Roman history were indirect before the Cinquecento is amply proved by those early collections. Pompey is depicted as a "wise and powerful king" in the first tale of the *Gesta Romanorum;* in subsequent stories both Pliny (91) and the legendary Greek lawgiver Zaleucus (50) are metamorphosed into emperors. Anachronistic encounters between famous persons of different periods abound in the *Gesta.* In Tale 57 Vergil (d. 19 B.C.) constructs a magic statue for Titus (r. A.D. 79-81). Philip of Macedon, who sends Socrates out to rid his land of dragons in Tale 145, was born about seventeen years after the famous philosopher was sentenced to death. Even more confusing is the sixty-first tale, in which Socrates (d. 399 B.C.), Alexander the Great (356-323 B.C.), and the Roman emperor Claudius (10 B.C.-

A.D. 54) are shown as contemporaries. The composer of the *Cento novelle antiche,* also using defective source materials, similarly converts Socrates into a Roman philosopher (Novella 61). In Chaucer's "Monk's Tale" Julius Caesar is described as both the emperor of Rome and the son-in-law of Pompey; his chief assassin is said to be "Brutus Cassius." Sercambi's forty-ninth novella has Vergil fall in love with the daughter of the Emperor Hadrian (r. A.D. 117-38).

Of the later novellists, Erizzo in Italy and Painter in England seem the ones most fascinated by ancient times. Several "avvenimenti" in the *Sei giornate* concern figures like Antigonus, Zaleucus, Cambyses, and Hipparchus. Painter's *Palace of Pleasure* embraces dozens of stories drawn from, among others, Herodotus, Quintus Curtius, Tacitus, Plutarch, and especially "that excellent Historiographer Titus Liuius, in whom is contayned a large campe of noble facts and exploites atchieued by valiaunt personages of the Romaine state." [21] More historically accurate than his mediaeval predecessors, Painter devotes novellas to such famous stories as the rape of Lucretia, Mucius Scaevola's stoic courage, the traitorous deeds of the proud Coriolanus, Timon's misanthropy, the unhappy life and death of Sophonisba, and the licentious behavior of the Roman empress Faustina—several of which, of course, served as plot materials for contemporary English poets and playwrights. Pettie seems to have had in mind modern counterparts to the ancient figures to whom he alludes. In his tale "Sinnorix and Camma," the Elizabethan writes, "If this mislike you in my discourse, that I make Camma, use the example of the countesse of Salisbury, the Dutches of Savoy, and such who were of later yeeres, ... you must consider that my Camma is of fresher memory ... and of fresher hew than the fairest of them." [22]

Oriental countries not only were seminal in the development of the novella itself, but also provided the tradition with a good supply of heroes and villains. From the first, Saladin, sultan of Egypt and Syria during the late twelfth century, came off extremely well. Novella 25 of the *Cento novelle antiche* relates how the Saladin once contemplated conversion to Christianity, but upon seeing the lack of civility in Christians changed his mind. In the third story of the *Decameron* Saladin is pictured as a valorous, just, and generous ruler who repays in full and with unexpected interest his debt to his creditor Melchisedech. In X:9 this "valentissimo signore"[23] lavishly returns in his own nation the kindness he received in Pavia from Messer Torello. A similar story is Bandello's "A Kindness Shown by Mansor, King of Morocco and Pontiff of Mohammedanism, to a Poor Fisherman, His Subject" (I,57). Separated from his entourage by violent weather during a hunt, the Saladin-like Mansor, although he never reveals his identity, is very well treated by a poor fisherman. The sovereign later builds for his benefactor an entire city as a reward for the peasant's goodness.

Side by side with such magnanimous characters is a sizable crew of barbaric and bloodthirsty Arabic figures. Bandello tells how Mohammed II of Turkey in order to demonstrate his worthiness to rule over his restless subjects allegedly beheaded in cold blood before an assembled audience the beautiful Greek captive Irenea, with whom in neglect of his sultanic duties he had for some time been amorously dallying. Retold by Pierre Boiastuau, François Belleforest, and William Painter before being dramatized by George Peele and others, Bandello's novella, entitled "Mohammed, Emperor of the Turks, Cruelly Kills His Lady" (I,10), is surpassed in barbarous atrocities by his own later "Mohammed, Emperor of the Turks, Kills His Brothers, His Nephews, and Their Servants with Unheard of Cruelty" (II,13). Painter includes in his *Palace of Pleasure* (II,34) an example of the heartless cruelty of Mohammed II's great-grandson Suleiman I. This so-labeled "enemy of Christianity" at the instigation of his favorite wife Roxelana has his innocent son strangled to death. In his "El amante liberal" by Cervantes, who himself fought the Turk at the famous Battle of Lepanto, thereby losing the use of an arm, the conflict between the Christians and the Turks seems to reflect, as Ruth El Saffar suggests, the internal struggles within the main characters of the *novela*: Alí Baja, Hazán, and the Cadí, the three Turkish leaders who destroy each other because of their greed and treachery, are for El Saffar no more than "representatives of man's weakness and perdition."[24]

The world of chivalry supplied the anthologist of the *Gesta Romanorum* with the legend of Guy of Warwick for Tale 172 of that collection. Stories about Merlin, Lancelot, Tristan and Iseult, and the Lady of Shalott are in the *Cento novelle antiche*. Sacchetti writes of Charlemagne in his Novella 125. The wide diversity of the *Canterbury Tales* is illustrated by its inclusion of, on the one hand, perhaps the most chivalric of novellas in the "Knight's Tale," and, on the other, in the tale of Sir Thopas probably the only parody of a romance in the novella tradition. Charlemagne figures in two novellas in Erizzo's *Sei giornate,* and Antonio Eslava's *Noches de invierno* offers a rare example of the use of chivalric materials by a seventeenth-century novellist, for Eslava has set down in his work two *novelas* belonging to the Carolingian cycle: one on the birth of Charlemagne himself, the other on the birth and youth of Roland.

Novellistic characterization, it is no doubt becoming evident, embraced nearly the entire spectrum of human experience. Indeed, sometimes within a single collection one finds personality types belonging to all the various "fictional modes" so conveniently outlined by Northrop Frye.[25] For instance, the mythical, romantic, and high mimetic strands seem to blend in the myriad of exemplary figures illustrious for their piety, selflessness, fidelity, humility, patience, and magnanimity. An early example of such a character is that "certain king" in Tale 30 of the *Gesta Romanorum* who upon the occasion of some great victory contrives for there to be for him as many unpleasant, even demeaning experiences as there are glorious ones. Boccaccio, of course, sets aside the entire last day of the *Decameron* to those whose personal behavior has been marked by liberality. In the third story of that day (the source of Lessing's *Nathan der Weise*) the generosity of Nathan elicits murderous envy and then deep shame in Mithridanes before the two men become lifelong friends. The fifth tale is devoted to the incredible liberality of Messer Ansaldo, who insists, as will Arveragus of Chaucer's "Franklin's Tale," that his wife Dianora keep the foolish bargain she has made with Gilberto. The husband's *quid* is matched by Gilberto's *quo,* for the ardent young man, shocked by Ansaldo's idealistic actions into recognizing his own dishonorable intentions, allows Dianora to return home a chaste wife. Then, in a veritable orgy of magnanimity, the magician responsible for making Dianora's garden as beautiful in January as it is in May refuses to accept Gilberto's payment for the necromantic services rendered. The famous friendship of Titus and Gisippus is the subject of the eighth novella, and the very last tale of the *Decameron*, immediately after that of Saladin and Messer Torello, concerns the remarkable patience of Griselda, a story translated by Petrarch into Latin and subsequently used by Chaucer as his "Clerk's Tale."

On a moral and spiritual par with the very patient Griselda is Lady Constance of the "Man of Law's Tale."

> In hire is heigh beautee, withoute pride,
> Yowthe, withoute grenehede or folye;
> To alle hire werkes vertu is her gyde;
> Humblenesse hath slayn in hire all tirannye.
> She is mirour of all curteisye;
> Hir herte is verray chambre of hoolynesse,
> Hir hand, ministre of fredam for almesse.

So, we are told, went the "commune voys" of those who knew her, to which the Man of Law adds, "And al this voys was sooth, as God is trewe."[26] The pious Constance, protected by heaven through thick and thin (especially through thick, as one can imagine) finally arrives at a happy and a holy end. In the General Prologue Chaucer presents the brave but humble Knight as a lover of chivalry, truth, honor, generosity, and courtesy; the Parson as a devout, kindly, and totally selfless pastor of his parishioners; and his brother the Plowman as a charitable Christian laborer who would thresh and dig ditches for his fellow man without pay.

On a somewhat lower plane, though nonetheless magnanimous in his own way, is the young Galgano in the first tale of Ser Giovanni Fiorentino's *Pecorone*. Finally bedding down with the beautiful wife of an acquaintance of his, Galgano learns from the woman of the very high regard her husband Messer Stricca has for the would-be cuckolder. Although unclothed and already embracing his equally unclothed lady, the youth upon hearing these words at once springs up out of bed, dresses, and promises ever after to treat Messer Stricca with the affection and reverence that are due him. In the *Palace of Pleasure* (I,46) Painter presents a more traditional exemplary figure in his account, derived from Bandello

(II,37), of the Countess of Salisbury. This virtuous heroine successfully resists the amorous assaults of the impetuous King Edward II of England and is rewarded for her impregnable chastity by becoming (at least in this story if not in real life) the wife of Edward and the queen of England.

Belonging also to the high mimetic mode—in which characters are superior in degree to other men, though remaining very much within the order of nature—are the assorted "tragic" figures widely dispersed throughout the novella tradition, many of which were conveniently to serve Renaissance tragedians, especially in England, with plots readily adaptable for dramatic presentation. An early example of such a novella is Tale 72 of the *Gesta Romanorum,* an exemplum on ingratitude in which a certain king, no doubt an ancestor of Lear, resigns his supreme command to his own son, but is then severely treated by the youthful monarch and ultimately thrown into jail. A group of noblemen, grown indignant at the ill usage of the old man, restores the father to his rightful throne and casts the ungrateful son into prison for the rest of his life. The twenty-seventh tale of the same work also deals with "just recompense" for the abuse of authority. An emperor who resolves to go to the Holy Land entrusts to a seneschal the care of his only daughter. The seneschal's negligence in fulfilling his duty, however, results in the death of the girl, and, upon the emperor's return, his own torture and violent death.

Day Four of the *Decameron,* ruled over by Filostrato ("Victim of Love"), with the single exception of Dioneo's story is entirely given over to "those whose love had an unhappy end." Two of these concern women who engage in premarital sexual affairs with lovers beneath their station. In the first, Ghismonda's father Tancredi, prince of Salerno, has his daughter's paramour Guiscardo strangled to death and sends Ghismonda the young man's heart. After kissing the lifeless heart an infinite number of times, Ghismonda ends her life with poison. Three dishonored brothers wreak a bloody vengeance on their sister's lover and thus cause her to die of grief in the famous novella of Isabetta and Lorenzo, the inspiration for Keats's *Isabella, or The Pot of Basil.*

Cinquecento novellists in particular composed—or collected— many novellas that were in every respect noble successors to

Boccaccio's "tragical" tales with their decided accent on downfalls of the powerful and the fortunate through the awesome effects of love. In Bandello's "A Husband Finds His Wife Committing Adultery and Forces Her to Hang Her Lover" (II,12), not only, as indicated by the title of the tale, does the husband discover his wife *in flagrante delicto* and then compel her to kill her lover; he also locks the adultress up in very narrow quarters with the paramour's corpse until her death several years later. The lustful passions of the Countess of Challant, whose story is recounted by the same novellist (I,4), lead to infidelity as well as to murder, and, ultimately, to the beheading of the countess herself. More familiar to students of Elizabethan tragedy are Bandello's novella of the Duchess of Malfi (I,26) and Da Porto's (or Bandello's or Belleforest's or Painter's) of Romeo and Giulietta.

Giraldi took one such tale of his own (II:2)—that of Sulmone, the king of Persia who murders the valiant though lowborn husband of his daughter Orbecche and their two children as well, only to be murdered himself by the vengeful daughter—and converted it into the highly successful tragedy *Orbecche*. But, ironically, he did not do the same with his companion story of the Moor of Venice (III:7), leaving the great dramatic potential of this character for Shakespeare to realize fully.

Since the novella was, as Vittore Branca has shown,[27] a predominantly middle-class form of entertainment, it is no wonder that a large number of tales in the tradition present characters belonging to the low mimetic mode (that is, neither superior nor inferior to but roughly on the level of the average man). Indeed, many may be properly described as "comic heroes"—common men and women who move from an unhappy to a happy state. Day Two of the *Decameron* concerns those who, after passing through various adventures, reached an unexpected happy end; Day Three, those who by their wits either acquired something greatly desired or recovered something lost; the fifth day, those who won happiness after grief or misfortunes; and the sixth, those whose witty remarks saved them from destruction or danger or scorn. Rinaldo d'Esti (II:2) and Federigo degli Alberighi (V:9) are two of Boccaccio's better-known comic heroes. Robbed of everything but his shirt and left by three highwaymen in a snowstorm, Rinaldo receives shelter from a beautiful woman, enjoys her favors that same night, and the next day both regains his stolen possessions and witnesses the execution of the three thieves. Although the penniless and desperate Federigo serves as dinner to his beloved Monna Giovanna the very falcon which her dying son longs to own, the widow is so impressed by her longtime suitor's greatness of soul in sacrificing for her sake something so valuable to him that she chooses Federigo to be her second husband.

As they did with tragical tales, Renaissance playwrights frequently transformed such comic novellas into dramas. Shakespeare was certainly no exception. Boccaccio's stories of Giletta di Nerbona and her bed-switching ploy to ensnare the affections—or at least the hand in marriage—of Beltramo di Rossiglione (III:9) and Zinevra's efforts to restore her falsely tarnished reputation to its rightful state and to win back the love of her duped husband (II:9) are the acknowledged sources (through Painter) of, respectively, *All's Well that Ends Well* and *Cymbeline;* the tale in Ser Giovanni's *Pecorone* (IV:1) of the Jew who demands a pound of flesh in lieu of a payment due him, but who is outwitted in court by a lady disguised as a lawyer contains the novellistic seed of *The Merchant of Venice;* and *Twelfth Night* and *Measure for Measure* are in large part dramatic adaptations of the respective accounts of Apolonius and Silla in Barnabe Rich's *Farewell to the Military Profession* and Promos and Cassandra in George Whetstone's *An Heptameron of Civil Discourses.*

Perhaps the bulk of novellas belong to the ironic mode of fiction, concerning themselves with characters presented as inferior in power or intelligence to that of the reader. One thinks here immediately of the abundant social and ecclesiastical criticism found in the tradition. Through most collections passes, as we shall see in subsequent pages, a veritable parade of corrupt lawyers and judges as well as lecherous and avaricious clergymen.

To the possible embarrassment of the modern reader, most women also received such ironic treatment at the hands of the novellists. In another chapter we shall see in far greater detail how the writers of novellas, with few exceptions, followed the wide-

spread mediaeval and Renaissance tradition of misogynistic or at best antifeminist literature.[28] Time and again in the novella we are presented with females who are either hopelessly libidinous or weak-willed, sexually aggressive or readily seduced; who are the eager victims—or victimizers—of students, priests, or any other convenient males; and who, always disobedient and self-assertive in their homes, are outrageously ingenious at playing tricks on or otherwise outwitting their already or soon-to-be cuckolded husbands.

To be sure, there are in the novella tradition too the Zinevras and the Griseldas, the Constances and the Countesses of Salisbury, but they are few and far between, and, in their way, offer as unrealistic a portrait of women as the menagerie of wayward wives does. Doubtless the most important figures in the tradition who attempted to liberate the literary depiction of women from the Janus-like stereotypes of the Saint and the Whore were the two famous women novellists Marguerite de Navarre and María de Zayas. With these two writers, as we shall subsequently demonstrate, one discerns the very conscious and deliberate attempt to direct the novellistic depiction of the female from the ironic toward the high mimetic mode of fiction, in the process bestowing upon women in the novella not just a more realistic image, but a more admirable one as well.

A final group of characters connected with the ironic mode which certainly merits our attention includes the assorted simpletons, scamps, and rogues who circulate throughout many a collection rubbing elbows as they do with emperors and queens, with popes and knights, and with courageous women and tragic heroes. In earlier collections, simpletons conveniently served as subjects for exempla. The *Gesta Romanorum* contains two such tales on avarice: one tells of the fool who collected so much wood that the extreme weight upon his shoulders made him fall into a deep pit (46); the other concerns the man who willingly blinded himself to receive benefits from the state, but being found out was turned away penniless (73). The famous second tale in Juan Manuel's *Conde Lucanor* about the father and son on their way to market with their donkey teaches a very practical lesson on the problem of relying too heavily upon the opinions of others. The simpleton *par excellence* in the novella tradition is Boccaccio's zany Calandrino, duped by Bruno, Buffalmacco, and other supposed friends into believing, among other things, that he possesses a magic stone which makes him invisible (VIII:3) and even that he is pregnant, a condition which Calandrino immediately attributes to his wife's predilection for the superior position in their lovemaking (IX:3). The carpenter John in Chaucer's "Miller's Tale," who awaits the second "Nowelis flood" while his wife is both being "swyved" *and* tricking the squeamish Absalom into imparting upon her person his famous "misplaced kiss," remains a symbol for the many foolish husbands in the genre.

In accordance with traditional morality, scamps in the novella are occasionally punished, an ironically tragic note being attached to such tales. In the *Decameron* (II:1) Martellino's pretense that he is a cripple miraculously cured by St. Arrigo is discovered and results in a sound thrashing and a jail sentence for the sacrilegious faker. The relatives of the naive Madonna Lisetta also uncover Frate Alberto's ruse as the angel Gabriel and have him imprisoned as well (IV:2). The three "rioters" in Chaucer's "Pardoner's Tale" similarly receive just punishment for their many sins, and in Marguerite de Navarre's thirty-third *nouvelle* both a lecherous priest and the sister whom he has incestuously impregnated (and publicly proclaimed a second Mary blessed by immaculate conception) are burned at the stake.

More often than not, however, quick-witted scoundrels—whether moral, immoral, or just amoral—tend to prosper and flourish in the tradition. Even the *Gesta Romanorum* has a few such characters. The pilgrim in Tale 106 who eats the one loaf of bread possessed by the company with which he is traveling has a convenient excuse for doing so: an angel in a dream commanded him to, and he piously complied with the celestial wish. In Tale 132 three inferior physicians do away with a more successful rival by pretending he has leprosy. From the *Cento novelle antiche* comes the memorable anecdote of the man who holds his piece of bread near a kitchen to let it soak up the steam being emitted therefrom, and when payment is avariciously demanded for this service, he tenders to his self-proclaimed creditor the ringing sound of a dropped coin (9).

Boccaccio left as a legacy to his successors an extraordinary gallery of such figures. First and foremost is the unrepentant blackguard Ciappelletto, who talked himself right onto the calendar of saints (I:1). Chichibio the cook devours a leg of the crane he is preparing and escapes punishment when, upon finding on the bank of a river a crane asleep in its natural sleeping position, he proves to his master that cranes do indeed have only one leg (VI:4). The first novella of Day Eight concerns one Gulfardo—he is called Don John in the version found in Chaucer's "Shipman's Tale"—who to enjoy a certain woman's favors lends her money which he (unknown to the lady) has borrowed from her husband; when he is asked to pay back the sum, Gulfardo replies that he has already returned the money to the foolish wife, who must admit this is so. In the fifth tale of that same day three rogues steal the breeches right off a judge while he is sitting on the bench.

So much a part of the Boccaccesque world are such practical jokes that in some of his stories tricks are contrived specifically to counteract or to avenge other previous tricks. Made to look foolish by Biondello, Ciacco gets the erstwhile trickster into trouble with the violently irascible Filippo Argenti, from whom Biondello gets a terrible beating (IX:8). When he discovers right in the middle of saying mass that some jokers have substituted a piece of coal for the feather he claims comes from the wings of the angel Gabriel, that great improviser Fra Cipolla announces to his congregation that through the will of God he has brought with him that afternoon not the angelic feather but instead, as a reminder of the coming saint's day, one of the coals which roasted St. Lorenzo, thereby reaping that day greater profits than he usually made (VI:10).

Few characters created by later novellists rivaled such scoundrels as these. In the *Canterbury Tales* we have, of course, the Pardoner with *his* false relics as well as the Miller with his celebrated "thombe of gold." The clerk in the thirteenth tale in the *Cent Nouvelles nouvelles* who pretends to be a eunuch in order to become the lover of his master's wife seems a not-too-distant relative of Masetto da Lamporecchio, and clearly a disciple of Frate Alberto is the hermit in the very next *nouvelle* who arranges for not overly intelligent women who wish to have popes for sons to lie with a certain angel who is infallible in such matters. With Cervantes' Rinconete and Cortadillo and their crowd from the seamy side of Seville the Boccaccesque scamp evolves into the more modern character-type: the picaro.

The variety demanded for the novella was also served by the regular introduction into the tales of subhuman and supernatural figures. Animal characters, traceable to such sources as Aesop, Phaedrus, Marie de France, and the *Roman de Renard,* are scattered throughout the tradition from the very earliest collections on. The seventy-ninth tale of the *Gesta Romanorum,* entitled "Of Presumption," tells of the ass who to gain favor with a certain dog-loving king imitates his canine companions by jumping upon the royal lap, thus further alienating himself from the king and receiving for his efforts nothing but a whipping. The fable of ingratitude (Tale 174) concerns a serpent that is freed from a painful predicament by an emperor. But no sooner is he liberated than the serpent bites his benefactor. For this bit of ophidian folly, the emperor has the serpent returned to his original circumstances and leaves him there to die. Included in Novella 94 of the *Cento novelle antiche* is the wolf who, having never seen a mule, finally encounters one and begs to know its name. Informed that it is written on the mule's hoofs, the curious wolf looks and becomes the recipient of a fatal kick. A nearby fox contributes the traditional moral tag when he ironically suggests that not everyone who reads is necessarily wise. There are several fables in the *Conde Lucanor,* including as Cuento 5 the famous one of the (as usual) crafty fox, the vain crow, and the much-coveted piece of cheese.

Boccaccio himself did not make use of such material in the *Decameron,* but his disciple Arienti included as the fiftieth tale of the *Porrettane* the fable of "The Fox and the Cock." Having been coaxed into pretending sleep, the gullible rooster is carried off by the fox to be consumed. However, at the very instant he cleverly induces his vulpine adversary to say something, the rooster immediately flies to safety. The fox complains, "It is bad to speak when there is no need to," to which the foolish fowl adds, "But it is worse to sleep when no one else is sleeping." [29] Another version of this fable is, of course, Chaucer's "Nun's Priest's Tale" of Chaunticleer and Pertelote, in which scholars have variously attempted to find, among just about everything else, political, social, and even religious allegory.[30] Borrowed from Ovid is the story related by the Manciple of Apollo and the tattling crow who informs the god of his wife's infidelity. As a reward for this intelligence, which arouses Apollo to kill his beloved spouse, the crow's beautiful song is taken away and his once-white plumage becomes forever black. The Manciple's moral goes on for more than fifty lines—"A wikked tonge is worse than a feend," "A jangler is to God abhomynable," and so on— and concludes,

> Whereso thou come, amonges hye or lowe,
> Kepe wel thy tonge, and thenk upon the crowe.[31]

In the Cinquecento Aesopic fables are rare. Straparola relates in *Piacevoli notti* X:2 how with boasts and threats an ass bested a timorous lion in a trial of strength. In his *Palace of Pleasure* Painter includes the "Fable of the Lark of Aesope" (I,20) with its admonition to the reader "to beware of lighte hope, and vaine truste, to be reposed in frends and kinsfolke." [32]

Another broad category of animal characters in the novella comprises what folklorists call the "benevolent beast." For instance, in Tales 99 and 119 of the *Gesta Romanorum* there are, respectively, a serpent who heals a knight by sucking out the poison his human friend has received from the bite of a venomous toad, and three separate beasts (a lion, monkey, and serpent) who richly reward a poor man named Guido who extricated the group from a pit. Aulus Gellius' famous story of Androcles and the lion found a place in both the *Gesta* (104) and Painter's *Palace of Pleasure* (I,22). A magic fish that aids the simple man who has caught it (III:1), a man whose animal friends—a lion, a bear, and a wolf—enable him to save and then marry a princess (X:3), and a cat that helps make his master a king (XI:1) are subjects of novellas in the *Piacevoli notti* of Straparola, whose last-mentioned story is credited with being the original Puss in Boots tale. Basile offers in the *Pentamerone* a variant of the Goose that Laid Golden Eggs (V:1) as well as his own versions of two tales from the *Piacevoli notti:* Basile replaces Straparola's lion, bear, and wolf with a beetle, a mouse, and a grasshopper (III:5) who combine to assist a young man in winning the hand of a princess; and the benevolent cat of the *Piacevoli notti* becomes in the *Pentamerone* the more famous feline Gagliuso (II:4).

With animals such as Straparola's and Basile's we are approaching if not already trespassing onto the world of the fairy tale. Fairies and other supernatural figures, though infrequent, are not altogether unknown in the novella tradition. There is a benevolent goblin in the *Gesta Romanorum* (Tale 161) who serves up an exquisite beverage to weary, thirsty travelers. The ugly, old woman of Chaucer's "Wife of Bath's Tale"—the familiar Loathly Lady of folklore—is, one recalls, a fairy who metamorphoses herself into the beautiful and faithful wife of a rather unknightly knight when she gains sovereignty in their marriage. Straparola revived interest in fairy tales by including several in the *Piacevoli notti.* In the first tale of the second day of storytelling, a queen's son, through the doing of a fairy, is born in the shape of a pig, but upon his third marriage changes into the proverbial handsome prince. In subsequent stories, Adamantina becomes a queen with the help of a magic doll that dispenses gold to its possessor (V:2), and Isabella flies to

Flanders on the back of a magic horse to rescue her husband from the snares of adultery (VII:1).

Almost all of the novellas in the *Pentamerone* are fairy tales. Indeed, Basile, though very much rooted in the novella tradition, is universally acknowledged as a prime force in the establishment of the literary genre that attracted the considerable talents of Charles Perrault, the brothers Grimm, Hans Christian Andersen, and others. Included within the *Pentamerone* are variations on many famous tales—not only Puss in Boots and the Golden Goose, but also Cinderella (I:6), Rapunzel (II:1), Sleeping Beauty (V:5), and Hansel and Gretel (V:8). Even the cornice of Basile's collection about the magic doll, a fairy's gift, that arouses in the treacherous Lucia an intense desire to hear stories, is, appropriately enough, the only framing fairy tale in the tradition.

III. Personages from Modern and Contemporary History

By the Renaissance the veneration of great men had become a more apparent function of education and literature. Following in the trend of Petrarch's *De viris illustribus,* Renaissance biographers such as Boissard and De Bèze held up great men as exemplars to be followed. Erasmus wrote counsel to Henry VIII on how to become a model king, while Aretino preached the same sermon to François I. A tide of books from Castiglione's *Cortegiano* to Peacham's *Perfect Gentleman* taught magnanimity with gentility, as did various manuals *ad usum delphini* and *de educatione principis.* English novella collections reflect this vogue of ethical propaganda in that period when the *Cortegiano* was one of the three most-read books at Cambridge.

A final group of characters recurrent in the genre—and one deserving of separate mention—is that which includes such personages from contemporary or at least modern European history. Sometimes presented as novellas are accounts of historical events in which famous people have participated. A good many others are simply amusing or interesting anecdotes—factual or apocryphal—about the well known and the celebrated.

Richard the Lion-Hearted and the Holy Roman Emperor

Frederick the Great were especially popular in the early collections. Novella 76 of the *Cento novelle antiche* relates how Richard outwitted a sultan, whereas the sheer physical prowess of the British king is the subject of the third *cuento* in the *Conde Lucanor*. Tale 54 of the *Gesta Romanorum* is no more than a very short description of a marble gate that Frederick had built. More than a half dozen stories concerning the emperor are numbered in the *Cento novelle antiche*. One of these deals with a gift received from Prester John (2), another with the capture of Frederick's hawk by his enemies (22); there are also tales showing him rewarding cleanliness (23), punishing prodigality (30), and—doubtless for the benefit of his human audience—putting to death a falcon that had killed an eagle, the king of birds (90). Even Frederick's son Conrad IV, shown as a somewhat unruly child on the brink of turning over a new leaf, has a novella devoted to him (48). The plot material for Novella 60 in this work pertains to an alleged love triangle involving Charles I of Anjou and a tournament forbidden by Louis IX of France. A greater degree of historical accuracy marks the two tales on the ambitions and the rebellious acts of Henry, the eldest son of King Henry II of England.

Boccaccio did not significantly increase the number, or, for that matter, the accuracy of such tales, but he did broaden for his successors the range of historical figures that could be successfully employed as novellistic characters and also extended the use of personages drawn from real life to include not just the individual tales but the frame-narrative as well. To be sure, political figures still predominate, but in addition to these one now notes historical characters connected both with the arts and with the author's personal life. Besides Saladin, who, as previously noted, appears in two novellas of the *Decameron,* Alfonso VIII of Spain is shown richly rewarding the valorous Messer Ruggieri (X:1). Charles I of Anjou makes an appearance as a monarch who overcomes his lustful longing for two beautiful girls and even arranges honorable marriages for them (X:6). In another novella (I:7) Can Grande della Scala, after some uncharacteristic parsimony, displays generosity toward the witty courtier Bergamino. On the sixth day Boccaccio also presents amusing anecdotes concerning the painter Giotto (5) and the poet Guido Cavalcanti (9). Finally, as some

Decameron scholars have suggested, Boccaccio has apparently placed his beloved Maria d'Aquino, natural daughter of King Robert of Naples, into the cornice of his collection as Fiammetta. If Boccaccio, unlike Sercambi and Chaucer, kept himself out of his cornice—choosing instead to write a little proem akin to the prologues of Renaissance comedy—nonetheless by the fourth day he jumps onto the stage to defend his tales from their critics, thus ironically holding up the tale to be recited by none other than Fiammetta herself.

Subsequent Italian novellists in general followed Boccaccio's lead in sprinkling historical tales throughout their works. The forty-ninth story in Masuccio Salernitano's *Novellino* tells of the enmity between Emperor Frederick Barbarossa and Pope Alexander III. Sercambi devotes two novellas to Dante (71 and 72) and one to Bernabò Visconti (92), the aggressive and bizarre ruler of Milan for some thirty years. In the *Porrettane* we are offered a story on the daughter of Edward II of England (Novella 22), and, more importantly, without making use of pseudonyms (as we suppose Boccaccio did) Arienti presents in the frame of his work a picture of Count Andrea Bentivoglio and his train on vacation.

Sacchetti and Ser Giovanni Fiorentino were two of Boccaccio's disciples who considerably raised the number of historical tales in their respective collections. The *Libro delle trecentonovelle* contains novellas about many local Florentines—politicians, clergymen, businessmen, and so on—as well several on more internationally renowned persons. Political figures, as usual, are well represented (e.g., Bernabò Visconti, Azzo VIII of Este, Obizzo III of Este, and Philippe VI of Valois). Men of letters and the arts, like Albertus Magnus, Dante, Guido Cavalcanti, and Giotto, are also in attendance among Sacchetti's tales, as are such popes as Gregory X, Boniface VIII, and Gregory XI. The case of Ser Giovanni is certainly a singular one. The first fourteen novellas in the *Pecorone* contain the customary occasional tale drawn from history. But from the fifteenth story onward, Ser Giovanni suddenly settles down and devotes the remaining two-thirds or so of his work solely to historical materials, often presenting no more than actual transcriptions of sundry chapters from Giovanni Villani's *Cronica*. Indeed, many a novella is more history than story. Instead of the

usual assortment of tales, the *Pecorone* offers accounts of the rise of
the Guelphs and the Ghibellines (VIII:1 and 2), the building of the
city of Florence (XI:1), the Pisan invasion of Majorca (XII:2), the
history of the Bianchi and Neri factions (XIII:1), the nature of the
power of the Tuscans (XVII:1), and the various kings of Italy
(XVIII:1).

Outside of Italy, in the meantime, interest in historical subjects
began to grow steadily, if somewhat more slowly. Chaucer's Monk
does not fail to include the falls of men like Count Ugolino della
Gherardesca, best known from his appearance in Canto 33 of
Dante's *Inferno;* Pedro El Cruel, King of Castille and León;
Bernabò Visconti; and Pierre de Lusignan, King of Cyprus. If the
arguments of certain critics are accepted, then many of the frame-
characters of the *Canterbury Tales* (e.g., the Man of Law, Franklin,
Shipman, and Host) may, like Chaucer the pilgrim himself, also be
based on historical figures.[33] The alleged storytellers of the *Cent
Nouvelles nouvelles* are unquestionably real-life personages, including
Philippe le Bon and Philippe Pot. A few stories from this French
collection are likewise taken from history, perhaps the most famous
of which (Nouvelle 5) deals with various experiences of John
Talbot, first Earl of Shrewsbury, the English military man who
served in France intermittently for well over thirty years. Nouvelle
25—the account of the young girl who lodges a complaint with the
provost of Le Quesnoy that she was raped, but under questioning
subsequently admits that she guided her attacker's maneuvers for
fear of otherwise receiving holes in her stomach—is related by
Philippe de Saint-Yon, the very provost of Le Quesnoy that
handled the case. Many such tales in the *Cents Nouvelles nouvelles,* in
the absence of sources and analogues, must be assumed to have
been based on authentic events and people.

Marguerite de Navarre, who consistently uncovered moral
teaching in historical stories, may well have been the first and only
novelist to use autobiographical material extensively in both
cornice and tales. The *devisants* of the *Heptaméron* have all been
identified by modern scholars and are said to include Marguerite's
mother Louise de Savoie (Oisille), her husband Henri d'Albret
(Hircan), and Marguerite herself (Parlemente). François I, Marguerite's brother, is the subject of the seventeenth story, in which

Oisille (its teller) wishes to show us that bravery springs from virtue. Count Guillaume, we are told, plots to kill the king while he is alone in the forest. Undaunted, François draws his sword and succeeds in frightening off his would-be assassin. There is some evidence that the less flattering Nouvelles 25 and 42 about a "young prince" are also based on events in the life of Marguerite's brother. In the former the prince contrives a way to enjoy the favors of the wife of an advocate; in the latter his amorous advances to a virtuous servant are flatly rejected. In the twenty-second tale the Queen of Navarre is herself portrayed assisting a nun escape the clutches of a lustful monk. Some believe the "Widow of Flanders" in Nouvelle 4, who fights off in her own bedroom an attack by a young man in the service of her brother the prince, is again none other than Marguerite. Finally, in the seventh day of storytelling Ennasuite relates the amusing incident concerning the time Marguerite's daughter and her husband, just recently married and asleep in bed together, were interrupted by an absentminded chambermaid who scolded them for their shamelessness.

The most conspicuous and most significant use of modern and contemporary history not only in the Cinquecento novella but in the entire tradition is surely to be found in the work of Matteo Bandello. All four parts of his *Novelle* are indeed suffused with a deep sense of the historical. Bandello does more than dedicate each individual novella to such celebrated Renaissance personalities as Ippolita Sforza, Isabella d'Este, Baldassare Castiglione, Francesco Maria Molza, Girolamo Fracastoro, Giulio Cesare Scaligero, Veronica Gambara, and even Marguerite de Navarre; he also asserts that all of the tales in his collection are factual—Bandello, we recall, like Marguerite, insists that his are not fictional narratives *(favole)* but "true histories"—and, furthermore, that he at one time or another heard all these *istorie* recited by often equally famous persons and subsequently decided to write them down for posterity. Whether one accepts Bandello's claim of being the dutiful secretary, or whether one accepts the contention of some modern readers that the novellist for the most part simply adapted material from works like Machiavelli's *Istorie fiorentine* or Jean Bouchet's *Annales d'Aquitaine*—a question that has engaged in our time a number of prominent scholars, including Letterio Di Francia, Gioacchino Brognoligo, Guido Manginelli, Giuseppe Toffanin, and Benedetto Croce[34]—there can be little doubt that Bandello was particularly fascinated by historical persons and events.

One finds, first of all, in the novellas of Bandello the traditional inclusion of narratives involving men of the arts. The poet Alain Chartier is honored by Margaret of Scotland in one tale (I,46), while in another (obviously gleaned from Vasari) the famous painter Fra Lippo Lippi is imprisoned by Moors but afterwards is liberated because of a work of art which he executed (I,58). Yet Bandello, like many of his predecessors, was primarily interested in the private lives of the noble and the powerful. Collected in his work are several anecdotes regarding the affairs (love and otherwise) and the witty conversations of figures like Louis XI[35] and Galeazzo Sforza.[36] In one of these (IV,13)—doubtless based on Nouvelle 25 of the *Heptaméron*—it is Galeazzo and not a "certain young prince" who deceives one of his counselors and thereby enjoys the man's wife sexually. Another story (I,39) apparently borrowed from Marguerite (Nouvelle 17) has Philippe le Bon— Duke of Burgundy and a prominent raconteur in the *Cent Nouvelles nouvelles*—rather than François I, escape great danger through courageous action. We also learn from Bandello's *Novelle* how Niccolò d'Este put his wife and son to death for their adulterous behavior (I,44) and how Emperor Otho III—actually it was Otho IV—arranged an honorable marriage for the virtuous Gualdrada (I,18). A more contemporary matchmaker is Alessandro de' Medici, who is also shown executing an act of justice against his favorite courtier (II,15 and 16). Still other tales offered by Bandello treat like topics, such as the confused marital affairs of Alfonso X ("El Sabio") of Spain (IV,9); the love of Edward II of England for Alice Perrers (II,37); the miserable death of Charles IV of Navarre (III,15); and the wives of King Henry VIII of England (III,60 and 62).

The presence in the novella of figures from modern history did more than just enhance the already extensive variety of the narrative offering in the typical collection. For one thing, the introduction of rulers and noblemen of past and present, elbow to elbow with fictional characters of lower rank, supported the writer of novellas, lacking a critical *droit de séjour,* in his efforts the more fully to legitimatize the all-too-popular genre in which he worked. Moreover, presenting historical personages alongside fictional counterparts lent a greater verisimilitude to the individual tales and a sense of historicity and authenticity to the whole, thus further buttressing the by now familiar "protective screen" of many a novellist that he is dealing not with frivolous untruths but with instructive factual material. Finally, novellas about contemporary historical figures, especially those of a Bandello, served to satisfy the perhaps natural curiosity of the common man for information concerning the carryings-on of the famous people of his time. This particular use of the genre seems to retain for the novella one of its earliest and most often overlooked functions: to provide its listener-reader with what we refer to in English as "news."

Notes

1. Booth, p. 9.
2. E. M. Forster, *Aspects of the Novel* (New York: Harcourt, Brace, 1927), pp. 103-12.
3. René Wellek and Austin Warren, *Theory of Literature,* 3rd ed. (New York: Harcourt, Brace, and World, 1962), p. 219.
4. Valency and Levtow, p. 19.
5. *The Early French Novella,* p. 41.
6. *The Short Story in Spain in the Seventeenth Century,* p. 21.
7. Booth, pp. 1-8.
8. ". . . egli era il piggiore uomo forse che mai nascesse," *Decameron,* p. 50.
9. ". . . non meno onesta che bella," ibid., p. 670.
10. Chaucer, *Works,* p. 17.
11. Ibid., p. 21.
12. Ibid.
13. Ibid., p. 22.
14. Ibid., p. 48.
15. Ibid., 150.
16. ". . . in brevissimo tempo, d'uno in altro pensiero pervenendo," *Decameron,* p. 583.
17. ". . . il suo fervore in compassione cominciò a cambiare," ibid., p. 1139.
18. Enrique Moreno Baez, Introduction, Don Juan Manuel, *El conde Lucanor* (Madrid: Editorial Castalia, 1970), pp. 11-12.
19. Chaucer, *Works,* p. 189.

20. Ibid., p. 25.

21. Jacobs, I, 4.

22. Pettie, I, 5. Appendix B of this volume is devoted to a consideration of the general question of the relationship between Elizabethan drama and the novella.

23. *Decameron,* p. 1191.

24. Ruth S. El Saffar, *Novel to Romance: A Study of Cervantes's "Novelas ejemplares"* (Baltimore: Johns Hopkins Univ. Press. 1974), p. 148.

25. *Anatomy of Criticism,* esp. pp. 31-67.

26. Chaucer, *Works,* pp. 63-64.

27. Vittore Branca, *Boccaccio medievale* (Florence: Sansoni, 1948), esp. pp. 3-8 and 71-99.

28. For a helpful discussion of the *querelle des femmes* in the Middle Ages and Renaissance, see Francis L. Utley, *The Crooked Rib* (Columbus: Ohio State Univ. Press, 1944), pp. 1-90; and Katharine M. Rogers, *The Troublesome Helpmate: A History of Misogyny in Literature* (Seattle: Univ. of Washington Press, 1966), pp. 56-134.

29. *Prosatori volgari del Quattrocento,* ed. Varese, p. 912.

30. See, for example, J. Leslie Hotson, "Colfox vs. Chauntecleer," *PMLA,* 39, (1924), 762-81; John Speirs, *Chaucer the Maker* (London: Faber and Faber, 1951), pp. 185-93; Mortimer J. Donovan, "The *Moralitee* of the Nun's Priest's Sermon," *JEGP,* 52 (1953), 498-508; and Charles Dahlberg, "Chaucer's Cock and Fox," *JEGP,* 53 (1954), 277-90.

31. Chaucer, *Works,* p. 227.

32. Jacobs, I, 87.

33. See in particular the classic study in this area, J. M. Manley, *Some New Light on Chaucer* (New York: Holt, 1926), as well as such later contributions as K. L. Wood-Leigh, "The Franklin," *RES,* 4 (1928), 145-51; and Margaret Galway, "Chaucer's Shipman in Real Life," *MLR,* 34 (1939), 497-514.

34. For a concise, useful summary of the debate, see T. Gwynfor Griffith, *Bandello's Fiction: An Examination of the "Novelle"* (Oxford: Blackwell, 1955), esp. pp. 1-22.

35. E.g., I, 48; II, 19; and III, 36.

36. E.g., I, 20; III, 32 and 45; and IV, 13.

CHAPTER 4

Images of Society:
Social Classes, Nations,
Races, War

Introduction: The Novella and Society

Just as the novella with its ideal of *brevitas* rarely delved into psychological complexity or extended depiction of environment of multiple plot structures, so it infrequently served as a vehicle for the presentation or discussion of profound philosophical ideas— Marguerite de Navarre's Platonism or Chaucer's Boethian ruminations on fortune being possible exceptions.[1] Instead, its economy of form rendered the genre perfectly suited for brief glimpses of and pungent comments on contemporary social matters. For Erich Auerbach the subject of the novella is, indeed, always society.[2] More specific is Georg Lukács' belief that the prime achievement of the genre is its bringing into focus the life of society through some extraordinary individual event.[3]

Of course, the conception of literature as a faithful mirror of society has been in recent times stringently attacked by René Wellek,[4] H.H. Remak,[5] and, in a more tempered statement, by Ian Watt.[6] Since the novellas (before Painter, Fenton, and the seventeenth-century Spaniards) usually illustrated realism unembellished with imagination, opinion, didacticism, or philosophical embroïderies, this genre conveyed as true a portraiture of society as literature has offered. To avoid what has been called the "mimetic fallacy," [7] we must acknowledge that the novellist's freedom to choose his subject matter and select his details may well result in an image of society inevitably reflecting his experience and social perspectives.[8] Even more important for our purposes hereafter than the manner and extent of the novella's reflection of society was its success as an active, objective corrective of that society.

In fact, current controversies on whether or how literature reflects society would hardly have interested the novellists of the age of Jean de Meung and his translator Chaucer, nor yet the giants of the age of Brant, Des Périers, Erasmus, Rabelais, Basile, and Quevedo. A wealth of satires and theories of satire deriving from Horace and especially Juvenal existed in the Renaissance, unanimously confirming the power of literature to correct society and taking for granted its inevitable reflection of society. Just as Sophocles had aimed to purge society through the individuals in his audience, so also did the novellists aim to *taxer* and correct and reform through their individual readers—or, as Addison was to put it, pass beyond the single foe to charge whole armies. How the novellists, like the contemporary satirists, played a collective role in weakening the textures of mediaeval conventions and institutions will become apparent from the images of society to follow. The composite of varied images about to occupy us in this and the subsequent four chapters provides the modern reader with an invaluable social document, rich in its diversity and complexity, yet unified by what was surely a sustained commonness of purpose.

I. Monarchy, Court Life, Class Structure, Feudalism

The social classes analyzed above as part of the fictive chain of being common to the tradition were rarely depicted in such a compartmentalized manner. Instead, dynamic interaction of and even bitter clashes among varied socioeconomic groups mark the representation of character in the novella, resulting in the copious heaping of praise or criticism at one time or another on figures of every stratum of mediaeval and Renaissance society.

The king of course was an institution difficult to attack. The power of the monarchy was immense. In our section on law (Chapter Six) we find that many wrongs could be righted and many wrongdoers punished only by the *lex regia,* a principle allowing and requiring kings alone to set entangled matters straight. In many areas, too, during the Cinquecento not only the *nihil obstat* of the Church, but the royal patent as well was required before a book could be printed. Hence, praise of monarchs is unsurprisingly abundant in the genre. Like many another novellist, Giraldi expresses admiration for kings and even spends most of his ninth *deca* indulging in a kind of tyrannophilia, making heroes of Ercole d'Este, Alfonso d'Este, Lorenzo de' Medici, and François I. María de Zayas introduces into a single one of her *Novelas amorosas y ejemplares* the monarchs of Hungary, England, and Germany.

Whatever antimonarchical sentiment we do find in the tradition is expressed in very particularized terms: individual kings who are tyrants, libertines, or fools may be criticized, but the idea of monarchy remained sacrosanct. The *Gesta Romanorum,* which normally idealized rulers, offers one bold indictment of a king. In Tale 144 a monarch incapable of dealing with his troubled kingdom asks his four wisest philosophers why his realm is declining in power and virtue. The first replies that the land is without law or honor. The second finds it without truth, faith, or devotion; the third, without decency, wealth, or prudence. The fourth sage completes this compound indictment of his arrogant and corrupt monarch with a judgment that anticipates a famous Nietzschean phrase:

The will is a counsellor; therefore the kingdom is ill ordered. Money gives sentences; therefore the kingdom is badly governed. God is dead; therefore the whole kingdom is full of sinners.[9]

In Italy the *Cento novelle antiche,* generally laudatory toward emperors and monarchs, particularly Frederick the Great, recalls for us in Novella 7 the biblical tale (I Kings, 12) of Solomon's son Rehoboam, who lost his kingdom because he listened to the wrong advisers and treated his people harshly. The less reverential Boccaccio presents several modern-day kings in a negative light. The ninth tale of the *Decameron*, for example, concerns Gui de Lusignan, King of Cyprus (r. 1192-94), described by Boccaccio as "dull and lazy" ("tardo e pigro"), a monarch who not only failed to avenge with justice the wrongs done to others, but also endured with shameful cowardice an infinity of insults to himself. However, when he is sufficiently shamed by a woman of Gascony, Gui undergoes the kind of sudden metamorphosis of character so typical of the tradition: "awaking as if from a dream," the king began by avenging the injury suffered by the lady, and from that day forward he became the "rigidissimo persecutore" of anyone who did anything to stain the honor of his crown.[10]

Marguerite de Navarre, a novellist with royal blood, wrote her collection of tales for her brother François I and even made him the hero of one of them (Nouvelle 17), depicting him as a gallant and understanding king, kind to the defenseless and forgiving of his enemies. Yet Marguerite has no sympathy for inept or tyrannical kings and dukes. In the third tale of the *Heptaméron* she applauds the Queen of Naples for indulging in some vengeful role-reversal by implanting the cuckold's horns on the head of her lascivious husband, King Alfonso V. Later, Marguerite totally approves of the murder of Alessandro de' Medici, Duke of Florence (r. 1531-37), by his cousin Lorenzaccio, supposedly for wishing to dishonor the bed of Lorenzaccio's sister (Nouvelle 12).

The sexual exploitation of women by the powerful clergy—which we examine elsewhere in this volume—was clearly rivaled by the kings and noblemen of the age, almost all of whom appear to have had at least a bit of Tarquin in them. Long before the attacks on the *droit du seigneur* by the eighteenth-century opponents of autarchy, including Beaumarchais, the novellists satirized and attacked this right of not only the first night but any night. As early as the *Conde Lucanor* (50) a vassal's wife complains to Saladin that great lords always promise much but leave a woman dishonored. The Marchioness of Monferrato (I:5), outwitting and curbing the lechery of King Philippe Auguste of France (1165-1223), became a legendary figure, still being praised in Painter's *Palace of Pleasure* (II,16). The *droit du seigneur* of King Juan of Aragon, who stole from the very altar the bride of his vassal, the Count of Prata (Bandello III, 54), led to the birth of Ferdinand of Aragon. A great king in the novellas who learned to master his sexual appetites was, of course, Edward III, whose passion for the Countess of Salisbury, recorded as early as Froissart, was familiar to Bandello, Shakespeare, and others. In the Painter version of the tale (I,46) there is praise for Edward's repression of his libido as well as a splendid script for the king to declaim on man's moral responsibility.[11]

Obviously, not all novellists were in a position to speak out their grievances against monarchs, especially those writers who enjoyed the favor of kings or were even of royal blood themselves. Nephew of Alfonso X, cousin of Sancho IV, and for five years beginning in 1320 co-regent during the minority of Alfonso XI, Don Juan Manuel was an expectedly strong supporter of feudal and Catholic values; he spoke well of Richard the Lion-Hearted and approved of Fernando III ("El Santo") and his son Alfonso el Sabio.

Chaucer, too, had connections with the crown. By 1357, when still in his teens, the English poet was a page in the household of the Countess of Ulster, the wife of Lionel, Duke of Clarence, a son of Edward III; a decade later he entered the service of the king himself. From the 1370s on, Chaucer enjoyed the favor of John of Gaunt (another of Edward's sons), to whose recently deceased wife the poet dedicated *The Book of the Duchess.* Although a witness to the deterioration of town and crown during the reigns of both Edward III and Richard II, the author of the *Canterbury Tales* did not join the chorus of critics. As Muriel Bowden has written, "... the polished work upon which he was then engaged had no place in it for London disasters."[12]

Although his sister was quick to attack corrupt foreign rulers, the *galant vert* François I was, as we have already suggested, protected and even idealized by Marguerite de Navarre in the *Heptaméron.* Modern historians, however, inform us that François in his early

teens was already "pursuing his first sexual adventures" and that
by 1512, when he was eighteen, his mother was writing of a disease
in her son's "secret parts." [13] When king, François had his own
personal seraglio, called *la petite bande,* and indulged in such male-
chauvinist activities as urinating behind bedroom firescreens on
hidden rivals and forcing potential female victims to ogle lascivious
scenes unexpectedly painted on the bottom of their soup dishes.
Finally, on the evidence of an unsigned letter written about 1521,
the nineteenth-century editor of Marguerite's letters François
Génin has even suggested the possibility of an incestuous relationship between the king and his older novella-writing sister,[14] a
contention which has been qualified to a certain extent by more
modern critics like Samuel Putnam.[15] Yet in the *Heptaméron* all of
these deeds—and rumors of deeds—are cloaked in silence. Instead,
François emerges as a gentle admirer of women, with only one
seduction recorded, and that anonymously (Nouvelle 25).

With some novellists criticism was deflected from the king to the
royal court. As satire of court life was a major theme of
Renaissance poetry (Wyatt, Du Bellay, Ronsard, and many
others), so the court, from which a mediaeval or Renaissance ruler
expected luxury, flattery, and obeisance, proved fertile ground for
novellistic attacks. Marguerite herself concludes her twenty-seventh *nouvelle* by censuring the courtiers who have such a superior
opinion of themselves that they attempt (often unsuccessfully) to
dupe lower-born rustics. In the *Ecatommiti* IX:10 Giraldi deplores
the inevitable adulators present in all courts. Bandello, who was a
familiar of the noble and wealthy, opines that envy is the
characteristic vice of courtiers (III,60). Agrippina in Pettie's tale of
"Germanicus and Agrippina" counsels her husband regarding "the
perils which princely state bringeth," primary among which are
"the falsehood in friends" and "the treason in nobility." [16]

Basile had much to say against court life, even though the
cornice of the *Pentamerone* has a royal setting. At the beginning of
the tale of Corvetto (III:7) he writes, "If anyone truly asked me
where hypocrisy and deceit could be found, I could not show him
any place comparable to the court, where people wear masks;
Backbiting wears the mask of Trastullo, Slander that of Graziano,

Treason that of Zanni, and Knavery that of Pollicinella, and where at the same time there is stabbing and salving, smashing up and putting back together." The eclogue that concludes the first day shows abject scorn for sycophancy and flattery in the trains of earls and knights:

> One nods to him from here, one bows to him from there,
> one doffs his cap, one says, "I am your slave." [17]

Often criticism of the powerful and the rich went hand in hand in the novella with indignation at the plight of the lower classes. In the very Prologue to the *Decameron* Boccaccio deplores the condition of the common people *(la minuta gente)* who suffered far more than other classes in the Florentine plague. Whereas victims from the upper classes were borne to church in biers, received the mass of the dead with candles, and were buried in consecrated ground, the common people "abiding in their own quarters, sickened by the thousands daily, and being untended and unaided, died almost without any recourse whatsoever. Many breathed their last on the open street both at night and during the day, while others died within their houses, to be discovered by neighbors only much later and usually through the stench of their rotting bodies." Such people were regularly buried not in family graves or even church plots, but by the hundreds in huge trenches just as bales are stowed away in the hold of a ship.[18] Boccaccio's sympathy for the poor was shared by Chaucer, who found a way to condemn the exploitation of the poor and peasants by attacking not only such corrupt clergymen as the Summoner and the Pardoner, but also figures like the Miller, who defrauded farmers and peasants with his famous "thombe of gold."

Although examples of the gross exploitation of the peasantry are numerous in the novellas, many tales were also introduced to illustrate that succor did exist. In Sacchetti's Novella 88 a nobleman of the Medici court is about to destroy the vines of a peasant, exercising his *andazzi,* or privileges of his rank, when Duke

Francesco de' Medici intervenes, encouraging Sacchetti to observe that feudal rights had lasted too long and had done too much harm. Bandello calls attention (III,25) to another defender of the lower classes, Duke Gian Maria Visconti, who heard that a priest was refusing to bury a townsman without proper payment from his widow. This surprising tale has a special significance to Bandello, as he explains in its Introduction. A liberal Catholic, he feels that the foibles of priests are strengthening the Lutherans and that the action of the Visconti Duke, whom the novellist does not particularly admire, might prove a lesson to other churchmen.

Peasants in the *Nouvelles récréations et joyeux devis* are usually presented as simple bumpkins and amusing clodhoppers, but Des Périers does include one *nouvelle* (70) in which a peasant unable to pay his *taille* has his cart and oxen cruelly confiscated. Like her literary valet-de-chambre, Marguerite's attitude toward the lower class also verges on conscious condescension. The fullest discussion of the lower class by the *devisants* of the *Heptaméron* follows Nouvelle 29. Geburon remarks that simple and low-class people ("les gens simples et de bas estat") have in them more malice by far than those higher born. "Just look at the thieves, murderers, sorcerers, counterfeiters, and all that kind of people, always stirring up trouble," he declares. "They are all of the lower class." Parlemente agrees that the poor are more malicious than others and further believes it impossible for a lofty passion like love to settle in a base heart ("ung cueur villain") such as theirs.[19] Yet the same Marguerite can show in her forty-second tale how a servant may set a virtuous example for her noble masters, for in the mystical Christian/Platonist phase of her split personality, the Queen of Navarre always insists that in the eyes of God and after death there is no class distinction at all.

We proceed now to the question of the nobility of rank and its relation to honor and nobility of soul. They would seem to be identified as one and the same by Don Juan Manuel, who placed a supreme value on *verguenza* (intense sense of honor, decency). However, Boccaccio, like Chaucer, seems to have believed that in life, too, nobility of rank did not necessarily result in nobility of soul. The author of the *Decameron* sets great value on nobility and virtue, but suggests that everyone is born with the opportunity of attaining them.

In defending her choice of Guiscardo, a man of low birth, for her lover, Ghismonda in IV:1 declares to her father,

> ... we all have the same mass of flesh; all souls were created by the very same Creator with equal powers, equal strengths, and equal virtues. It was virtue which first introduced differences among us who were born and are born equal: those who were most virtuous were deemed noble, the rest accounted otherwise. And although contrary custom has obscured this law, it has not yet been discarded by either nature or good manners. Therefore he who lives virtuously manifests himself noble, and if anyone calls him otherwise, the fault lies not with him but with his detractor.[20]

Chaucer's Parson warns against pride arising from the "goodes of fortune," which include "richesse" and "hyghe degrees of lordshipes." Such pride, he says, is "ful greet folie," for sometimes one's wealth is the "cause of his death." Moreover, often a man who is "a greet lord by the morwe" is by night no more than "a caytyf and a wrecche." The Parson even suggests that "ofte tyme the gentrie of the body binymeth [diminishes] the gentrie of the soule." Everyone, he believes, must come to the conclusion that we all are born of a mother and a father and that all of us, "bothe riche and povre," are by nature "roten and corrupt." True "gentilesse' for the Parson is signified by "eschewynge vice and ribaudye and servage of synne, in word, in werk, and contenaunce"; he deems a "noble herte" one that attains to "heighe vertuouse thynges." The carpenter John in "The Miller's Tale" may be wealthy and possessed of a young and desirable wife, yet he is nothing but a "riche gnof," whereas the Plowman and the patient Griselda belong, so to speak, to an aristocracy of the spirit.[21]

The inevitable clashes in the novella between upper and lower classes often show the latter as superior to their social betters not just in virtue but in native wit as well. In Day One of the *Decameron* both Bergamino and Guglielmo Borsiere with clever remarks change the avaricious ways of the lords whom they are serving, respectively, Can Grande della Scala and Ermino de' Grimaldi. The baker Cisti and the cook Chichibio outwit their masters on the sixth day of storytelling; and in III:2 a groom is able through trickery both to enjoy his queen's favors and to frustrate the cuckolded king's efforts to learn the identity of the culprit. The *Cent Nouvelles nouvelles* contains several such stories, including those of the miller who progressed from cuckoldee to cuckolder by repaying a knight in his own coin (3) and of the virtuous woman, the near-victim of rape, who literally trips up her nobleman-assailant and runs away (24).

Several novellists apparently viewed upward mobility as a desirable possibility. After listening to the Monk's interminable recital of the moral and social "falls" of men, the Knight interrupts with "Hoo! . . . good sire, namoore of this!" He would prefer to hear contrary stories,

> As whan a man hath been in povre estaat,
> And clymbeth up and wexeth fortunat,
> And there abideth in prosperitee.
> Swich thyng is gladsom, as it thynketh me,
> And of swich thyng were goodly for to telle.[22]

Painter's generation, on the other hand, seems scornful of the young picaresque types moving up the social scale. The ambitious servant in his tale of Ariobarzanes (II,4) is warned "to beware how he doth compare in those noble vertues with Princes and great men, which beyng ryght noble and pereles vppon yearth canne abyde no Comparisons." Fellow countryman Fenton was to write in his ninth "discourse": "And trulye the domesticall servant, in credit or truste with his maister, and evil gyven or affected towardes his lord, is more to be feared then a whole armye of ennemies standynge in battaile araye in the felde." [23] Upstairs and downstairs in England would keep their identity until the Edwar-

dian period. After all, Fenton dedicated his collection to Lady
Mary Sidney, and Painter was dedicating his volumes to such
notables as the "Right Worshipful Sir George Howard Knight,
Maister of the Quene's Maiestie's Armarye."

Rastell anticipates the attitudes of the Elizabethan novellists,
although he has more sympathy for his peasants and finds them
amusing: "They that be brought up withoute lernynge or good
maner shal never be but rude and bestely, althoughe they have
good naturall wyttes," he concludes in his very first tale. Thus, a
plowman's son mistakes a lute for a goose (45), a butcher's friend
named Philip Spencer hears the word *Philippenses* during a sermon
and interrupts the service with a ridiculous comment (52), and so
on, *même jeu*. This simple bumpkin type of peasant is the
descendant of Boccaccio's Calandrino.

In two different tales from the *Ecatommiti* (IV:8 and X:10),
Giraldi lashes out at the lower class, the members of which, he
contends, have an evil soul, are incapable of gratitude, and, in fact,
make it a point of honor to harm their benefactors. The
contemporary work *Sei giornate* by Sebastiano Erizzo is another
collection perpetrating class bias. A nobleman, senator, and
member of Venice's Council of Ten, Erizzo features in his stories
kings, princes, and wealthy burghers. They inhabit a world of
unquestionable magnanimity, justice, loyalty among peers, and the
devotion of servants. As Di Francia observed, "It is enough just to
glance at the index of the book to see the kind of subjects and
personages which the Venetian senator almost always treats:
Charlemagne, the Young King of Hungary, Edward III of
England—these are the names we encounter." [24] As the narrators
themselves are wealthy young noblemen enrolled in the University
of Padua, their class prejudices are hardly concealed.

A half-century or so later Basile in the first eclogue of the
Pentamerone writes bitterly of the *servitore*, the manservant, who
appears polite, clean, industrious, and selfless, but who upon closer
inspection proves to be just the opposite:

> You will discover him to be a traitor, a coward for his life, a
> first-class pimp, a swindler, a glutton, a gambler. If he spends,

it is only for personal gain; if he feeds the mule, he thins the oats and keeps the rest; he corrupts the maid-servant, rummages through your pockets, and finally, to top it all off, one fine day he makes a clean sweep of everything, clears out of your house, and runs away.

The essence of Basile's social theory is perhaps best expounded in Prince Taddeo's speech on "degree" that precedes II:8—"In truth, every man ought to work at his own craft, the lord as lord, the groom as groom, and the constable as constable; for just as a street urchin becomes ridiculous when he takes the role of a prince, so it is with the prince who plays the part of a street urchin." [25]

Qualified demophilia seems in contrast to exist among seventeenth-century Spanish novellists. Cervantes' warmth for peasants, which we know from his great affection for Sancho Panza, extends in the *Novelas ejemplares* to lowlifes and gypsies, whose weaknesses and misdemeanors the novellist indulgently forgives. Tirso de Molina shared this sympathy for the humble classes, but there is in both the *Cigarrales de Toledo* and Cervantes' *novelas* the common assumption that any individual of merit must be an aristocrat. Even though Tirso's Dalmao and Dionisia hide their true identity in the country under the guise of *villanos,* the villagers recognize their inherent superiority regardless of their costumes. In the rustic village games, for example, Dalmao is always the winner because gentlemen are, of course, superior to the *aldeanos.*

Nowhere was the clash of classes more keenly felt in the novella than in its treatment of marriage. A staunch supporter of the feudal marriage with all of its caste conventions was the anonymous compiler of the *Gesta Romanorum.* The very first story of that mediaeval collection pinpoints several aspects of the feudal marriage which were in future times to be thought intolerable and outrageous. It concerns a runaway princess who without parental consent wishes to consort with a man below her station purely for reasons of self-interest (that is, love).[26] When the prodigal daughter, sufficiently sobered and repentant, is welcomed home by her family, one gift she receives is a ring on which is significantly engraved, "Thou art noble, despise not thy nobility."

The code against marrying beneath one's class was to remain inviolate for centuries. This is demonstrated in Marguerite's oft-cited Nouvelle 42 when a prince (presumably François) falls in love with a girl of lower station. Although the young woman is said to be possessed of a "grace which surpassed that of her rank" and to seem more a *gentil femme* or *princesse* than a *bourgeoise,* she fully comprehends that marriage is out of the question. She says to the prince,

> My lord, I am not so foolish or so blind as not to see and understand well the beauty and grace that God has placed in you, and not to believe that she who will possess the heart and person of such a prince will be the happiest of women. But how does that concern me, since this is not for me or for any woman of my rank, and even for me to desire it would be perfect folly?

Marguerite held marriage to be "the most beautiful state that exists in the world" and strongly felt that love must be an essential component of the marital union. But the Queen was adamant on the issues of unequal marriage and parental consent. At the conclusion of her tale of Rolandine (40), Parlemente remarks,

> I pray to God, ladies, that this example may be so profitable to you that none of you will wish to marry for your own pleasure, without the consent of those to whom you owe obedience.

Concurring, Oisille hopes the story will suffice to make ladies have "such reverence toward their parents so as to marry according to their will." [27]

Boccaccio, the liberal on so many social questions of his time, seems to turn all the conventions of the feudal marriage on their heads. At the beginning of I:5 Fiammetta states her belief that it is always wise for a man to seek a wife from a higher level ("di più alto legnaggio") than himself.[28] What she—or rather Boccaccio—quite possibly had in mind was that it was permissible for a middle-class scholar-banker (Boccaccio) to fall in love with the niece of a king (Fiammetta's apparent alter ego, Maria d'Aquino, natural daughter of the king of Naples). Such upwardly mobile young men who marry above their stations frequently appear in the *Decameron*. The penniless prodigal Federigo degli Alberighi so impresses the wealthy, recently widowed Monna Giovanna with the depth of his love for her that she chooses him over the objections of her family as her next husband (V:9). The feminine counterpart to Federigo is Giletta di Nerbona, the physician's daughter who contrives to marry the son of a count, Beltramo di Rossiglione, despite the young man's initial aversion to such a match (III:9).

One particularly intriguing tale from the *Decameron* concerning a man who marries above his rank is II:3, which also directly challenges another important marriage convention: parental consent. The King of England's daughter, on her way in disguise to Rome to be married by the Pope, falls in with and becomes enamored of the debtridden Alessandro. At an inn where they stop for the night, the princess reveals her feelings to the young man, and before enjoying each other sexually, they perform their own marriage ceremony in bed, complete with vows and ring. When they reach Rome, the girl—and Boccaccio doubtless shares her thoughts—explains to the pontiff that she did not want to marry her intended, the old King of Scotland, for fear that the weakness of her youth might have caused her to do something contrary to the laws of God and to the honor of her royal family. Instead, she has chosen for her spouse Alessandro, whose virtues and manners are worthy, although his blood may be lacking in *la nobilità*. The Pope grants the lady's request, and her royal father, after some reluctance, forgives his daughter and welcomes her husband.

Boccaccio obviously held the arranged marriage somewhat in contempt, favoring instead marital union based on mutual love. For him love and marriage were of a pair. Indeed, in his tales love—in its most physical manifestation—often precedes marriage, as in the clever story of Messer Lizio's finding his unwed daughter Caterina in bed with the young family friend Ricciardo, the former even in her sleep clutching her beloved "nightingale," and then

with little effort his persuading the lovers that they should marry
that very day (V:4).

Tale 57 of the *Cent Nouvelles nouvelles* is a Boccaccesque-like story
concerning a marriage between a shepherd and a noblewoman.
This unorthodox match created a scandal, of course, but the
bride's brother welcomed the shepherd as a brother-in-law, and,
recalling the humble origins of his own family, explained to his
shocked peers that he would rather have his sister married to a
herdsman whom she loved than to some *grand maistre* who
displeased her.

Chaucer's views on marriage are first introduced at the conclusion of "The Knight's Tale." Theseus urges Emily to marry
Palamon with regard only to his devotion to her and not to his
station in life:

> Lat se now youre wommanly pitee.
> He is a kynges brother sone, pardee;
> And though he were a povre bacheler,
> Syn he hath served yow so many a yeer,
> And had for yow so greet adversitee,
> It moste been considered, leeveth me;
> For gentil mercy oghte to passen right.[29]

Palamon weds his beloved, and his feelings are requited ("Emelye
hym loveth so tendrely"), the chief ingredient of a happy marriage
for Chaucer.

Illustrious examples, on the other hand, of loveless marriages in
the *Canterbury Tales* include those of John and Allison in "The
Miller's Tale" and January and May in "The Merchant's Tale."
The root of the unhappiness of these unions lies in the marked
incongruity of the spouses in terms of not social rank but age. As
the Miller says of the carpenter,

> He knew nat Catoun, for his wit was rude,
> That bad man sholde wedde his simylitude.
> Men sholde wedden after hire estaat,
> For youthe and elde is often at debaat.[30]

Both "The Wife of Bath's Tale" and "The Cleric's Tale," according to George Lyman Kittredge, also offer less than perfect marital relations, the former representing female dominance, the latter absolute male dominance in the marriage. But it is "The Franklin's Tale," argues Kittredge, that treats what to Chaucer is the ideal marriage because, as in the union between Palamon and Emily, it is based on love rather than convenience, on interdependence rather than dependence:

> It was the regular theory of the Middle Ages that the highest type of chivalric love was incompatible with marriage, since marriage brings in mastery, and mastery and love cannot abide together. This view the Franklin boldly challenges. Love *can* be consistent with marriage, he declares. Indeed, without love (and perfect *gentle* love) marriage is sure to be a failure. The difficulty about mastery vanishes when mutual love and forbearance are made the guiding principles of the relation between husband and wife.[31]

Of course, Boccaccio had earlier made use of the Griselda story—which Chaucer's Cleric says he got directly from the Latin version by "Fraunceys Petrak, the lauriat poete"—seemingly with much the same general purpose in mind as the English writer. Dioneo, the storyteller himself, describes Gualtieri's actions in the tale (X:10) as "agre e intollerabili" and his treatment of his wife as an example of nothing but "una matta bestialità." Boccaccio also seems to wish to show us here yet another instance of the exploitation of the peasant class. The Marquis simply goes unannounced to the home of Griselda's father and without any hesitation declares, "I have come to marry your daughter"; in Chaucer's version the serf, though "astonyed," "abayst," and "quakynge," can only respond, "Lord ... my willynge/Is as ye wole." [32] The heinous behavior of Gualtieri, bordering on sadism, is held possible and even acceptable in the story only because of Griselda's humble, peasant origins, which also make it easier for the Marquis to set up a potential divorce or annulment of his marriage with Rome's complete consent (see also below, Chapter Eight).

Many of Boccaccio's sympathies seem to be reflected in Bandello's tragical tale of the Duchess of Malfi (I,26), the high-born lady who secretly married and bore children to her majordomo Antonio Bologna. The Duchess, true, was of the Ragona family, an international oft-crowned dynasty; but Antonio was no peasant. Bandello makes it clear that Bologna was a "very gallant and worthy gentleman," not only handsome in appearance but an accomplished horseman and lutanist, and a more than moderately lettered man. What is more, the two loved each other deeply. Yet the Duchess's brother the Cardinal Ragonese, incensed by his sister's behavior, did not cease his persecution of her until she, Antonio, and their children were all cruelly murdered, with their assassins escaping unpunished. It is interesting to note that the more class-conscious Painter tags on to his version of the story (II, 23) the following conclusion: "You see the miserable discourse of a Princess loue, that was not very wyse, and of a Gentleman that had forgotten his estate"—along with an appropriate moral, "We ought neuer to climb higher than our force permitteth, ne yet surmount the bounds of duty." [33]

Another consequence of marriage between classes surfaces in Painter's story, derived from Bandello and Boaistuau, of Didaco and Violenta (I,42). It concerns the double tragedy of a woman of low rank ("a Goldsmithes doughter") who married a nobleman. Although she acknowledges that she is "inferiour" to Didaco "in merites, goodes and vertues," Violenta nevertheless agrees to the marriage, but with the understanding—or warning—that her husband must never "exchaunge my persone for a greater Ladie, what so euer she be." [34] When Didaco does precisely that, Violenta ("like another Medea") lives up to her name with a vengeance, stabbing Didaco, dismembering his body, and tossing it piece by piece out of the window into the street. (The tale ends with the execution of the murderess.) By way of contrast, the same author's account of Rolandine the Chaste (I,62), a tale borrowed from the *Heptaméron*, has its heroine fall in love with a bastard but wisely avoid the hazards of an "unequal" marriage.

In general the English novelists of the late Renaissance frowned upon marriages which crossed social boundaries. Fenton appears to find even the thought of such an alliance annoying, if not downright disgusting. He deems the villainous Pandora (derived from Bandello) odious not so much for murdering her own child, so it seems, but for allowing a mere servant—"Monsieur le Page"— to be her first lover. With a sense of outrage he writes, "She had payd the fyrste frutes of her virgynytie to one no lesse unworthy of th'offering then to enjoye the possession of so deare a jewell, beinge already vowed to another by them that by most ryght ought to dispose of it." As for Ginevra, who in his last tale rejects Don Diego to marry someone of lower station, Don Roderigo (no doubt with Fenton's approval) upbraids her for "refusing the friendship of a nobleman, famous by wealth and vertue, and the verey parragon of the wholle contrey, for the society of a pore companion, whose parentes beynge unknowen argued a doute of hys discente, and she altogether a straunger to hys dispocition." [35]

A final example of the very real dangers of a *mésalliance,* at least according to a novellist, concerns the question of interracial marriage. We speak, of course, of Giraldi's famous novella (III:7) of the Moor who married the Venetian Lady Disdemona. As the Iago figure, the Ensign, slowly works his psychic poison on his gullible master, we are assured that Moors are of "so hot a nature" that every little trifle moves them to anger and revenge. The upshot, more ignoble and ignominious here than in the Shakespearean treatment, is the foul murder of the ever-chaste and faithful Disdemona.

With this celebrated Giraldian novella we see how demophiliac and demophobic sentiments were matched in the tradition by manifestations of both xenophilia and xenophobia.

II. Nationalism, Patriotism, Xenophobia, Racism

The novella, flourishing as it did during an age of growing nationalisms, offers a fairly generous catalogue of prejudicial portraits and comments on several nationalities and races. The prime targets included non-Christians and non-Europeans (Turks, Moors, Jews, gypsies, and African blacks), but there are also numerous diatribes or at least caustic remarks against the French, Italians, Spaniards, and even, curiously enough, the Welsh.

The Turk did not become a bogeyman to Europe until the seizure of Constantinople in 1453, an event described in Bandello's novella (I,11). The Ottomans remained a frightening specter until their defeat at the naval battle of Lepanto in 1571. As we noted in the previous chapter, sympathetic depictions of Turks regularly appeared in such early collections as the *Cento novelle antiche* and the *Decameron.* In Chaucer's "Man of Law's Tale" we learn that a marriage between a Christian and a Moslem would be looked down upon by both cultures, and we detect the Western European hope that all those devoted to "mawmettrie" would be converted, like the Sultan of Syria in the story, to "Christes lawe deere." [36] However, the mass beheadings undertaken by the Turkish armies after 1453 brought panic to a disunited Europe, watching with dismay as the Turks marched along the Danube. Probably no mass murders of the time equalled the slaughter of some 1,500 Hungarians on 29 August 1526, only a day after the other bloodbath at Nohatz. Even Henry VIII noted the potential danger to England, observing to the Spanish ambassador Chapuys that Emperor Charles V should stop killing Christians and start killing Turks.

The Hungarian attempts to check the Turk are mentioned in the tale of Sultan Mahommed (II,13) by Bandello, who composed several novellas against the "more than barbarous" Turks. He recounts how Mahommed, on sacking Constantinople, took as mistress the Greek girl Irenea, only to have his janizaries mock him for idling with her (I,11). Mahommed therefore "seized her by the hair, took a knife, and slit her throat." Irenea was to relive in tales by Boaistuau, Belleforest, and Painter. Bandello also retells a story (IV,18) heard from a friend who had been for forty years a Turkish captive. A Greek maiden named Marulla, fighting alongside the Venetians in the Aegean area, strikes terror among the Turks, who attempt to flee; these so-called "dogs," unable to make it to their ships, are cut down "a filo di spada."

Painter (II,34) tells us that Mustapha, the son of Sultan Suleiman, is like his father a "Furiose Enemy of God":

And lyke as this unhappy Father was a deadly Enemy vnto Chryst and hys Church, so this yonge Whelpe was no lesse a sheder of Christian Bloud. No doubt a very froward Impe, and a towarde Champion for the diuel's Theatre.

This novellist also mentions that sultans cultivated harems to satisfy their libidinous appetites and excel over all other nations in vileness. The Turk is not only an enemy to our country and our life, but "also to our Soules." When everyone at last comes to this realization, he concludes:

. . . it will not be so hard a matter to withstand the force of this enemy of Christendome, as if we doe not, it wyll be daungerous through our continuall discorde to giue him occasion to inuade the rest of Europe, and so with his tiranny bring the same to vtter destruction, which God that is omnipotent forbid, who bring vs to vnity through his Sonne Iesus Christe, Amen.[37]

Attitudes toward the Moors were not so fixed, even though they kept a strong foothold in Europe until 1492. (Chaucer's Knight had fought them successfully at Algeciras in 1344.) Whereas the

Turk remained the enemy and the villain, the Moors, several of whose countries enjoyed diplomatic relations with England, Spain, and other European courts, were viewed with mitigated respect. Hence, to the novellists the Moors, though as pagan as the Turks, were not always so sadistically cruel.

The Spaniards knew the Moors best, and nearly half of the fifty-one tales of the *Conde Lucanor* either concern them or are derived from their literature. In Exemplo 9 we learn of the Infante Enrique, whom the King of Tunis tried without success to feed to lions. Other tales in the collection record a knight's fear at the approach of a Moorish army (15), the generosity of a Moorish king holding Spanish territory (28), a re-creation of the splendor of life in the eleventh-century Muslim courts at Seville and Cordoba (30), and an evocation of the Caliph Al-Hakam, who improved the design of flutes and expanded the Mosque of Cordoba (41). Although the novellist Don Juan Manuel thus held the Moors in a certain respect, he becomes the chief protagonist in Bandello's tale III,39, spending a year fighting Islamites and killing seven in single combat. The episode of his entering a lion's cage to retrieve a woman's glove becomes the source of Schiller's ballad, *Der Handschuh.*

After being held captive in North Africa for five years, Cervantes wrote tolerantly of the Moriscos in *Don Quijote,* Part II. Yet in the *Novelas ejemplares* of the same period the Moors are depicted as "rabble" in the "Coloquio de los perros." The dog Berganza, recalling a time when his master has been a Moor, says of the race:

> It would be a miracle if you could find among them one who believes firmly in the sacred law of Christianity. Their only purpose is to accumulate and hoard money, and to accomplish this they will labor without eating; . . . so that by always earning and spending nothing they have come to amass the largest amount of money that there is in Spain.[38]

Since the Arabs loved to tell tales about themselves, even inserting them in such marginal works as the *Perfumed Garden,* it is no surprise that other novellists than Don Juan Manuel retell them. Bandello (II,52) recalls the clemency of King Saich toward

Mahomet of Dubdú, who plotted unsuccessfully against him. He retells (IV,3) how the King of Tunis was blinded and killed by his cruel son Amida. His tale I,57 recalls the generosity of the Mahommedan King Mansor to a simple sailor who praises the monarch without recognizing him. The plundering and kidnapping on the part of the Barbary pirates, tracked down by such sea hawks as Andrea Doria (a hero of Lepanto), is fully discussed in Bandello's tale III,68.

Doña María de Zayas, like Cervantes, held ambivalent opinions about the Moors. Sometimes she makes them kindly and chivalrous, but her Catholic conscience leads her to make excuses for them. On the one hand, we find her continually creating scenes in which Moors are about to become Christians, ready to convert at an opportune time. On the other hand, we note the statements in her first *novela* that when Moors settle in a city, highborn Spaniards seek to settle elsewhere. As an apparent partisan of the caste system of marriage in Spain, the novellist Castillo Solórzano believed fervently that a Christian should not be contaminated by marriage outside his faith. Hence, in his *Niña de los embustes,* Teresa, a *pícara* no less, disdains to wed a rich Moorish chieftan.

The skin coloration of Moors, darker than that of Europeans, intrigued some novellists. Sacchetti wrote a tale (99) of a man married to a Moorish woman who made every effort to lighten her complexion, only succeeding in aging and drying her skin. Likewise, in Giraldi's famous tale, the villainous *alfiero* hopes that Disdemona may be tired of the *nerezza* of the Moor's skin. It is noteworthy that Cinzio, like Bandello, stresses honorable and civic-minded qualities in the Moorish character. Shakespeare's curious transformation of the Moor of Venice leads to his Othello becoming one of the most generous and sympathetic portraits of an African black in Renaissance literature. A final sympathetic portrait of a Moor is Bandello's tale (I,58) wherein the painter Fra Lippo Lippi was kidnapped off the shore of Ancona by Berber pirates and taken prisoner to North Africa. For over a year he rowed galleys and worked as a gardener. One day, however, he drew on a wall a charcoal portrait of his master Abdul Maumen. The Arab, much impressed, commissioned several paintings and eventually sent the artist back free to Naples, without the usual ransom demanded, for example, by the abductors of Cervantes.

The fortunes of Jews during the Diaspora fluctuated in the Middle Ages and the Renaissance. Spain first sheltered and honored the great Hebrew scholars in the Middle Ages, but then instituted the brutal pogroms of the fifteenth and sixteenth centuries, including burnings at the *autos-da-fé*. The novellas lead us to conclude that the same ambivalence shown toward the Arabs applied to the Jews.

As early as his second tale, Boccaccio shows great sympathy for the Jew Abraam, on whom the Italian lavishes such adjectives as *diritto, leale, valente, savio*, and *buono*. A righteous man confirmed in his Jewish faith, Abraam witnesses the fraud, envy, avarice, lust, and other sins of Christians in the Holy City itself. Ironically, though, Abraam decides that since Christendom continues to flourish despite its wickedness, it must have the full support of the Holy Spirit—hence he decides to get baptized and convert to Christianity. In the very next tale we meet another noble and worthy Jew, Melchisedech, a character already known to Europe through the *Cento novelle antiche* (73) and other mediaeval works. In this tale, when asked by Saladin which religion—Judaism, Moham-medanism, or Christianity—is the true religion, Melchisedech replies with the famous anecdote of the father who on his deathbed gave each of his three sons a beautiful ring: one of these was the family heirloom, the other two being almost perfect copies. Each son claimed to have the genuine ring, but no one knew for certain. Melchisedech thus concludes:

> And so, my lord, concerning the question which you asked me about the three Laws given by God to the three peoples, I say this to you: each one believes that it has the inheritance, the true Law, and carries out its commandments, but who does have it, as with the rings, is a question still unanswered.[39]

Less than two centuries later Protestantism was a fourth major religion. One wonders if, allowed the opportunity, Melchisedech (and Boccaccio) would have then revised the tale, giving the wise father four sons and as many rings.

The admirable lack of prejudice displayed in Boccaccio's tales

and their sources was not always displayed in later novellas.
Chaucer, who most likely knew the tales about Abraam and
Melchisedech, was apparently never tempted to retell them.
Instead, we have in his "Prioress's Tale" the depiction of the
martyrdom of a pious little boy at the hands of Jews. The extreme
anti-Semitic tone of the tale swells at several points, such as:

> Ther was in Asye, in a greet citee,
> Amonges Cristene folk, a Jewerye.
> Sustened by a lord of that contree
> For foule usure and lucre of vileynye,
> Hateful to Christ and to his compaignye:
>
> Oure firste foo, the serpent Sathanas,
> ... hath in Jues herte his waspes nest.[40]

Students of the *Canterbury Tales* continue to be challenged by the
question of Chaucer's intention in including this tale, especially as
he has assigned its narration to the vain, worldly, and hypocritical
Prioress.

The principal source of Shakespeare's Shylock is to be found in
Ser Giovanni Fiorentino's *Pecorone* (IV,1). The Jewish moneylender
here, we are told, would rather collect his "pound of flesh" than
the actual money owed him, for in this way he can bring about the
death of Ansaldo, the greatest of Christian merchants.

In the *Trecentonovelle,* dating from 1392 to 1400, Sacchetti betrays
not so much a prejudice as a scorn for the Jews as objects of humor.
Almost at the outset, in a tale (24) of very bad taste, he tells how
the poet Dolicibene, imprisoned in a Jewish temple of Jersualem,
commits a nuisance during the night and convinces his credulous
captors that his turd is their God, vanquished by the Christian
God. In Novella 190 Gian Sega of Ravenna detaches a young
Jewess from her fellow travellers, pretends to save them from
assailants, lodges the males in a redolent public toilet, and spends
the night in bed with the girl. Sacchetti piously concludes that
such things deserve to happen to those who "so pertinaciously
oppose the faith of Christ." Tale 218 of Sacchetti concerns the
mother of a short child who gives a Jew eight florins for a secret
formula which will cause her son to become taller ("Let him stand

up on a tree trunk"). Sacchetti moralizes: "It often happens that people today will believe a Jew more than a thousand Christians; Christians are now so *tristi*, with so little faith, to their own harm." Tale 219 is a variant of this theme. Two wives of brothers, eager to have children, pay a Jew a large sum for a beverage to encourage pregnancy. This David (synonym for Jew) supplies them with two bottles of a potion containing snake eggs. The wife who takes the potion finds herself expelling serpents. Again the refrain above: "It's amazing how Christian men and women would trust a Jew more than a hundred Christians." Northern Italy during the mid-fourteenth century was mistrustful of Jews, but the great pogroms were to take place elsewhere.

Bandello, a century and a half later, would seem to illustrate the more enlightened clergy. His tale about the rabidly anti-Semitic Frate Francesco (I,32) notes that after the pogroms in Spain had sent many Jews and marranos into Naples, Francesco tried to persecute and expel them in every way, only to be punished by life imprisonment by King Fernando. Yet, as a novellist, Bandello can forget the *caritas* of a prelate in describing the student Peretto (III,38), who is mocked by the girls of Modena for his Jewishness:

Now I shall digress briefly here so that you the reader may take great pleasure in the tale. Peretto was a tiny fellow with a face more Jew than Christian. And his manner betrayed more the rabbi than the philosopher. He went around always shorn and tonsured. His speech sounded like a German Jew trying to speak Italian.

In his third *Cigarral*, Tirso de Molina marvels at the patience of the Lord Jesus "in the hands of the Jews, under the power of Pontius Pilate." So often, as this passage demonstrates, anti-Semitism leaned on the easy rationalization of the Crucifixion to justify itself. Basile chides the habit of fear which Jews have acquired from the persecutions and pogroms to which they have been subjected. Indeed, they were expelled from Naples in 1541. One of Bandello's more offensive references is to a "Giudeo cacabrache."

Like Painter, Fenton was ironic about the Jews awaiting another

messiah than Christ. A brimming vessel of prejudice and
xenophobia, as will be further demonstrated below, Fenton refers
to the violent actions of Pandora as evidences of "her Jewishe
creweltie" and the avaricious persecutor of Charles in Discourse I—
merely "un riche Citoyen" in his source, Belleforest—he transforms
into a "longe nosed marchaunte." [41] Indeed, the novellas show,
with their additional comment on Egyptians, Turks, Tunisians,
and Moors, that anti-Semitism had less to do with religion than
with the run-of-the-mill xenophobia of the time, a xenophobia
which extended to closer neighbors as well.

Probably the most unwanted people in Europe during the
lifetime of the novellas were the gypsies; whose nomadic incursions
were viewed as plagues. The gypsies, it was believed, brought with
them violence, theft, fraud, and even kidnapping—a reputation
that lasted well into the twentieth century. Henry VIII ordered
them out of England in 1538, giving them the ultimatum to depart
from the nearest port within forty-eight hours or be hanged.
France followed suit in 1560, Spain in 1591.

The novellists wasted little affection—or creative energy—on the
gypsies. Cervantes alone gives us a memorable portrait of them
and their ways. In the "Coloquio de los perros" we learn from
Berganza how gypsy thieves sell an ass with a false tail to a simple
peasant, steal it back from him, and immediately, before he
discovers his loss, resell it without a tail to the selfsame peasant.
The canine narrator tells us that the only thoughts to enter the
gypsy mind concern cheating and stealing, acts they learn, both
male and female, almost from the time they are able to walk.
Gypsies marry among themselves, so Berganza informs us, so that
their evil ways may not become known to others. His summation:
"Finally, they are an evil race, and although many wise judges
have condemned them, still they do not reform."

Although the depiction of the gypsies in "La gitanilla"—a
subject to which we return in our final chapter—is far more
romanticized, Cervantes admits even here to their thievery and to
their simple, unorthodox code of justice. For example, when a wife
is unfaithful, the husband does not go to court for justice, but is
himself judge and executioner.[42]

African blacks make their first notable appearance in the famous tale of "The Emperor's New Clothes" in the *Conde Lucanor* (32). Unlike more modern versions, such as those of Hans Christian Andersen and others, this *exemplo* reasons that whereas all the courtiers and citizens would have much to lose by exposing the king's self-deception, an African Negro, at the bottom of the social scale in the fourteenth century, had the least to lose by speaking out. Subsequent appearances of blacks in the novellas are scant. There is some question whether the deceitful Lucia, the "grasshopper-legged slave" who marries Taddeo by trickery in the *Pentamerone* frame, is a Moor or an African black. The *nera* used to describe her could denote either; yet her curious "broken Italian" (e.g., "non mi stare cullo gnamme-gnamme") might well be meant to suggest some African pidgin. A true literary relative of Lucia appears in María de Zayas' tale, "Tarde llega el desengaño," which concerns a perfidious black servant girl who informs Don Jayme that his wife had been unfaithful. He imprisons the woman and replaces her at table with the servant. When the black girl finally confesses her lie, it is too late. The wife has already died. Shakespeare's novella-derived Othello, on the other hand, a synthesis (whether through ignorance, confusion, or design) of Giraldi's Moor and the African Negro, emerges as we have stated above, as one of the most sympathetic figures of the African black in the literature of the Renaissance.

Xenophobia in the novella not only embraced other races and other religions, but extended to other European nations as well. The Italians, who indulged in their share of xenophobia, often found themselves the butt of this prejudice. Boccaccio had been aware of it early, mentioning in the *Decameron* (II:1) a German judge who had apparently "some aversion toward Florentines." [43]

Despite its creator's dependence upon Italy for much of her inspiration and literary art, the *Heptaméron* is nevertheless turgid with anti-Italian sentiment. In her fourteenth *nouvelle* Marguerite tells of a Milanese lady who learns that Frenchmen not only are better lovers but are also "wiser, more persevering, and more discreet than Italians." Both Saffredent (16) and Hircan (17) comment on Italian cowardice in fighting. Simontault states at the end of Nouvelle 39 that for the Italian "the greater the sin, the greater the pleasure." Oisille's story of how the Duke of Urbino killed a potential daughter-in-law of whom he disapproved prompts animated discussion of Italians by the *devisants*. "Do not be surprised at this cruelty," Simontault remarks, "for those who have been in Italy have seen such unbelievable acts than what we have just heard is but a trifle." Geburon endorses this view with an anecdote concerning an Italian captain who tore out the heart of a man he hated, roasted it, and ate it, then killed the man's wife, tore out the fetus in her womb, and stuffed the bodies of the three with oats for his horses to eat. Hircan sums up matters with his unswerving belief that Italians "make their God out of things contrary to nature." [44]

The laureate of Italophobes was Fenton. As with Marguerite, it is ironic and perhaps paradoxical that his ample plagiarizing from the tales of an Italian—the very worldly and talented Bandello—did not prevent him from infusing them with a scorn of most things Italian. A lengthy catalogue of these sentiments could be compiled; we include only a brief sampling. A tacit assumption throughout the *Certain Tragical Discourses* is that Italians are corrupt, cowardly, lascivious, disorderly, and generally inferior. He disdainfully refers to the Italian soldiery as "ferfull Italyans" and mentions "th'Ytalian inclynacion touching the desier of the fleshe." At the beginning of Discourse I he signals Italy's fame as "the market place of tumultes and suborned trobles." The story of the adultress Pandora, recalled above, leads to the exclamation, "Ah las! have th'Ytalian mothers no other tombes for their children, then to bury them in the belly of a dogge? . . . Is this the curtesy of Italye, or a creweltie derived of the barbaric nacion?" To understand these and the many other expressions of anti-Italianism in Fenton, we must realize that by 1567 an anti-Italian current had swept into England, which would eventually erupt with Queen Elizabeth's refusal at the end of the century to let young Englishmen study in the schools of Italy.[45]

Fenton's xenophobia was, moreover, fostered by a kind of superpatriotism. The English army is composed, of course, of only "courageous Englishmen." As contrasted with the false prophets of Catholicism, English clerics are "th'undowted and faithfull mynisters of Godes worde." [46] When Fenton so often plays *traduttore/ traditore* in translating Belleforest, it is usually to the benefit of the

English, or the discredit of another nation. Belleforest's fulsome "ce victorieux et illustre Ferdinand le jeune, fils d'Alphonse, Roy d'Aragon" [47] is totally suppressed by Fenton. Yet when Belleforest mentions simply "ce vaillant et hardy capitaine Tallebot," Fenton must aggrandize his fellow countryman to "the onlye flower of chyvalrye of the tyme and valyant capteine, the Lorde Talbot." [48]

Sometimes Fenton's chauvinism borders on the laughable. Belleforest praises Philiberto for his decision to journey to France, "which, since antiquity has been the solace and refuge of the wretched, as much for its serene and mild environment, its land rich and abundant in all things, as for its people, more courteous, good-natured, and affable than any other nation under the moon." Fenton dismisses all of this, stating only that France was a "countreye moste meete for hys abode." [49] Finally, when Belleforest in a long account of nearly a hundred words describes a battle between French and English during the Hundred Years War, indicating the valor of the French and their glorious victory, Fenton condenses it to a grumpy few words: "In the skirmish (if a man may credit a French bragge) the Pyemontoyse and Talbot unhorsed each other." [50] A *caveat lector,* however: when considering Fenton's chauvinism, one should keep in mind Stephen Gottlieb's warning about the Elizabethan writer: "His early nationalism may not all be genuine, for Fenton was exceedingly ambitious, and dedicated his translations to his political designs." [51]

Often the prejudicial comments and characterizations that we find in the novellas were merely repetitions of clichés and stereotypes. Bandello, for instance, mentions (II,18) that Germans like to drink at length. An earlier story from the *Cent Nouvelles nouvelles* (80) concerns a simple German girl, recently married, who, when comparing it to that of a six-month-old donkey, is sorely disappointed with the *baston* with which her young husband is equipped. "You see the situation with the girls of Germany," the tale concludes. "If God pleases, they will soon be like that in France." [52]

A definitive thesis on the motivation of xenophobia and xenophilia among the novellists would probably bring to light the many shifting political trends of the age, from which of course no nation was exempt. María de Zayas was prejudiced against the

Flemish, but the Flemish were costing the Spanish crown a fortune by their resistance. Straparola betrayed a hatred of Spain, but he wrote not long after the Spaniards has sacked Rome and tried to pillage Florence. And so it went. Tirso held some grudge against the Catalans. The *Hundred Merry Tales,* printed by John Rastell, hammered away at the Welsh for their ignorance and brutality. Such sentiments as these carried the seeds of the ultimate expression of xenophobia: war.

III. War

Still known to the Middle Ages as the fiercest horseman of the Apocalypse, war obviously disturbed the novellists. It is said that the incessant series of wars sustained by the city-states and monarchies—the most sustained between the Roman and the Napoleonic Empires—were made possible by a financial policy of soft money,[53] a policy already condemned by Dante (*Paradise,* XIX:122-23). Wars were made further possible by the payments, ransoms, and booty provided by the defeated armies and populations. The chief wars mentioned in the novellas after the Hundred Years War were the long struggles of the Angevin and Aragonese crowns for Italy and Sicily, the expulsion of the Arabs from Spain, the skirmishes between Portugal and the North Africans, the land and sea migrations of the Turks up the Danube Valley and across the Mediterranean, strife between England and Spain in the New World, the unfortunate campaign of England against the Spaniards and Flemings in the Lowlands, and the continuing struggles between France and Emperor Charles V and his Hapsburg son, John of Austria.

Outright condemnation of war by the novellists appears slow in getting started. Boccaccio, especially through his closeness to the court of Naples, could recognize wars merely as conflicts between the powerful and the ambitious. He must have marveled that his friend Petrarch could devote an entire military epic to the Punic Wars. Military battles among the Swabians, Angevins, and Aragonese serve as the backdrop to the tale of Madonna Beritola (II:6). Boccaccio's attitude toward the nature and consequences of

war are reflected in the novella's opening line: "Sad and pitiful are
the various revelations of Fortune. . . ." [54]

One looks in vain for a condemnation of war in Chaucer. Yet as
Nevil Coghill has written, "Plague, schism, the Peasant's Revolt,
and the clashes between Richard II and his nobility, that were to
end in deposition and regicide, have no place in his poem of
England. Jack Straw's massacre of the Flemings in 1381 was
poetically no more to Chaucer than the flurry in a farmyard
aroused by the rape of Chanticleer." [55] Actually, his glowing
portrait in the General Prologue of the Knight, a "worthy man"
who had successfully fought in Alexandria, Prussia, Lithuania,
Russia, Granada, Algeria, Turkey, and elsewhere, would indicate
that Chaucer fully endorsed his nation's military campaigns and
those of its allies.

Wars against an aggressor or a religious proselytiser—seen either
as "crusades" (fought on behalf of an ideal) or as "just wars"
(fought on behalf of justice)[56]—were generally not condemned in
the novellas. To Don Manuel, who as a young man had taken up

arms against the Moors in 1294, the avoidance of war would have seemed dereliction and cowardice. His thirteenth tale, in which Don Juan himself figures, has Patronio tell Lucanor that his Catholic duty is to wage war on the Moors. Cuento 3, also affirming the righteousness of fighting religious wars, concerns the conversation between hermit and angel explaining that, despite all of Richard the Lion-Hearted's cruelties, his courageous leap into the sea to attack the infidels first won glory for God and pardon for Richard. It is hard therefore to agree with Giménez Soler's claim that Juan Manuel's warrior life-style constitutes a contradiction to his inherent religious piety.

Few novellists understood better the risks of soldiering than Luigi Da Porto—completely incapacitated in battle—or Cervantes, who reminds his readers in the Prologue to the *Novelas ejemplares* that he had been a soldier for many years, over five of them spent as a prisoner. He was, he says, proud to have joined the struggle against the Turk, even though it cost him his left hand, "a wound which, although it appears hideous, he considers beautiful because he received it on the most memorable and lofty occasion that he had seen in past centuries, or that he could hope to see in future ones." [57] Like Don Juan Manuel, Cervantes accepts the necessity of warring against an expanding infidel empire. In the "Licenciado vidriera" a captain enlists the young student into the army by omitting to tell him of "the bitterly cold nights standing guard, the peril of attacks, the horror of battles, the famine during sieges" which are the constants of war.

Obviously, by the time of the Renaissance, with its many conflicts listed above, other novellists would join the chorus of condemnation and satire of war, as old as Aristophanes. One finds Des Périers sympathizing (Nouvelle 67) with the victims of roaming armies of regulars and mercenaries: "They pillage, they ruin, they destroy all." [58] When this was published in 1558 the religious wars were raging in France. Not long afterward the future Henri III wrote from the battlefield a letter deploring these increasing ravages of the civil population.[59]

In the oft-invaded Italy several novellists spoke out. Leaning on Valerius Maximus the aristocratic Erizzo devoted a tale to the destruction of wars of aggression. It records the change of heart in the conqueror Aratus Sicyon, who so destroyed the Greek city of Lokris that he wept for his victims and forbade further destruction. Giraldi Cinzio reflected sadly (X:4) on how men, once girded with a sword, shed all humanity and freely indulge in thieving, treachery, wantonness, dishonesty, and every other imaginable evil. By far the most fiery and outspoken denunciation of war is to be found in Basile's *Pentamerone*. The steward Iacovucci in the eclogue concluding Day One pities the young man who idealistically goes off to war only to encounter disillusionment, anguish, suffering, and often death:

> He is stiffened by cold, wasted by heat, devoured by hunger, broken by fatigue. Danger is ever by his side, rewards far away. The wounds are in cash, the repayment on credit. The ills are long, the comforts short. Life is uncertain, death is assured. At last, worn out by great suffering, he runs away, but is caught after three steps and put to death by rope or firing squad; or else he remains and is slaughtered in battle, or he returns a cripple and receives but the companionship of a mange or a subsidy to purchase a crutch. Even when the evil is least, he fills an empty bed in the hospital.[60]

Travel was difficult in the Middle Ages and Renaissance. Chaucer was unusual in getting all the way from England to Italy. We know from Erasmus that it was a veritable exploit to get from Holland to Paris, and from Cellini how difficult and dangerous was the route from Florence to Paris. In such a world the antidote of travel was less available to dispel the clichés of xenophobia. Most of the travel in that world was carried on for war or conquest, and such travel is an antidote for nothing.

Notes

1. The theme of *fortuna* pervades the novella tradition as it does most other mediaeval and Renaissance literary genres. Besides Chaucer, see also, for example, Bandello's tale of Diego and Ginevra (I,27) and Fenton's tireless preaching on the subject in his *Certain Tragical Discourses*. Fenton's belief that those punished by harsh fate are invariably those who lack virtue—"Neither hathe she [Fortune] anye to followe the chariot of her victorie but the caitiffe or cowarde, and suche as are denied the assistaunce and benifet of trewe vertue" (I, 166)—seems a British

response to the Machiavellian compromise between fortune and free will that whereas one cannot stop the flood of a mighty river, one could nonetheless devise dikes, channels, and the like to reduce its impact by half.

2. *Zur Technik der Frührenaissancenovelle in Italien und Frankreich,* p. 1.

3. *Deutsche Literatur in zwei Jahrhünderten* (Berlin: Luchterhand Verlag, 1964), p. 374.

4. Wellek and Warren, *Theory of Literature,* p.95.

5. See, for instance, H. H. Remak's comments from the symposium "The Comparative Method: Sociology and the Study of Literature" published in *Yearbook of Comparative and General Literature,* 23 (1974), 27, hereafter cited as *YCGL.*

6. "Literature and Society" in *The Arts in Society,* ed. Robert N. Wilson (Englewood Cliffs, N.J.: Prentice-Hall, 1964), p. 308.

7. See Jean Alter's remarks in *YCGL,* p. 22.

8. Wellek and Warren, *Theory of Literature,* pp. 95 and 103-04.

9. *Gesta Romanorum,* trans. Charles Swann, rev. Wynnard Hopper (1876; rpt. New York: Dover, 1959), p. 251. For other royal tyrants or fools in the *Gesta,* see among others, Tales 25, 48, 72 and 91.

10. *Decameron,* p. 110.

11. Jacobs, I, 345.

12. Muriel Bowden, *A Reader's Guide to Geoffrey Chaucer* (New York: Farrar, Straus, and Giroux, 1964, p. 14.

13. Desmond Steward, *A Prince of the Renaissance: The Life of François I* (London: Constable, 1973), p. 33.

14. See François Génin, *Nouvelles lettres de la Reine de Navarre* (Paris, 1842; rpt. New York: Johnson Reprints, 1965), pp. 1-24. The poem itself appears on pp. 25-27.

15. Samuel Putnam, *Marguerite de Navarre* (New York: Coward-McCann, 1935), p. 137.

16. Pettie, I, 101.

17. Giambattista Basile, *Il Pentamerone,* trans. Benedetto Croce, rev. ed. (Bari: Laterza, 1957), pp. 300 and 114.

18. *Decameron,* pp. 22-24.

19. Jourda, p. 920.

20. *Decameron,* pp. 470-71.

21. Chaucer, pp. 241-42 and 48.

22. Ibid., p. 198.

23. Jacobs, II, 208; and Fenton, II, 104.

24. Di Francia, II, 104.

25. Basile, pp. 124-25 and 207.

26. For a helpful discussion of the conventions of the feudal marriage as well as some of the reactions to it, see Bernard I. Murstein, *Love, Sex, and Marriage through the Ages* (New York: Springer, 1974), pp. 173-204.

27. Jourda, pp. 981, 960, and 968.

28. *Decameron,* p. 86.

29. Chaucer, p. 47.

30. Ibid., p. 49.

31. *Chaucer Criticism,* p. 157.

32. *Decameron,* pp. 1218 and 1232; also cf. *Decameron,* p. 1222, and Chaucer, p. 104.

33. Jacobs, III, 43.

34. Ibid., I, 223.

35. Fenton, I, 132, and II, 292-93

36. Chaucer, p. 64.

37. Jacobs, III, 396, 402, and 415.

38. Cervantes, p. 1021.

39. *Decameron,* p. 78.

40. Chaucer, pp. 161-62.

41. Bandello, II, 446-47; Fenton, I, 161 and 241; also cf. Fenton, I, 29 and Belleforest in *The French Bandello: The Original Text of Four of Belleforest's "Histoires Tragiques,"* ed. Frank S. Hook (Columbia: Univ. of Missouri Press, 1948), p. 160.

42. Cervantes, pp. 1021 and 789.

43. *Decameron,* p. 133.

44. Jourda, pp. 809, 965, and 1021-22.

45. Fenton, II, 59 and 131; I, 21; and I, 161. This phenomenon of anti-Italianism in England has been analyzed in a penetrating volume by George B. Parks, *The English Traveler to Italy* (Rome: Edizioni di storia e letteratura, 1954).

46. Fenton, II, 59, and I, 265.

47. *French Bandello,* p. 83.

48. Cf. *French Bandello,* p. 75; and Fenton, II, 201.

49. Cf. *French Bandello,* p. 72; and Fenton, II, 200.

50. Cf. *French Bandello,* p. 76; and Fenton, II, 201.

51. Stephen A. Gottlieb, "Fenton's Novelle," *Revue de la littérature comparée,* 40 (1966), 122.

52. Jourda, p. 294.

53. See Robert S. Lopez, "Hard Times and Investment in Culture," in *The Renaissance: Six Essays* (1953; rpt. New York: Harper and Row, 1962), p. 34.

54. *Decameron,* p. 193.

55. Nevill Coghill, *The Poet Chaucer,* 2nd ed. (London: Oxford Univ. Press, 1967), p. 93.

56. See Roland Bainton, *Christian Attitudes toward War and Peace* (New York: Abingdon, 1960), esp. pp. 14, 39 and 95-96.

57. Cervantes, p. 769.

58. Jourda, p. 504.

59. *Renaissance Letters,* ed. Robert J. Clements and Lorna Levant (New York: New York Univ. Press, 1976), pp. 330-31.

60. Basile, pp. 118-19.

CHAPTER 5

Images of Society:
Trades, Professions, Money,
Medicine, Sciences
And Pseudo-Sciences

I. Trades and Professions, Money, Usury

Since the novella was essentially a middle-class genre aiming to please the rising burgher class, it is not surprising to find great prominence given to the *uomini mezzani,* sometimes for satirical ends, sometimes for praise. Among the professions and trades flourishing in both the countryside and the rising towns of Europe, especially singled out in the novellas, were, to name but a few, members of guilds, millers, merchants, physicians, and alchemists.

For Chaucer with his characteristic upper-class bias, guild members were little more than hopelessly crass *nouveau riche* figures, straining for a kind of life they neither understood nor appreciated. His Guildsmen—a Haberdasher, Carpenter, Weaver, Dyer, and Tapestry-Maker—possess all the requisite status symbols of their time: knives mounted with silver, well-wrought belts and pouches, and their very own Cook (even though he did have a "mormal" on his shin). John the Carpenter in "The Miller's Tale," as we recall, is merely a "riche gnof" who enters into a loveless marriage with a

127

vivacious and shapely girl of eighteen. An ancestor of the inevitably cuckolded John is the "very wicked and very covetous" carpenter in the *Gesta Romanorum* (109), admittedly the symbol of "worldly-minded man," whose misplaced money is ultimately distributed among the poor. Chaucer is also very critical of millers. Robin in the frame-tale of the *Canterbury Tales* is not only a drunkard, boor, and dimwit—knocking doors off their hinges with his head—he is also a cheat:

> Wel koude he stelen corn and tollen thries;
> And yet he hadde a thombe of gold, pardee.

The miller in the Reeve's tale is clearly a blood relative, if not the alter ego of Robin:

> A theef he was for sothe of corn and mele,
> And that a sly, and usant for to stele.[1]

A more sympathetic attitude toward a miller's cleverness is exemplified in the previously mentioned story from the *Cent Nouvelles nouvelles* (3) in which a Burgundian miller makes a cuckold of a knight who is himself given to placing horns on other husbands' heads by trickery.

There is a memorable description of the butcher's trade in Cervantes' "Coloquio de los perros." Berganza tells us of the violence and immorality of those who work in the slaughterhouse. "First you must believe that all who work in it, from the youngest to the oldest, are men of little conscience, inhuman, without fear of either the king or his justice. Most of them live with concubines and are carnivorous birds of prey. They maintain themselves and their mistresses by what they steal. . . . Yet nothing astounded me more or seemed worse than to see that those butchers with the same ease kill a man as they do a cow. For the least straw, they plunge a knife into the belly of a man, as if they were slaughtering a bull." [2]

A daily concern of the middle and lower classes in the age of the novella was money. None was more insistent. Money was the incentive of the mercantile boom of the Trecento, and many are the tales about merchants in this period, not all of which are complimentary. In one extravagant tale of the *Cento novelle antiche* (97), retold by Straparola (VIII:4) in the mid-Cinquecento, the Genoese merchant Bernardo, like his counterpart in Chaucer's "Shipman's Tale," found Flanders a most promising area for trade, earning two large sacks of golden crowns there by selling watered-down wine to the Flemings. But just as he was sailing home with his unusual profit, justice was served when a monkey kept aboard hurled one of the bags of gold into the sea. In the novellas (see also Sacchetti, 154) the most successful merchants were often Genoese, for Genoa was a banking center.

In every age there will be those who look askance at "persons in the trade," called by Fenton "peltynge [contemptible] marchaunts." This English novellist would bar them from holding office in the commonwealth and from sitting in judgment on those "whose harts by nature abhorre to be tryed by the barbarous voice of so vile and base people." The eclogue that closes Day Four of Basile's *Pentamerone* also condemns conniving merchants intriguing

to become wealthy: "The merchant never loses his hat in a crowd.
. . . He swears, vows, affirms that what is rotten is fresh, what is
worn is new, and with beautiful words but evil deeds he deceives
you and shows you white for black, so that you always discover
some flaw in his merchandise." [3]

Chaucer and Cervantes were more ambivalent in their attitudes
toward merchants. Supposed by some to be Gilbert Maghfield,[4]
the Merchant in the *Canterbury Tales* is said to be energetic and
expert at currency exchange, but Chaucer adds that he spoke
pompously ("solempnely"), discussing "alway th'encrees of his
wynnyng." Yet, despite his shrewd financial maneuvering, the
Merchant was "in dette." Again, the novellist concedes, "For sothe,
he was a worthy man with alle," then hastily concludes, "But,
sooth to seyn, I noot how men hym calle." [5]

Cervantes' Berganza in the "Coloquio de los perros" tells us that
a very wealthy merchant was among his many masters. Although
Berganza speaks of "the delightful and ordered life" spent with the
merchant, a period of his life he characterizes as calm and restful,
his canine companion Scipio remarks that many merchants of
Seville as elsewhere love to make a great show of their wealth and
importance not in their own persons but in those of their sons,
sardonically explaining:

> Merchants show their authority and wealth . . . through their
> sons because they are greater in the shadow than in them-
> selves. And as they rarely attend to anything but their trade
> and their contracts, they behave modestly. When they long to
> show off their ambition and wealth, they do it through their
> sons, maintaining them as if they were princelings. Some even
> acquire titles and wear on their breasts the emblems that
> distinguish men of rank from the masses.[6]

Boccaccio emerges among the novellists as the great champion of
merchants. Perhaps because his early days in Naples found him
physically counting and changing money, Boccaccio could admire
the honest enterprises and ambition of merchants and bankers,
since they reaped benefits not only for themselves but for society,
and of course, the Church as well. One observes Boccaccio's

sympathies in the story of Rinaldo d'Esti (II:2) or Andreuccio da Perugia (II:5); the latter went to Naples to buy horses at a good price, underwent several misadventures to which a merchant could be exposed, and returned having "invested" his 500 florins in a ruby ring worth much more, as the ex-banker Boccaccio makes explicit. A parallel story (VIII:10) demonstrates his compassion for Salabaetto, the merchant bilked by a seductress, whose business acumen gets him back his warehoused goods. Finally, perhaps recalling his own resistance to his father's putting him into a bank, Boccaccio whimsically sympathizes (VII:7) with the wealthy Parisian merchant who refused to let his impractical son Lodovico inherit the business and instead sent him to the royal palace to be a *mignon* of the king. He obviously knew, as did Chaucer's merchant, that one must be sharp in money matters to survive.

Money drove some adventurous types into counterfeiting. The ecologue with which Basile closes the third day of his *Pentamerone,* "La Coppella," takes its name from the cupel used for gold and silver in the act of counterfeiting, a special enterprise of the Neapolitans. Money led others into beggary, like the baron of mendicants Tailleboudin, whom we meet in Du Faïl's *Propos rustiques* (7). An ancestor of the gentleman-beggar in *Deus lhe Pague* of Brazilian dramatist Joracy Camargo, Tailleboudin learns that he can earn more in a day before a church than in pushing a plow for three days. Money was seen to corrupt the rich, making them all the more avaricious. This embittered Fenton, who wrote in Discourse XII that the wealthy "not only close their eares against the lamentable cries of the needie, but also make no conscience to dispoile theim, either by awe, feare, or flattery, of that litle which their fortune hath lefte theim."[7] Money could drive those addicted to gaming to the loss of their entire patrimony, as one learned from Bandello's tale (I,14), the source of Fenton's aforementioned Discourse XII. And money bred misers, like Rastell's tightwad merchant dying in London (17), who lay on his deathbed with "ten or twelve pounds in nobles" stuffed into his mouth.

Worst of all, money also bred usurers, one of the most despised groups in the novellas. In the *Cento novelle antiche* (26) a housewife eager for a new *cotta* drives her husband to borrow ten marks from a usurer at 20 percent, only to have the magus Merlin revile her for

driving her man to a usurer. She removes the coat and gives it to
Merlin to shrive her for her sin. In Don Juan Manuel's tale (14) of
St. Dominic and the usurer, after a greedy Lombard moneylender
has died, his heart cannot be found in his body, for it has fled,
decaying and rotten, to his money-chest.

During the Middle Ages the Church forbade Christians to lend
money at any amount of interest whatsoever, since this was seen as
a blatant violation of the Christian virtue of charity. We recall that
Dante included usury in Circle Seven of *Inferno* as a sin of violence
against God and nature. Usury is the product, as we learn from the
Gesta Romanorum 109, of another, deadly, sin—avarice. A usurer on
trial before an especially vindictive mediaeval court could even
find a charge of sodomy added to the indictment to ensure his
being found guilty.[8] However, with the rise of capitalism in the
Renaissance, northern Protestants initiated money-lending at a
modest rate. Calvin approved interest of 5 percent as ethical (lower

for needy borrowers), and the Puritans agreed with Francis Bacon's essay "Of Usury" that usury should be reduced to "five in the hundred."

In Sacchetti's amusing Tale 32, a Dominican who usually preaches to an almost empty church conceives a way to attract the parishioners of his confreres. He announced a sermon which will prove, after his long study, that usury is not a sin. To the large congregation he explains that moneylending *(usura)* is not a sin. The point is that collecting interest is the sin. In Tale 100 a preacher is reproached by a wise old peasant for sermonizing to his poverty-ridden flock on usury; the priest wisely shifts his theme to the "Beati pauperes." In Tale 128 a usurer is dying and even his friend the bishop of Florence refuses him a Christian burial until he has repaid the collected interest shown in his financial ledgers.

Another amusing tale against usurers is Bandello's III,53. When the great preacher Fra Bernardino of Siena is giving sermons in Milan, a rich usurer Tomasone Grasso reproaches him for not having sermonized against the terrible vice of usury. Tomasone's subtle motivation is his hope to see his competitors reform after hearing the "canonical and civil" condemnations of lending. In the novella "Belfagor," Machiavelli explains that his devil-hero settled in Florence in preference to other towns as most favorable for his making a living by usury.

Yet the tale about a usurer which won worldwide fame is in Ser Giovanni Fiorentino's *Pecorone* (IV:I). It was from this novella that Shakespeare took for his *Merchant of Venice* such details as the bond and the rings, the setting of Venice, and the alternate locale of Belmonte, home of Portia. The fact that Christian businessmen could not for many years lend money—whereas Jews could do so with impunity—makes it perhaps inevitable that a villainous Jewish usurer would make an appearance in a novella as well as on the dramatic stage. The horrendous "pound of flesh" aside, it is not clear what extreme percentage was being charged by the usurers in some of the novella collections. Certainly the 20 percent mentioned in the *Cento novelle antiche* of the thirteenth century sounds almost as frightening as a pound of flesh.

II. Scholars, Medical Men

Not many of the novellists were, like Painter, teachers or schoolmasters. Therefore "bookful blockheads," as Pope will call them, will occasionally be taxed in the novellas. These include teachers and students. A serious charge against the schools in both the Middle Ages and Renaissance seems to have been that diplomas were often bought rather than earned. In Straparola (XIII:10) we encounter the most inept student ever to enter the University of Bologna. Nevertheless, through "money, luck, favor, and connections" he received his doctoral bonnet. Like Boccaccio's Master Simone, graduates considered their diplomas and academic robes a sign of high social rank (VIII:9). Their pretensions become ludicrous when encountering the unlearned, matter-of-fact middle and lower classes, and the novellist is always on the side of the latter. The brother-in-law of the learned and modest Thomas More, Rastell, is proof of this sympathy. In the eighth of the *Hundred Merry Tales* an Oxenford pedant takes his shoes to a cobbler to have them cleated. "Cobbler, I pray thee set me two triangles and two semicircles upon my subpeditals and I shall give thee for thy labour." The bewildered shoemaker answers, "Sir, your eloquence passeth mine intelligence, but I promise that if ye meddle with me, the clouting of your shoon shall cost you three pence." Let us not forget that the learned Doctor from Bologna was a standard comic role in Renaissance comedy.

As for students, they do not fare much better than teachers and scholars as objects of the novellists' satire. Calling only Des Périers as witness, one finds him (54, 59, 65, 76, 84) testifying to students' immorality, duplicity, stupidity, and criminality—they are capable of stooping to such depths as stealing a poor tailor's shears. In Nouvelle 76 a student practices public speaking before cabbages. When he is faced with a real audience, like Rabelais' young giant after a Scholastic training, he is incapable of uttering a syllable. The Church, which administered the schools and seminars almost entirely, stands accused of failure both educationally and ethically.

Of all the learned professions, medicine was probably most often the butt of satire. So primitive was mediaeval medicine and so poor the patients that a current joke asked, "Why pay so dearly for death when it costs nothing to die?" With its belief in humors, its clumsy surgery, its faith in herbs and stones, mediaeval medicine was a natural target. Anatomies and dissections were long forbidden by the Church.

Several physicians are lampooned in the *Gesta Romanorum.* Tale 76 concerns two foolish medical men who attempt to discover which is the superior physician by plucking out each other's eyes and trying to restore them. The collection also contains the familiar story (132) of the three doctors who connive to destroy the practice of a young colleague of whose success they are envious. Another physician early mocked is Taddeo di Alberotto of the Studium of Bologna, whom the *Cento novelle antiche* (35) shows accepting a ridiculous proof as demonstrating a ridiculous theory (that eating eggplant for nine days causes madness). The dishonesty of a doctor who will poison another's patient is depicted in Tale 11 of the same mediaeval work.

If Boccaccio had developed an antipathy to physicians equal to that in his friend Petrarch, we might find some lively satires against medicine in the *Decameron.* Such is hardly the case. Two doctors, Mazzeo della Montagna of Salerno and Simone de Villa of Florence, are among the few Ser Giovanni includes. The former, "un grandissimo medico in cirugia," appears in the role of cuckold in IV:10. Simone is invited by the pranksters Buffalmacco and Bruno into a fictitious honorary society (VIII:9). Boccaccio manages briefly to deride Master Simone, whose medical expertise is said not to go any further than "curing babies of milk-sickness." He is also given to boast, "I have the finest books and the handsomest gowns' of any physician in Florence," and he takes pride in the fact that as a student at Bologna he spent more evenings wenching than poring over books.[9]

Chaucer uncovered the weaknesses of mediaeval medicine more fully. In the "Nun's Priest's Tale" we learn from Pertolote that enemas were the prescribed cure for the "vapors" of melancholy and choler. The "Doctour of Physick" in the General Prologue is one of Chaucer's best-known character portraits. The books he has allegedly read catalogue the ancient medical authorities known to Chaucer's age: Dioscorides, Hippocrates, Galen, Avicenna, Averroes, John of Gatesden, and others. Like other medical men of his time, Chaucer's physician was grounded in astrology and magic, believing that they helped one choose the time and nature of appropriate cures. He also conceived of the body as composed of the four elements in varying proportions, the precise makeup of which could determine a patient's "humour." Chaucer also utilizes his "parfait praktisour" of medicine to satirize the connivance between doctors and chemists, a theme so cleverly dramatized centuries later in Jules Romains' spoof *Knock, or the Triumph of Medicine*. Chaucer's medic dealt with a tribe of apothecaries, and "ech of hem made oother for to wynne." [10] Greed seems indeed to be the most unethical trait of the Physician, enamored of gold and eager for the sums he could acquire during pestilences.

The *Trecentonovelle*, immediately after the *Canterbury Tales*, picks up this theme. Tale 155 contrasts the greatness of the physician Dono del Garbo (also in Tales 26 and 70) with a medical charlatan Gabbadeo of Prato (also in 155, 168), who cannot carry a urinal without spilling its contents all over himself. Having bound up a child's hand, which was twisted and swollen, another charlatan Dolcibene (156) boasts of this as a medical triumph. One final impostor, Gonnella in Tale 173, collects money from a group afflicted by goiters, only to skip off with their cash.

Nor did physicians escape the earthy satire of the *Cent Nouvelles nouvelles*. Tale 2 deals with a friar-physician who attempts to cure a woman of piles, but manages to blind himself instead. Another *nouvelle* (20) illustrates the humorous side of diagnosis by urinalysis. At the instigation of the parents involved, a benevolent doctor predicts that a recently married but still virginal young wife will die unless she has sexual intercourse with her backward, inexperienced husband. (The youth good-heartedly supplies the cure.) In the variant novella which directly follows, it is an abbess who risks death. Both tales are variants of the mediaeval *conte* of the *vilain mire* (rustic doctor), with its preachment that the cure for an ill woman is a man. Another mediaeval tale concerning doctors, known as "La Comédie de celuy qui espousa une femme muette," concerns a husband who has a physician return the power of speech to his mute wife, only to beg in vain for her to be rendered mute again. It is retold in Rastell's edition of tales (62) of 1526.

Returning to the rich lode of satire in the *Cent Nouvelles nouvelles*, we come to the physician (79) who prescribes a single remedy—the ubiquitous enema—for all maladies. Through a misunderstanding he prescribes it to a simpleton who has lost his donkey. When the donkey is fortuitously recovered, it wins great fame for the doctor. Tale 87 tells how a medical man blindfolds a knight whose eye he is treating in order to make love freely to the knight's doxy. The physician, by the way, automatically deems the knight's blindness incurable, for, we are told, "that is how doctors usually diagnose, so that after effecting a cure, they gain more fame and profit." [11] Incidentally, in Tale 22 of the *Gesta Romanorum* a knight's unfaithful wife blindfolds him similarly so that he cannot observe the presence of her lover.

Like all sciences, medicine made rapid strides in the Renaissance, breeding pioneers like Vesalius, Eustachio, Falloppio, Rabelais, Amboise Paré, and other precursors of Harvey. Surgery advanced once doctors freed themselves of the Church's opposition to dissections. Yet so baffling were such prevalent diseases as gout, sweating sickness, the stone (gallstones), and plagues that Aretino was able to write scornfully of physicians that the sum and substance of their knowledge of the art of Galen is to give mallow-water as enema. Traditional mediaeval cures subsisted. In Du Faïl's *Propos rustiques* we learn how a blind faith in herbals passes from father to son. In Tale 4 Huguet advises that if one falls into some illness, he should not resort to purges, blood-lettings, and such, but should seek the remedy in his garden.

In the *Piacevoli notti* (VIII:6) Straparola amusingly illustrates that rich and famous doctors are often inferior to unassuming, poor confreres and have much to learn from the latter. Des Périers *Nouvelles récréations* abounds in cynical observations on Renaissance medicine. A bogus doctor and an apothecary get rich as they talk their Latin à la Molière and make all the villagers undergo urinalyses (59). When the bogus doctor gets so rich that he decides to study medicine in Paris, it is assumed that his diploma will merely make him a worse physician than before. (This tale reemerges with few changes in the *Mirrour of Mirth* of 1583.) In Tale 89 the mockery shifts from urinalyses to blood-letting and enemas. By mistake a patient's monkey takes the prescribed purgative, and its wholesale soiling of the man's home makes him laugh so hard that he is permanently cured. Rastell adopts this plot with only slight variations (7), concluding that "medicines taken at adventure" are often more fruitful than those prescribed by a physician. In Des Périers's eleventh novella we learn, incidentally, that the local barber not only serves as surgeon, as was to be expected, but also diagnoses maladies, applies unguents, dresses wounds, and fulfills the function of a general practitioner. Similarly, we learn from the *Trecentonovelle* (106) that blacksmiths served as dentists for the extraction of teeth.

Fenton keeps alive in England Chaucer's ridicule of the physician's purported greed or covetousness—especially when the king is footing the bill:

Then mighte a man see suche a mooster of phizisions and chirurgions, with their appoticaries carienge their bagges and boxes of all confections, that their rowte seamed rather a newe supplie of power, to assiste the kinge against his enemies, then a convocation of gownesmen to consulte of the disease . . . not so muche for the glorye of the acte as gaine of the moneye (without anye helpe notwithstandinge to the sickman). . . .

But a bargain demanded by a certain king—that *he* will get paid by anyone who undertook the cure and failed—left the physicians and their "mistical crewe" in full retreat, cursing Galen, Hippocrates, and Avicenna, for not leaving them with the means of a sure cure, "a sufficient net to fysh so great an honor," that would have earned them ten thousand francs.[12]

In his *Cigarrales* Tirso de Molina is amused and bemused at the masses' credulity with respect to the medical profession. In a scene from the third tale during which an innkeeper's wife lies helpless with a stomach ailment, Carrillo rejects the services of a doctor: "The ignorant place faith in medicine more than in anything else, although barbarians practice it." He himself concocts in the kitchen a plaster learned from his mother. Feeling it applied to her stomach, the woman hops out of bed screaming, to the effect that everyone cries, "Milagro!" Finally, in the eclogue concluding the

Pentamerone's fourth day, Basile divides physicians into these two categories:

> The doctor, if he is an evil one, lengthens out one's sickness and has such an understanding with the apothecary. If he is a good doctor, still he will show that among his many prescriptions he knows also the secret of stretching his hand behind his back for payment.[13]

A good deal of skepticism concerning medicine was directed, as we have seen, toward apothecaries. In Nouvelle 68 of the *Heptaméron* Marguerite presents a philandering apothecary who prescribes a new "wonder drug" for a wife whose husband is faithless. But the apothecary's own wife overhears the conversation and administers to her husband a large dose of the drug, which almost kills him. The Queen of Navarre's apothecary is sent for, and, curing his wayward colleague, censures him sharply for "making another take drugs which he would not himself take willingly." Cervantes is the most severe, considering the apothecaries at least as criminal as doctors. For when they are out of a medicine requested on a prescription, they substitute something similar which produces the reverse effect of the right one. It is also Cervantes who rises to the ultimate charge in the "Licenciado Vidriera" that physicians are murderers whose crimes are never discovered, since the bodies are quickly deposited under the earth— "Only the physicians can kill us without fear of any punishment, without unsheathing any other sword but a prescription." [14]

III. Astronomy, Sciences, and Pseudo-Sciences

Other branches of sciences and pseudo-sciences also came under attack in the novellas. Astrologers and astronomers, for instance, the nature of each often confused, appear with great frequency. The *Cento novelle antiche* (38) dutifully relates the traditional tale of how the famous astronomer Thales wandered star-gazing at night, only to fall into a ditch and be rescued by a scolding shrew, but it refers to the famous Greek as an "astrologer." The same confusion of terminology occurs in Tale 29, where a fool mocks a group of learned "astrologers" and demonstrates that they know no more than himself about what lies beyond the planets.

Chaucer, like his own Physician, was "grounded in astronomie," yet even physicians sometimes cast the horoscopes of their patients. It may be said that astrology in the late Middle Ages attained the popularity of psychoanalysis in our own age. The Wife of Bath's character, she is convinced, is formed by virtue of her "constellacioun":

> For certes, I am al Venerien
> In Feelynge, and myn herte is Marcien.
> Venus me yaf my lust, my likerousnesse,
> And Mars yaf me my sturdy hardynesse;
> Myn ascendent was Taur, and Mars therinne.
> Allas! allas! that evere love was synne!

The Man of Law curses the "crueel firmament" that shapes our ends, and blames the failure of Constance's marriage on the heavens: "That crueel Mars hath slayn this marriage,/Infortunat ascendent tortuous." "The Franklin's Tale" illustrates how a magician searches the skies for auspicious omens:

> His tables Tolletanes forth he brought,
> Ful wel corrected, ne ther lakked nought,
> Neither his collect ne his expans yeeris,
> Ne his rootes, ne his othere geeris,
> As been his centriz and his argumentz
> And his proporcioneles convenientz
> For his equacions in every thyng.[15]

Chaucer shows, too, how astrology could easily be perverted to serve one's own selfish ends. Nicholas in "The Miller's Tale" convinces the carpenter on astrological evidence of his own invention that a flood far greater than that of Noah will soon arise.

While the credulous husband, asleep in a barrel, awaits this terrible calamity, the student makes love to his wife.

Rastell's tale (84) of the astronomer of Oxenford teaches us that "the cunning of herdsmen and shepherds as touching the alterations of weather is more sure than the indicals of astronomy." For the herdsman knows that it will rain within a halfhour after his dun cow "danceth and holdeth up her tail."

Even though Nostradamus and other astrologers were subsidized by kings, the novellists were prone to view them as fraudulent. Sacchetti (151) mocks the *astromaco* Fazio da Pisa, claiming that none of these would-be Ptolemies or Alfonso Tenths can foresee the future. During the first day of the *Pentamerone* Iacovuccio delivers a diatribe against the popular astrologers and astrolobes:

> The astrologer is besieged from all sides by innumerable demands. This one wants to know if his baby will be a boy; that one, if he will be happy; another, if he will win his lawsuit; still another, if he will have bad luck. This one wants to know if this lady loves him, that one if an eclipse is on its way. And he gives reply, to demonstrate his worth, guessing half, and making a hundred errors.

Like poor Thales, adds Fabiello, the astrologer lets the stars lead him into misfortunes: "Always ready to foretell to others, he does not know what falls upon his own back. He gazes at the stars and tumbles into a ditch." [16]

Along with astronomers and astrologers, alchemists fascinated people in the Middle Ages and Renaissance, but since there was never any evidence that they were getting on with their discovery of the fifth essence, they were a less influential group. As early as the fourteenth century Juan Manuel begins to satirize alchemy. In his twentieth exemplum, derived from the earlier *Caballero Zifar*, a rogue convinces a king that he has access to *tabardie*, his name for the fifth essence. He bilks the monarch out of a large sum of money before disappearing from the scene. Chaucer makes of the "Canon Yeoman's Tale" a pretext for an extended diatribe directed against alchemists with their tireless quest for the "philosopher's stone."

Thanne conclude I thus, sith God of hevene
Ne wil nat that the philosopheres nevene
How that a man shal come unto this stoon,
I rede, as for the beste, lete it goon.
For whoso maketh God his adversarie,
As for to werken any thyng in contrarie
Of his wil, certes, never shal he thryve,
Thogh that he multiplie terme of his lyve.[17]

Two consecutive *nouvelles* of Des Périers are aimed at alchemists, their arcane language, their promises, and claims of knowing things about nature unknown to others. They are said to be like the milkmaid who going to market compounds in her mind the earnings and purchases she will make, only to drop and break the crock of milk. "Thus the alchemists, after they have set up their furnaces, lit the coals, distilled, calcinated, congealed, fixed, liquefied, vitrified, purified, one needs only to break the alembic to liken them to the good milkmaid." Nouvelle 13 attributed the discovery of the philosopher's stone to King Solomon, who used it to constrain demons, which at length he penned up in a huge copper vault. But lately these goblins have escaped and are preventing the alchemists from discovering the *pierre philosophale*. Now the alchemists must set themselves ever more zealously to "conjure, adjure, excommunicate, anathemize, exorcize, cabalize, ruin, exterminate, confuse, and destroy those demons." [18]

By the 1630s, well after Ben Johnson's *Alchemist* illustrated the eventual disbelief in this pseudo-science, Fabiello and Iacovucci in the *Pentamerone* concur that everyone is now agreed that the bankrupt alchemists have failed once and for all in transmuting metals to gold:

He goes hunting after secrets and is hailed by all as mad. In searching for the prime matter, he loses his own form. He believes he will multiply gold, but diminishes the little that he already has. He imagines that he will heal all the sick with metals, but it is he who winds up in the hospital. Instead of collecting quicksilver, which has value and can be spent, he wears himself out and thus squanders his very life. And while he thinks he will transmute baser metal into pure gold, he only transforms himself from a man into an ass.[19]

Lastly, necromancy and chiromancy (or palmistry), if not taken seriously, at least lend some variety to a few collections. In the *Cento novelle antiche* (21) three necromancers win the support of Emperor Frederick of Sicily by making rain, thunder, and lightning appear at their behest so suddenly that all the courtiers disappear in terror. Through illusionism they subsequently lead the Count of San Bonifazio to believe that he has married, had children, and fought battles over the course of forty years. In Cuento 11 of the *Conde Lucanor* the Dean of Santiago Cathedral learns necromancy from the soothsayer Don Illán. In a dream sequence, the two narrative planes of which may well suggest reality and black magic, the Dean, as he ascends through the hierarchy from bishop to cardinal to pope, refuses all favors to Don Illán. Indeed, he even threatens the latter with a charge of heresy and witchcraft, when, all too soon, the illusion is ended. In *Gesta Romanorum* (102) a necromancer in love with a knight's wayward wife tries in vain to kill her husband in effigy.

In the *Decameron* (X:5) a necromancer precipitates a marital crisis by acceding to a whimsical desire to make a garden as beautiful in January as it is in May. In Chaucer's "Franklin's Tale" he removes ugly and dangerous rocks from the shoreline. Reminiscent of Ariosto's later *Negromante* Boccaccio's lying scamp Bruno (VIII:9) has no necromantic powers, but he nevertheless brags of his connections with the necromancer Michele Scotus, the widely known astrologer and alchemist in the Court of Federico II who is credited by Dante in the *Inferno* (XX) with having learned the "game of magical frauds."

In the mid-Cinquecento Straparola amusingly adapted both necromancy and chiromancy in his fictions. In VIII:5 Lauretta tells of a tailor who secretly practiced necromancy, specifically the art of enabling a man to convert himself into a horse, a fox, or a cock. We meet a Spanish king in IX:1 who depends on the counsels of his chiromancer. In the *scène à faire*, so to speak, the counselor discovers that his royal master is a cuckold: "The chiromancer took the king's hand and diligently scrutinized every line in it. Having looked, he fell silent and paled." [20]

It is safe to conclude from these paragraphs on astrology, alchemy, necromancy, and chiromancy, that the novellas from the thirteenth to the seventeenth centuries did not merely record a growing disbelief and rationalism, but actually played a role in the gradual discrediting of all pseudo-sciences and magic.

Notes

1. Chaucer, pp. 22 and 56.
2. Cervantes, p. 999.
3. Fenton, I, 33-34; and Basile, p. 457.
4. See, among other studies, Edith Rickert, "Extracts from a Fourteenth-Century Account Book," *Modern Philology*, 24 (1926), 111-19 and 249-56.
5. Chaucer, pp. 19-20.
6. Cervantes, pp. 1006-07 and 1004.
7. Fenton, II, 230.
8. For a discussion of usury in the Middle Ages, see Benjamin Nelson, *The Idea of Usury*, 2nd ed. (Chicago: Univ. of Chicago Press, 1969), pp. 3-28.
9. *Decameron*, pp. 977-81.
10. Chaucer, p. 21.
11. Jourda, p. 311.
12. Fenton, II, 203.
13. Tirso de Molina, *Cigarrales de Toledo*, ed. Victor Said Armesto (Madrid: Biblioteca Renacimiento, 1913), p. 182; and Basile, p. 457.
14. Jourda, p. 1085; and Cervantes, p. 884.
15. Chaucer, pp. 82, 65, and 141.
16. Basile, pp. 138-39.
17. Chaucer, p. 223.
18. Jourda, pp. 397 and 401.
19. Basile, p. 141.
20. Straparola, II, 95.

CHAPTER 6

Images of Society:
Law, Justice, the Courts,
Crime and Punishment

I. Contemporary Law and Jurisprudence, Types of Law

The profession perhaps most frequently depicted in both jest and earnest in the novellas was the law, with its judges, attorneys, and other officials. Deep interest and concern with law and justice are reflected therein. A few novellists knew something of the law, especially canon law. François Belleforest was probably the most erudite in this field, having attended the law classes of the Scotsman George Buchanan at Bordeaux in the company of an indolent youth who bore the name of Michel Eyquem (de Montaigne). Other novellists, like Cervantes and Painter, fell afoul of the law.

In mediaeval and Renaissance times Roman jurisprudence served as the basis for the *ius gentium,* which applied for universal legal purposes. The early Augustan laws, which Andrea Alciati and others wished to revive in the Renaissance, had been superseded by the Emperor Justinian's commentaries (533-34): the *Institutiones,* the *Pandectae,* and the *Codex.* The importance of these compilations for mediaeval law can be evaluated by the canto-long

145

apologia for Justinian's law in Dante's *Paradiso* VI. Canon law was devised during the Middle Ages from Roman law, tribal customs and precedents, the writings of the patristic fathers, biblical exegesis, and various other sources, from all of which Gratian of Bologna compiled and published around 1150 the *Concordantia discordantium canonum.*

In England beginning with William the Conqueror legal issues were logically separated into civil and canonical classes. A system of hierarchical Church courts (archdiaconal, episcopal, provincial) was established to deal with all matters "which, by any exercise of clerical ingenuity, could be claimed as pertaining to the cure of souls: all matters in which a cleric was interested, all offences against divine law, all claims of Church dues, all questions affecting matrimony (a sacrament of the Church), all disputes concerning the validity or meaning of wills . . . or the distribution of property for pious uses. . . ." [1] All other matters were in the province of civil law. In the other countries of Europe under the influence of the Church of Rome there was a similar tendency to accept this separation of authority. However, as Alan Harding states, civil law increasingly assumed more and more control. Even larceny from a church was made "non-clergyable." [2]

An indication of the extent of Church jurisdiction in the Middle Ages can be gleaned from the opening lines of Chaucer's "Friar's Tale," describing the duties of a summoner:

> Whilom ther was dwellynge in my contree
> An erchedeken, a man of heigh degree,
> That boldely dide execucion
> In punysshynge of fornicacioun,
> Of wicchecraft, and eek of bawderye,
> Of diffamaciaoun, and avowtrye,
> Of chirch reves, and of testamentz,
> Of contractes and of lakke of sacramentz,
> Of usure, and of symonye also.
> But certes, lecchours dide he grettest wo;
> They sholde syngen if that they were hent;
> And smale tythers were foule yshent.

If any persoun wolde upon hem pleyne,
Ther myghte asterte hym no pecunyal peyne.[3]

The narrowing of cases punishable under canon law by the early
Renaissance is traced by Lauro Martines, who found the Church
responsible for "marriage, oaths, and manifest usury; cases concerning clerics, the materially destitute, sacred grounds, and those
affairs in which sin was critically involved or where lawyers were in
doubt. Everything else fell under the aegis of civil and temporal
law." [4]

Novellists repeatedly demonstrate, however, that the inherent
values of both civil and canon law tend to become inoperative in
the hands of their executors. Thus the novellas show a contemporary belief in other categories of law, such as divine law, natural
law, the law of the just or Solomonic ruler, and the *lex talion* or
Hammurabian (or Mosaic) law of an "eye for an eye."

Chaucer was probably the leading spokesman among the
novellists for the existence of divine justice, whether Hellenic,
Hebraic, or Christian. In "The Knight's Tale" Saturn states
categorically that the only real justice is divine justice:

Myn is the prison in the derke cote;
Myn is the stranglyng and hangyng by the throte,
The murmure and the cherles rebellyng,
The groynynge, and the pryvee empoysonyng;
I do vengeance and pleyn correcioun.

Again in "The Man of Law's Tale" Chaucer makes it clear why
Lady Constance was able to survive likely death, drowning, and
starvation:

Wel may men knowe it was no wight but he
That kepte peple Ebrayk from hir drenchynge,
With drye feet thurghout the see passynge.

Finally, a Christian God executes the law in this same tale when

King Alla maneuvers a false knight into committing perjury with his hand on the Gospels:

> A Britoun book, written with Evaungiles,
> Was fet, and on this book he swoor anoon
> She gilty was, and in the meene whiles
> And hand hym smoot upon the nekke-boon,
> That doun he fil atones as a stoon,
> And bothe his eyen broste out of his face
> In sight of every body in that place.[5]

The concept of an ordained justice is voiced in Boccaccio (III:7) by Tedaldo, who explains to Monna Ermelina that her husband has been unjustly imprisoned for murder because of *her* indiscretions: "This then is that sin which divine justice, which metes out all its operations with righteous scales, has not permitted to go unpunished." Later, when the husband, the simple Aldobrandino, is exonerated from all charges, he too expresses belief in this idea of an ordained justice: "In truth, I never committed the crime for which people say I was to be sentenced to death. All the same I have committed plenty of others, and these are probably what brought me to this pass." [6]

The ideal of natural law, independent of human statutes, was occasionally recalled in cases where codified justice was honored only in the breach. Thus in Giraldi's tale of the unlucky Felice (II:4), forced by a public official to confess a murder he has not committed, the novellist comments: "Laws in themselves are decreed and accepted for the common weal. If they are enacted with equity and prudence rather than harshness and rigor, they serve the public welfare. This is tantamount to saying that it would be better to have no laws at all than such as were administered by this judge, and that if man accepted only natural laws as his guide, he would never in following them fall into a similar error." [7]

Natural law was not, of course, based on a Plinian nature, impulsive and unfair, but on a harmony supposed to exist in universal nature. It was the law proposed by the early Humanists as an answer both to the divine law, of which there was no certainty, and to the laws of laymen or churchmen, so often unenforced or unenforceable. The mistrust of man-made laws is voiced in Cervantes' "Coloquio de los perros": "Today a law is made and tomorrow it is broken, and perhaps it is fitting that this should be so. There is indeed a great difference between saying and doing."[8]

The novella tradition, like those of the sermon and the Christian and Oriental books of exempla, often assumed the presence of the wise ruler like Solomon, who is himself evoked several times in the *Decameron* alone. Thus, the *lex regia,* which may be simply defined as the monarch's taking the law into his own hands, is another code often found in the novellas. In "The Wife of Bath's Tale" King Arthur is obliged by law to condemn to death a knight who has raped a girl.

> By verray force, he rafte hire mydenhed;
> For which oppressioun was swich clamour
> And swich pursute unto the kyng Arthour,
> That dampned was this knyght for to be deed,
> By cours of lawe, and sholde han lost his heed—
> Paraventure swich was the statut tho.[9]

But the king invokes the *lex regia* and turns the decision over to his charitable queen, who gives the knight a riddle to solve in place of the chopping-block.

Monarchs in the novellas often meet a situation so deplorable that it is impossible to be merciful. When this does happen, however, the reader is led to understand that the *lex* cannot be abrogated to encourage villainy. In "The Man of Law's Tale" the king is obliged to condemn to death his own mother, "For that she traitour was to hire ligeance." In *Gesta Romanorum* (50) a king is required to blind his own villainous son, at length issuing the unhappy order, "Pluck out therefore my own right eye and let him surrender his left." The *Decameron* (II:8) demonstrates that *lex regia* could also be reversible. By *lex regia* a king sentences an innocent count to death and all his descendants to perpetual exile, but when the truth comes to light, Gualtieri the Count is not only saved, but "raised to an even higher estate." [10]

The novella collection most interested in *lex regia* is probably the

Gesta Romanorum. Many of its tales start with the historical or pseudo-historical presentation of a monarch's law or decree which creates the subsequent moral dilemma of the plot:

> The Emperor Titus made a law, that whosoever provided not for his parents should be condemned to death. (2)

> A certain emperor decreed that if any woman were taken in adultery, she should be cast headlong from a very high precipice. (3)

> An emperor established a law that every judge convicted of a partial administration of justice should undergo the severest penalties. (29)

> Valerius informs us that the Emperor Zelongus made a law by which, if anyone abused a virgin, he should lose his eyes. (50)

The *Gesta* offers many more such background laws, inevitably infracted, leaving it up to the ruler to exercise *lex regia* to resolve a troubling moral problem of his own creation.

The fourth type of law operating beyond the civil or canonical is the *lex talion*, decreeing an eye for an eye. One example of several that comes quickly to mind is that of King Guglielmo in *Decameron* (IV:4), whose grandson tries to abduct the girl he loves, succeeding only in causing her death. "The old king, full of mighty wrath on learning how it had happened, saw no way of denying the retribution justice demanded"—a life for a life. He has his grandson beheaded, "preferring to die without issue rather than be thought a dishonorable king." [11]

II. Law and Social Classes

In the age of the novellas, as in all other times, the existence and workings of law did not necessarily result in justice. One of the most surprising texts attacking the doctrine of equality before the law came from the pen of Henry Peacham in 1634. He wrote:

Noblemen ought to be preferred in fees, honors, offices, and other dignities of command and government before the common people. We ought to give credit to a Noble before any of the inferior sort. His punishment (if guilty of offense) ought to be more favorable and honorable upon his trial and conviction; and that to be by his Peers of the same noble rank.[12]

The prerogatives which Peacham demanded for noblemen were easily granted by the society of the Renaissance, and even more easily by the society of the feudal period. The novellas themselves stand as testimony to the relation of law to social classes, as described by Alan Harding: "The law emphasized class distinctions, and to a great extent was the custom of the aristocracy. The villein was marked out by legal disabilities; since he could not own land, he could not use the real actions. The Common Law was the law of the freemen—or rather freeholders. In a system worked by the corruption of juries and the 'grace' of officials the rich had an overwhelming advantage. ... Justice might be described as the morality of class relationships, but it was in the control of the gentry. ... The cost of the law remained one of the chief grievances of the poor." [13]

This excessive cost of justice was one of the most widespread themes of the mediaeval and Renaissance novella. A well-known tale (43) in the *Cent Nouvelles nouvelles* concerns a husband and his wife's lover who haggle at length to determine an *emende* to pay the husband, but agree that they could not possibly take their disagreement to court, for the court costs would be exorbitant. The implication here and in many stories is that the judge himself will pocket the money. The same collection presents details of a canonical trial, complete with "promoteurs, scribes, notaires, advocatz, et procureurs," and the local bishop as presiding magistrate. The tale (96) depicts canonical judges as being as "avaricious" as civil judges. A well-to-do curate is sentenced to prison by the bishop for having buried his dog in the cemetery. Before being committed, he tells the magistrate that his pet made out a will just before expiring which left fifty golden crowns to the bishop. Accepting the coins, the bishop praises the "good sense of the worthy dog" and frees the curate.[14]

The judges in the Renaissance were no less greedy than Rabelais' Bridoye, if we accept the evidence of the novellas. In "La gitanilla" of Cervantes the gypsy grandmother of Preciosa urges her to accept 100 golden crowns from her lover, remarking, "If any of our sons, grandsons, or relatives should fall by some misfortune into the hands of justice, will he have any aid so useful in reaching the ears of the judge and the court clerk as these coins as they approach their purses?" Again in "La ilustre fregona" Cervantes counsels "no lack of ungent to anoint the palms of all the ministers of justice, for if they are not anointed, they grumble worse than a cart drawn by oxen." Basile heightens his criticism of this situation by having Palmiero (IV:2)—found guilty although innocent—cry out that no one listened to the poor on trial, that there was no justice, that decisions were made by chance, and that because he had not anointed the judge's palm, fed the clerk, bribed the magistrate, and shown favor to the prosecutor, he was being sent to meet his fate at the gallows.[15] Rastell indicts in Tale 94 an impaneled jury for both ignorance and corruption; bribed by a mere groat, these jurymen approved a verdict that Jesus of Nazareth was as much a thief as Barabbas.

The manipulation of the legal system by the powerful and the wealthy and the allegiance of the justices to the high-born are historical facts. Writes Alan Harding, "It may be doubted whether respect for the law was not a form of social subservience to justices who promoted nothing so much as the dominance of their classes." [16] Cervantes, who had been jailed and thus had a special grievance, inserts in his writings such comments as, "It was unlikely that the rigor of justice would be executed upon the son-in-law of the Corregidor" ("La gitanilla"). Straparola's tale II:3 shows how through fear of the powerful and evil Carlo d'Arimino a judge fawns on the guilty nobleman while promising to punish others for the crimes of which Carlo is guilty. Small wonder that Straparola (IV:1) can become caustic about highborn "thieves who have robbed others of thousands of florins standing and enjoying in the public square the sight of some poor wretch being led off to the gallows for perhaps stealing only ten florins to buy bread for

himself and his family." Boccaccio's two young noblemen Gian di
Procida (V:6) and Teodoro (V:7) both are saved from the pyre
after committing adultery, when they are recognized as scions of
noble families. In the *Novelas amorosas y exemplares* María de Zayas
notes cynically of the murderer Don Juan, "since he had money
and favor, it was not a difficult thing for him to gain freedom
within a month." [17]

III. Judges, Lawyers, Law Officials, Crime and Punishment

Boccaccio has this explanation in VIII:5 for the number of
grasping judges in towns like Florence: "Potestates come here from
the Marches, the most paltry people imaginable and so extremely
miserly and covetous that they have brought fellows along with
them as judges and notaries who seem to have been plucked from a
plowshare or a cobbler's last rather than from schools of law." [18]
The English novellists left us with two famous reproaches of
judges, each uttered by an outraged female. The first is St. Cecilia's
outburst at the judge Alamachius in the *Canterbury Tales,* para-
phrased thus: "Oh foolish creature! You have said no word which
does not show your folly and that you are in every way an ignorant
official and a vain judge." The second upbraiding, from the
Hundred Merry Tales (20), is directed at the circuit judge Vavasour,
who after enjoying the hospitality due him by a family, has his
servant place the leftover bread and meat in his pouch. The irate
housewife pours pottage over his pouch and robe, with the
sarcastic reproach, "For if I should keep any thing from you that ye
have paid for, peradventure ye would trouble me in the law
another time." [19] Both Bandello and Painter are shocked that
when the murderers of the Duchess of Malfi and Antonio walk the
streets of Milan, no one dares denounce them, for they are
protected by the powerful Ragona family and even, if we can
believe Painter, by Pope Julius II. Des Périers derided judges,
including one who has a young boy hanged by mistake (61) and
the provost-judge La Voulte, who hanged twelve innocent bystan-
ders to a crime (80).

We have recorded Basile's charge that not only judges but minor

courtroom officials as well must be bribed. But bribes went out through the whole civil body, if we believe Monipodio, the gang leader in Cervantes' "Rinconete y Cortadillo," who assures the novices, "Among our benefactors we count the attorney who defends us, the sheriff who tips us off . . . and the court clerk, thanks to whom, if he is on our side, no criminal is found guilty, no sentence entails much pain." The practice of bribing witnesses is alleged by Fenton in his Discourse I. The minute an accusation against Charles was published, the prosecutor "hadde at his elbowe double choise of perjured witnesses." In the "Ilustre fregona" Cervantes puts into the mouth of a mule boy this impassioned observation:

> How many poor wretches are chewing mud for no other reason than the anger of a tyrannical judge or a corregidor, ill-informed or overemotional! Many eyes have double vision, and the poison of injustice does not so quickly affect many hearts as it does one alone.

Again in the "Licenciado Vidriera" Cervantes has Tomás, the "glass law student," score a judge who passes savage sentences on the ironic pretext that he therefore leaves the field open for the Lords of Council to play merciful by moderating the sentence (should they be in the mood). In the same *novela* is Cervantes' characterization of a harsh judge—perhaps similar to one before whom he had himself appeared: "I'd bet that judge bears vipers in his breast, pistols in his belt, and thunderbolts in his hands in order to destroy anyone who comes within his jurisdiction." [20]

The tale of the wicked and uxorious judge Appius goes back to Livy. It appeared in the Middle Ages in Gower, Chaucer, Ser Giovanni's *Pecorone*, and in the sixteenth century in Painter (I,5), whose version spawned several tragedies on the subject. It is a tale loosely parallel to the myth of Amphytrion and Alcmena, for while Icilius is away at war, Appius Claudius abuses his powers as judge to summon and attempt to have his way with Virginia, daughter of Virginius. (In Chaucer's version, the "Physician's Tale," the judge's legal maneuver is to have a conspirator present him with a petition alleging that Virginia is a runaway slave.) The maid asks her father to kill her to preserve her chastity. He consents, and ultimately, as the wicked Appius is imprisoned, Virginia's spouse makes a highly rhetorical speech—"Is authoritie geuen thee, libidinously to abuse our wyues and children?" [21]—denouncing Appius' misuse of judicial and political power.

The novellas have bequeathed other examples of judges who abused their office to get at available women. There was the evil magistrate in Boccaccio's tale of Andreuola (IV:6). When Gabriotto dies in the arms of his Andreuola, an autopsy is demanded by the judge. Although Gabriotto's death by suffocation did not inculpate the girl, the judge made a pretense of offering her the freedom that was not his to sell, saying that he would release her if she ceded to his desires. His persuasions proving worse than useless, he tried to do her violence. When others learned of his action, the judge praised the young woman's constancy and implied that he had simply meant to test her virtue. In the *Decameron* V:1 Lisimaco, the chief magistrate of Rhodes, has Cimone released from jail in order for the two to abduct the women they love.

In Giraldi Cinzio's *Ecatommiti* (V:6) a judge permits the wife of a tailor condemned to death for homicide to stay in the tailor's cell. The potestate finds her attractive and offers to release the husband in return for her favors. She denounces him to the Duke of Florence, who dismisses him and compels him to pay the freed husband in an effort of consolation. A more calculating judge at Lucca, introduced by Bandello (II,28), manages to jail a husband to get at the latter's young wife. Unlike his often foiled legal colleagues in other tales, Judge Buonaccorsio manages both to win the friendship of the young man he jails and later liberates and to keep the wife as mistress even as he rises from judge to *podestà*. The cynical last line of the novella reads, "And in such high esteem did young Fridiano hold Messer Buonaccorsio that he not only remained in ignorance of who had had him arrested, but even if he saw the two of them lying in bed and embracing, he would not have believed his eyes." [22] Lest we forget that such abuses did in fact occur, we are reminded by Harding's history of law of the mediaeval judge who held up the action of an abbess "until one day she brought with her the more good-looking nuns of her house." [23]

As an antidote to such uxorious judges as Chaucer's Summoner and his band of harlots or Tirso's churchmen who will sometimes grant annulments with the proper persuasion, it is refreshing to find Boccaccio's comic judge Ricciardo da Chinzica of Pisa (II:10), who is seeking not more but less sexual activity. He sets up a calendar of saints' days and shows it to his wife Bartolomea: "There was not a day that was not devoted to a saint ... out of reverence to whom men and women had to abstain from such sins as intercourse. As if these were not enough, he piled on fast days, ember days, vigils of the Apostles and a thousand other saints, as well as Friday, Saturday, the Lord's Sabbath, the whole of Lent, certain phases of the moon, and other exceptions." [24] He ends up as that comic character of farce, the cuckold, with Bartolomea happily spending the rest of her life with a lusty pirate.

By the time of the Renaissance, lawyers had become familiar targets of satire, as Rabelais, Sebastian Brant, Erasmus, and, of course, the novellists probed further this rewarding vein. And the historian Harding assures us that their satire was justified. Concerning the income of lawyers, he writes that the "greatest

legal incomes had a wide margin where fees merged into bribes. . . .
When documents and procedures were paid for by length, delay
was the lawyer's business." [25] Among the legal rogues, Harding
mentions one Gilbert Sherman, attorney at the Common Law,
who was arraigned for starting lawsuits against his neighbors and
then accepting payment to leave them in peace. The contemporary
evaluation of the integrity of lawyers is illustrated in the fiftieth of
the *Hundred Merry Tales.* A friar-limitor, seeking alms at the home of
a rich man, is rudely treated by the housewife. He vindictively
predicts that her first child will be a beggar, her second a thief, and
the third a homicide. He shortly afterward redefines the first and
last of these as a friar and a physician, the middle one as a man of
law.

Chaucer, who had some knowledge of law and lawyers after
studying at the Inns of Court,[26] chose not to exploit the satirical
possibilities posed by his important creation, the Man of Law.
Instead, he is content to smile at his attorney, a sergeant of the law
who received a regular retaining fee and who was something of an
arriviste or "operator" ("Nowher so bisy a man as he ther nas,/And
yet he semed bisier than he was.")[27] In his *Propos rustiques,* Du Faïl's
lawyer Perrot Claquedent follows the pattern of his colleagues in
Rabelais by impoverishing his clients completely, "indifferently
and without great concern." Des Périers's lawyers in his *Récréations*
(8, 10, 14, 25) are naive, stupid, and inconsiderate, being duped by
clerks and servants, and speaking unintelligible Latin.

Fenton offers this blistering indictment of many members of the
legal profession:

> Besides, howe many are to be seene, who, puffed up with a
> little smatteringe skil in eyther of the lawes, which rather
> settes abroche the humour of their vanity then confirmes them
> in good order or integritie of judgement or lyving, do trade
> only in corrupting the good and sound partes of every one,
> indusing some to sedicion, other to thefte, perjurye, and false
> witnes, bearing others to habandon their countrey and
> parentes, with the societie and felowshippe of all their frendes.

Fenton's indictment also covers men of law other than merely the
practicing attorneys, and indeed the novellas arraign many law

officials of varying stature and function. To offer a representative sampling, we may begin with a lofty procurator mentioned by Marguerite de Navarre in the first tale of the *Heptaméron*. In this tale the procurator of Alençon murders in ambush the young lover of his scheming wife. The King of England intercedes on his behalf and obtains remission of this murder. Succeeding events finally lead to the man's downfall, but the point is made that a procurator is able to murder the son of a nobleman and get away with it. That constables are corruptible is illustrated by Cervantes and others. In "Rinconete y Cortadillo" Monipodio obliges Cortadillo to return to the constable a purse pickpocketed from a relative of the constable. Monipodio explains that the corrupt constable deserves this courtesy, since "It is not much to offer to one who gives you an entire chicken a leg of it." [28]

Chaucer is more severe on his minor law officials, civil and canonical, than on his sergeant of the law. In the "Friar's Tale" his corrupt bailiff lives admittedly by extortion, by tricks and violence. Nor is his Summoner, out for wealth no matter how acquired, any less corrupt: "He wolde suffre for a quart of wyn/A good felawe to have his concubyn/A twelf month, and excuse hym atte fulle." [29]

Among the many targets of Basile is the policeman in the street. He leaves the impression that the populace must bear swords not against criminals, but against the *sbirri*. A vivid portrait of one is to be found in Cervantes' "Coloquio de los perros." One of Berganza's myriad of masters is a police officer who together with an attorney and two prostitutes ran a thriving confidence game:

> They were always going hunting for foreigners, and ... whenever a greasy one fell in with one of those harpies, she would send word to the police officer and the attorney of which inn they were going to, and these two would then surprise the pair and arrest them for immorality. Yet they never took them to jail because the foreigners always liberated themselves from the problem with money.[30]

Trial by jury—the jury being convoked by an accused man to support his oath in a folk-moot—existed early in England, replacing the trial by combat which Chaucer re-creates in the "Knight's

Tale." The grand jury, of Norman origin, was convoked by the monarch himself. Tale 94 of the *Hundred Merry Tales* concerns a jury impaneled in Middlesex by the king to inquire into indictments, murders, and felonies. "The persons of this panel were foolish, covetous, and unlearned—for whosoever would give them a groat, they would assign and verify his bill whether it were true or false, without other proof or evidence." By their careless handling of a bill written in Latin, they "indicted Jesus of Nazareth for stealing an ass." [31] Even this branch of the law is condemned as callous and corrupt.

The obtaining of confessions preceding a trial was often equally corrupt. Both Boccaccio and Chaucer in the fourteenth century refer to the practice of confession by torture. In the *Decameron* (II:1) a magistrate "was so incensed that he ordered Martellino to be trussed up and had given him a good trouncing to make him confess what he was charged with so that later he might be strung up by the neck." The assumption of guilt was a correct one in this case, as it was in IV:10: "Ruggieri . . . was immediately put to the rack since he was known as one of bad character, and he confessed . . . whereupon the provost sentenced him to be hanged as soon as possible." In *Decameron* V:7 young Pietro's torture is succinctly told: "Sent to the torture, he confessed everything." In Boccaccio's time torture was obviously an accepted part of the legal system. The judge Varro in the novella of Tito and Gisippo (X:8) asks Gisippo, who had confessed out of depression over the marriage of his former betrothed to Tito, "How could you be so foolish to confess, without any torture, a crime which you did not commit?" Chaucer also takes it for granted that the mediaeval practice of torture existed in ancient times. When Theseus in the "Knight's Tale" condemns Palamon and Arcite to death, he tells them,

> This is a short conclusioun,
> Youre owene mouth, by youre confessioun,
> Hath dampned yow, and I wol it recorde;
> It nedeth noght to pyne yow with the corde.[32]

The Renaissance novella mentions torture even more frequently. In a novella of Grazzini (I:5), Fazio of Pisa had robbed a dying man, stabbed by highwaymen. Without contrary evidence, Fazio was accused of the stabbing. "They put him to torture. He confessed whatever they wished to hear. He was sentenced to be quartered alive, while the state appropriated his possessions." We recall that Giraldi's Moor of Venice (III:7) was exceptionally able to withstand torture even though an accomplice in the murder of Disdemona. "But the Moor, bearing with unyielding courage all the torment, denied the whole charge so resolutely that no confession could be drawn from him." He was released, but "slain by the kinfolk of the lady, as he merited." [33]

From Renaissance novellas we learn the specific types of torture used in both eliciting confessions and inflicting punishments. From one of Straparola's tales (XIII:4) we learn of a system of torture called the *strapado,* consisting of a pulley which raises a man and then lets him crash to the ground. An old gypsy in Cervantes' "Gitanilla" obligingly enumerates to Andrés the tortures which threaten them and which they endure in silence. "Cords do not twist our courage, nor pulleys intimidate us, nor gags stifle us, nor racks subdue us. Between yes and no we do not make any distinction when it suits us. We are always prouder of being martyrs than confessors." In "Rinconete y Cortadillo" Monipodio hopes the two young initiates possess the courage "to endure, if it were necessary, half a dozen water tortures without unsealing your lips." The hangman's rope is also curiously recalled in the same tale in the singular custom of Monipodio and his gang of thieves not to steal on Friday, and to give something of what they steal as alms to the Church, for the "Virgin of the Lamp" who protects them under *ansias* (tortures) and gives them the strength to stand the *primer desconcierto* (the first turn of the cord given by the torturer to one on the rack).[34]

Punishments were cruel, then, and sometimes inventive, such as that inflicted on Ambriguolo in the *Decameron* (II:9); he was smeared with honey and left to the attacks of bees. But decapitation, quartering, burning, and hanging were more normal punishments depicted by Boccaccio and his fellow novellists. When the illicit lovers Pietro and Violante must be punished (IV:7), the governor orders the young man to be whipped through the town and then hanged; Violante is to die by poison or the knife, as she

chooses: "If she refuses, say I'll have her burned in the marketplace before the townspeople, as she has well deserved. When you have done this, take the newborn child and dash its brains out against a wall. Then give it to the dogs to eat." [35] Two other lovers, Gianni and Restituta (V:6) caught *in flagrante,* are chained back-to-back, to be taken naked to the marketplace, then burned alive. In each of these tables the pair is exonerated because of revelations of their noble births, but again we see what justice is capable of in the Trecento.

The habit of exhibiting culprits being punished in the public square was widespread in the centuries from Chaucer to Cervantes. Prisoners in the "Cook's Tale" on their way to jail were preceded by minstrels. And in the Spain of Cervantes they were mounted on asses with faces toward the tail and flogged through the streets. Whether this was a deterrent to crime remains, as with most issues of crime and punishment, uncertain. To the old gypsy in "La gitanilla," who found the marks of a whip emblems of distinction, punishments were not deterrents. "Yes, it is great fun to go out in the morning with nothing and to return to the camp in the evening loaded down. . . . The actions of a thief may lead to the galleys, to whippings, and to the gallows, but just because one ship runs into a storm or even sinks, it does not mean that others should stop sailing." [36]

Whether deterrent or not, there remained the general feeling that if a person was guilty of a cruel and unjust crime, the punishment, as we observe in Bandello (I,42), should be commensurate. Thus Violante and Giannica, paying for a life with their own lives, "each went to death just as happily as though they were going to a party." Death might prove just as welcome as life in some of the prisons described by the novellists. Straparola thus depicted daily life in one prison (X:5): Inmates wore "tenacious chains" and were each day given "only three ounces of bread and three of water." [37]

Notwithstanding his determination to record the injustice and social inequalities of his time, the novellist was under the Horatian obligation to entertain as well as instruct. Hence, as we have seen above, an act of forgiveness or a change of heart or a reprieve often brought about a happy ending. This reprieve could result from the discovery that the person indicted was of a noble family. It could result from the news that additional evidence exonerated that person. It could result from the changeable nature and capricious impulses of the authority in power, as demonstrated by Emperor Octavius in *Decameron* X:8 who reprieved three prisoners at a time, one of them the acknowledged murderer.

The parallel systems of civil and canon law provided for excessive power without redress, that absolute power that corrupts absolutely. If the novellists rarely depict for us those stern, upright magistrates we see in Holbein's painting, nevertheless there were obviously in the Middle Ages and Renaissance conscientious and just judges, lawyers, and legal officials. Such a judge is encountered in *Gesta Romanorum* 58, making a confessional of the courtroom and dismissing sinners after a sincere confiteor and display of penance. Another is the well-intended judge in Boccaccio (IV:7) who goes to extraordinary lengths to determine the cause of Pasquino's death. Ironically, his good intentions cause the death of Pasquino's sweetheart. Messer Rubaconte of Florence (whose name for a while was applied to the Ponte delle Grazie) delivers in the *Trecentonovelle* (196) four brilliantly logical decisions for which Sacchetti parallels him to Solomon. In tale 139 Sacchetti reminds us in passing that an honest judge could exist, but might well end up in debtor's prison.

Cervantes depicts a just judge Francisco, who cleared Seville of thieves and criminals with such vigor that he was named *puñonrostro* (Fist-Face). Yet justice will not triumph, for "he will soon resign the post of presiding judge because he does not relish being at drawn-daggers with the gentlemen at court." Cervantes' Scipio offers this final defense of just men of law:

> There are many, very many, attorneys who are good, faithful, law-abiding, and eager to please without giving pain to a third party. Not all of them delay lawsuits, nor advise both parties; nor do all charge more than the proper fee. Nor do all go searching and inquiring into others' lives in order to catch them in the web of the law. Nor are they all in collusion with the judges. . . . Nor do all police officers have understandings with vagabonds and card-sharps, or keep mistresses as decoys. There are many—very many—who are nature's noblemen and have noble qualities.[38]

The performance of such men, however, does not make for as interesting fiction and satire as that of their more colorful colleagues. They exist in the background, leaving center-stage to their ambitious, ignorant, greedy, dishonest, servile, and concupiscent colleagues.

Notes

1. Edward Jenks, *A Short History of English Law* (London: Methuen, 1912), p. 21.

2. Alan Harding, *A Social History of English Law* (Baltimore: Penguin, 1966), p. 82.

3. Chaucer, p. 89.

4. Lauro Martines, *Lawyers and Statecraft in Renaissance Florence* (Princeton: Princeton Univ. Press, 1968), pp. 92-93.

5. Chaucer, pp. 41, 67 and 69.
6. *Decameron,* pp. 392 and 395-96.
7. Giraldi, p. 108v.
8. Cervantes, p. 1008.
9. Chaucer, p. 85.
10. Chaucer, p. 72; and *Decameron,* p. 274.
11. *Decameron,* p. 512.
12. Quoted in William S. Davis, *Life in Elizabethan Days* (New York: Harper and Row, 1930), p. 21.
13. Harding, p. 244.
14. Jourda, pp. 331-32.
15. Cervantes, pp. 783 and 930-31; and Basile, p. 366.
16. Harding, p. 245.
17. Cervantes, p. 805; Straparola, I, 167; Zayas, p. 393.
18. *Decameron,* pp. 914-15.
19. Chaucer, p. 212; and *A Hundred Merry Tales and Other English Jestbooks of the Fifteenth and Sixteenth Centuries,* ed, P. M. Zall (Lincoln: Univ. of Nebraska Press, 1963), p. 85.
20. Respectively, Cervantes, p. 841; Fenton, I, 31; and Cervantes, pp. 925 and 884.
21. Jacobs, I, 37.
22. Bandello, I, 977.
23. Harding, p. 211.
24. *Decameron,* p. 296.
25. Harding, pp. 209-11.
26. F. E. Halliday, *Chaucer and His World* (New York: Viking, 1968), p. 26.
27. Chaucer, p. 20.
28. Fenton, II, 103; and Cervantes, p. 843.
29. Chaucer, p. 23.
30. Cervantes, p. 1009.
31. Zall, pp. 144-45.
32. *Decameron,* pp. 131-32, 563, and 1185; and Chaucer, p. 34.
33. Salinari, I, 281; and Giraldi, p. 163v.
34. Cervantes, pp. 789, 842, and 839.
35. *Decameron,* p. 652.
36. Cervantes, p. 791.
37. Bandello, I, 507-08; Straparola, II, 153.
38. Cervantes, p. 1010.

CHAPTER 7

Images of Society:
Women and Marriage

I. Status of Women and the *Querelle des Femmes*

The eternal feminine has occupied us in these pages—for example, we have discussed woman's role in the class sytem, including the inability to choose one's mate under that system—and will occupy us again when we later consider the relationship between women and the Church in the Middle Ages and Renaissance. But until now we have only touched upon our present subject, novellistic depiction of women in relation to what the Renaissance knew as *la querelle des femmes*. It may seem hard to believe that the antifeminism voiced in Boccaccio's *Corbaccio* or in Petrarch's final denial of Laura to Saint Augustine could be taken seriously in the enlightened Renaissance. Or that, for example, Rabelais' Doctor Rondibilis could still define woman as "the excrement of nature." In the sixteenth century there is still an active antifeminist literature, but it was in fact being vigorously challenged by a growing body of feminist writings. As one might expect, both movements are reflected in the novellas.

To comprehend at a glance the general type of woman depicted in novellas composed by men, especially the earlier ones, we need only to recall the perennial Widow of Ephesus or Hans Carvel's faithless wife (both dealt with below) or Don Juan Manuel's untamed shrew (Cuento 35), a probable source of Shakespeare's subsequent comedy. Or the tales of Day Seven of the *Decameron* on the tricks played by wives on their foolish husbands. Or the dozens of accounts of promiscuous females in the *Cent Nouvelles nouvelles*. Or the ribald narratives related by Chaucer's Miller, Reeve, Shipman, and Merchant. Or, at the end of the tradition, the deceptions of the scheming Estefanía in Cervantes' "El Casamiento engañoso," who not only relieves Campuzano of all his worldly possessions but also gives the ensign, a heartless conniver in his own right, a potent case of syphilis as a memento of their brief "marriage."

Boccaccio clearly shows us the contemporary notion that a woman's "natural" condition was complete subjugation to men. Emilia, queen of the ninth day, explains at the beginning of IX:9 that women should be "humble, patient, and obedient, besides being virtuous. . . . If custom had not taught us of this, nature very manifestly would show it to us." [1] This subjection is dramatized in the subsequent story in which Solomon indirectly counsels Giosefo that the only way to treat a woman is to beat her like a donkey, a corrective which Giosefo uses successfully on his wife.

Although he believes that Juan Manuel's women may be offered as favorable alternatives to "the vain and adulterous chimeras of the false Breton and Provençal idealism, profanations of the feminine type," Menéndez y Pelayo nevertheless admits that a reading of the *Conde Lucanor* convinces one that the "natural law" of female dependence and inferiority was universally accepted in mediaeval Spain.[2] This "natural law" also finds echoes in the *Canterbury Tales,* of course, as in Lady Constance's acknowledgment: "Women are born to thraldom and penance,/And to been under mannes governance." And in Griselda's abject lines to her husband:

Lord, al lyth in youre plesaunce,
My child and I, will hertely obeisaunce,
Been youres al, and ye mowe save or spille
Youre owene thyng: werketh after youre wille.[3]

After hearing the Merchant's narrative, Chaucer's Host utters an extreme mediaeval broadside against women: they are subtle in their deceptions, they ensnare men, they babble too much, and have other vices as well. Tale 19 of the *Hundred Merry Tales* nicely sums up the Host's point of view in comparing women to the elements; water is in her eye, wind in her tongue, and fire in her heart.

One of the most enduring tales of wifely infidelity is of course "Hans Carvel's Ring," coming out of the thick Gothic night and still eliciting belly laughs in Rabelais. It emerges as a novella in the *Annulus* of Poggio and the *Cent Nouvelles nouvelles* (11). It makes a late, crude appearance in *Tales and Quick Answers* of 1567, printed by Henry Wykes. While Hans Carvel tosses sleepless in his marital bed, alongside his flirtatious and unfaithful young wife, God appears to comfort him. In this vision God promises to give him forthwith a ring which, if worn night and day on his finger, will always assure Hans that his wife is not cuckolding him. Hans is of course overjoyed and grateful. The coarse humor is revealed when Hans awakens to find his ring finger penetrating the vagina of his sleeping wife (or "arse" by 1567).

Noel Du Faïl, like Boccaccio's Solomon, believed in the therapeutic effects of wife-beating. In the fifth *nouvelle* of his *Propos rustiques* Lubin assures his friends that every time his wife speaks offensively, "I beat her with a stick, and it's been going on like this for nineteen years." Superficially evocative of Hitler's banishment of women to kitchen, chamber, nursery, and church is the idea of Du Faïl and others that woman's role is to sew and spin. In the seventh tale of the *Propos* Du Faïl's Thenot orders his mother back to the spinning wheel: "You have nothing to do here, go do your sewing."[4]

William Davis paints this picture of an antifeminist England during the Renaissance: "The legal status of women is such as will make their champions in another age cry out with horror. Unmarried, a woman is almost completely in the power of her father, elder brother, or other guardian. Married, she is as completely in the power of her husband. . . . Her property is for practical purposes at his entire disposal. She is lawfully in a state of perpetual tutelage and minority. Husbands have kept their wives locked for years. If they use the lash or rod on them it is hard to find a legal remedy." [5] All this was of course applauded by the likes of Pettie and Fenton. At the conclusion of his "Admetus and Alcestis" Pettie complacently defines the role of women and wives as follows:

> This seemeth strange unto you, Gentlewomen ... that you should die to yourselves and live to your husbands; that you should count their life your life, their death your destruction; that you should not care to disease yourselves to please them; that you should in all things frame yourselves to their fancies. ... If they be solemn, you should be sad; if they hard, you loving; if they delight in hawks, that you should love spaniels; if they hunting, you hounds; if they good company, you good housekeeping; if they be hasty, that you be patient; if they be jealous, that you should lay aside all light looks; if they frown, that you fear; if they smile, that you laugh ... etc.

Fenton, like Du Faïl, ascribed to the woman "the indeavor of the needle," a recreation for widows and all honest matrons.[6]

In his *Certain Tragical Discourses* Fenton further lectures that women, derived of the imperfections of men and ordained from the beginning to be their vassals, are like infants unable to distinguish between "the value of an aple or figge and a jewel of gret price." Obviously he counsels at great length the strictest surveillance of wives and daughters, to avoid "wepinge in the villeinie of wives and daughters, utter ruine and subvercion of so many houses." [7] Yet, ironically, even as Fenton was worrying about the freedom which might be accorded women, the world around him had indeed passed him by, as a queen was ruling the new British empire with a fist of iron.

In the seventeenth century Basile's antifeminism often seems more literary than real, a pretext for humor and not to be compared with his apparently heartfelt social and political criticism. Still, through Iacovucci he does rail at the "blood-sucking female" and at the inordinate use of cosmetics by women who are nothing but enameled dolls or newly plastered walls: "The hair is false, the eyebrows tinted with lampblack, the cheeks redder than a vermilion bowl, with purest chalk and varnish. She smoothes and rubs her face, then whitens it, daubs it, and paints it with cosmetics, ointments, pastel color-sticks, dyes, and powders." Such a woman, Fabiello immediately adds, is like a chestnut: handsome on the outside, but with a worm within. Finally, in the eclogue at the end of the third day Giallaise likens the bonds of marriage to a convict's chains, and Cola Iacopo responds, "An unlucky gardener is he who marries! For only one night does he sow contentment, and afterwards reaps a thousand days of torments." [8]

The extremes to which antifeminist novellists could go is illustrated by Erizzo and Pettie, both of whom treated the theme of feminine participation in bestiality. In his *Sei Giornate* Erizzo recalls that Attila's mother had slept with dogs. Pasiphae and the bull became a tale realistically chronicled in Pettie's *Petite Palace:* "At length her lust grew to such outrage that she felt in herself an impossibility to continue her accursed life without the carnal company of the bull." [9] Their lustful sisters, Messalina and Romilda, who stopped just short of bestiality, are of course recalled in the novellas. Romilda (Bandello, IV, 8) was punished in a sadistic way, by having twelve robust soldiers rape her for an entire day and night and then impale her "in Turkish fashion."

Once the novellists had decided to assign antifeminist classifications to their stories, the *querelle des femmes* was perpetuated. Once Boccaccio had chosen as a principal theme the treasonable stratagems of wives or Marguerite de Navarre the "tricks played by men on women, or women on men," women stood to be degraded. Expressions of sympathy for the woman's lot are rare in the tradition before the sixteenth century. An interesting transformation of the stereotype is Boccaccio's Filippa de' Pugliesi (VI:7). Having fulfilled her assigned literary role by cuckolding her husband with another man, risking a death sentence in doing so, Monna Filippa, a liberated heroine, when brought to court complains of the double standard. This woman *di gran cuore* argues to the lord provost: "Laws ought to be alike for all, and made with the consent of those whom they concern. Now in this law of yours, it is quite otherwise, for it is binding on only us poor women, who are able to satisfy many more than men can; besides, no woman ever gave her consent about this law, and so it deserves to be called inequitable."

With all the freethinking resolution of a Wife of Bath, Monna Filippa pursues the point with a now-famous defense: "And if my husband has always taken of me that which was needful and pleasing to him, what, I ask you, was I or am I to do with that which remains over and above his requirements? Should I cast it to the dogs? Was it not far better to gratify withal a gentleman who loves me more than himself than to leave it to waste and spoil?" The members of the court, we are informed, "almost with one voice shouted that the lady spoke well and was right." Not only is Filippa acquitted, but the law is changed.[10]

If this novella seems to justify a law of promiscuity to woman, an illustrative tale from the *Cent Nouvelles nouvelles* upholds the logic of masculine promiscuity. A young knight, seemingly content with his beautiful new bride, continues to seek illicit rendezvous with ladies of dubious virtue. The knight's squire, obedient until now, refuses to undertake the arrangement of these assignations. To convince his squire of the need of periodical deviations of routine, the knight inquires of the young man his favorite dish. The answer is *pâté d' anguilles*. From that day on the master has him served an exclusive diet of eel pie. After a month the squire summons the courage to state that despite his fondness for eels, he would like some other meat to recover his lagging appetite. "Now you can understand," replies the knight, "that I am as surfeited in my own way as you are of the eel pies." The servant grasps the point, gets his change of diet, and arranges for his master to follow suit. Yet the vast majority of novellas show that for a woman to experiment with such a variety of diet brings only disaster.

Cervantes gave a unique twist to the endless novella theme of the attempt to keep a wife faithful and chaste. Don Felipe de Carrizales, the title character of the novela "El celoso extremeño," keeps his thirteen-year-old bride in the custody of both a duenna and a Negro eunuch. Not even a male cat or dog is allowed in the house. Any inveterate reader of novellas could predict that the child bride would somehow end up in the arms of a younger man. But what he would not predict is that Don Felipe would offer her the chance of marrying the young man and inheriting his fortune upon his own death. Nor would he predict that the girl, convinced finally of his generous love, would turn down his offer and instead enter a convent at his death. Perhaps Don Felipe and his author sensed that women given such a narrow role in life could be easily led astray, thus fulfilling both the husband's fears and his expectations. In his *Lecciones sobre Tirso de Molina* Karl Vossler theorizes how the contemporary universal belief in the gullibility of women actually permitted her to be taken advantage of and how, "according to both Aristotelian and ecclesiastical teaching and the dominant opinion and customs of Spain at that time," the woman, "a second-grade creature, denied autonomy," was therefore "susceptible to all types of temptation." [11] It is uncertain whether Tirso himself was influenced by the Marianic cult or the current sentimental strain in literature, or whether he simply followed his own personal inclinations—in Spain, then as in other ages, the plight of woman was probably worse than elsewhere in Western Europe. Nevertheless, he found it easy to sympathize with characters such as Serafina and Victoria, treated as chattel and used to further the financial and social aspirations of their households. One might even view Tirso's play on Don Juan Tenorio as a tract on the abuse of women during the Siglo de Oro.

After discussion pro and con of the role of women, Girolamo Parabosco's *Diporti* concludes with praise of women. Yet the novelist at that period who most staunchly defended women was, of course, Marguerite de Navarre. Citing her feminism and her strong belief in the Christian doctrine of grace, the Professors Cholakian write of Marguerite:

> She therefore told many stories which prove that . . . it is the women who are virtuous, while the men are completely lacking in any sense of decency. Indeed, she puts the record straight and proves that women are often innocent victims, while society through its double standard permits in men what it castigates in women.[12]

Marguerite's *nouvelles,* especially those recited by her female *devisants,* staunchly defend women from every station in life. Thus on separate occasions the matron Oisille relates how the virtuous wives of both a muleteer (2) and a judge (46) aggressively resist the lustful approaches and even physical attacks of men. Ennasuite tells a similar story about a princess, possibly Marguerite herself (4). Parlemente, the author's *porte-parole,* tells, among others, of the married Floride, who, though genuinely enamored of the soldier Amadour, rejects the young man's proposal of an extramarital sexual relationship and eventually fights off his desperate attempts to rape her (10). Parlemente tells also (13) of the pious and faithful young wife of an aged man who, though loved by a younger, more handsome captain of a galley promptly forwards the diamond ring he gives her to his wife waiting back home. All the discussants agree that the heroine did right in returning the diamond, although Nomerfide demurs for a while, "Are you all saying that a beautiful stone worth two hundred crowns *(escuz)* isn't worth anything?" In this *nouvelle* Marguerite returns to her poetic vocation and includes a splendid chivalric poem of a *loyal serviteur* of some 160 verses. Parlemente later (42) tells of the servant girl Françoyse, in love with and herself much loved by a young prince; despite entreaties, arguments, stratagems, and bribes, she remains irresolutely chaste, eventually more properly accepting in marriage another servant. Parlemente's commentary firmly buttresses the arguments illustrated in her tales. The story of Rolandine ends with the comparison between the love of man and that of woman: a woman's love, says Parlemente, is founded "on God and on honor" and is "just and reasonable," but the love of most men is founded on "pleasure". Likewise, a man's honor is said to be augmented by "wrath and concupiscence," whereas the foundation of a woman's honor is "sweetness, patience, and chastity." Women's sins are grounded in pride, and therefore no one suffers for them. Parlemente argues elsewhere to the men in the company that "your pleasure consists of dishonoring women, and your honor of killing men in battle, which are two things absolutely against the law of God." [13]

Some of the *nouvelles* of the *Heptaméron* based on contemporary *faits divers* or court gossip were retold in the *Vies des dames illustres* and *Vie des dames galantes* by the chronicler Brantôme (Pierre de Bourdeille), who was born in approximately 1540 and died in 1614. His stories or *témoignages,* which parallel the novella tradition, stress the libertinage of the late Cinquecento; one recalls more easily the *galantes* than the *illustres* of his women.

Still more militant in her feminism than Marguerite was María de Zayas. A major theme of her *Novelas amorosas y exemplares* is not merely that "men are worse than women," according to Edwin Place, but that "women are oppressed and men are the oppressors." [14] In the second part of her collection, in such *novelas* as "El verdugo de su esposa," "Tarde llega el desengaño," "La inocencia castigada," "Amar solo por vencer," "El traidor contra su sangre," and "La perseguida triunfante," a series of virtuous women are beheaded, or are starved or bled to death, or have their eyes torn out of their heads, or are otherwise tortured and cruelly murdered by sadistic husbands, brothers, and fathers. Zayas strikes the keynote of her literary design in the very Prologue to Part I of her work, in which she explains why there are so few women writers and scholars:

> By what right do men claim to be learned and presume that women cannot be so? The only answer it seems to me is that through their wickedness and tyranny they keep us locked up and do not give us teachers, and thus the true reason why women are not learned is that they lack not intelligence, but the opportunity to apply it, for if in our childhood they gave us books and tutors instead of lace-making and embroidery, then we would be as competent for positions of state and for professorships as the men are. . . .

For her age, as Lena Sylvania has observed, "Doña María was a woman of advanced ideas, advocating general education for women, recognition of the equal rights of both sexes, and respect for women in the eyes of men." [15]

II. Marriage, Divorce, Abortion, Prostitution

Marriage, Giulietta's or that of hundreds of other young women, was a sacrament which afforded plots of every sort, every mood, in the novella. Indeed, the *Quinze Joyes du Mariage* was a highly successful Quattrocento collection of tales exploring this theme thoroughly and pessimistically. Within the novellas themselves the tricks of husbands against wives and wives against husbands were sometimes announced as the twin topics consuming two of the days of storytelling.

Unfortunately, the perfect marriage seemed to have less entertainment value than imperfect ones. Too many wives in the novellas won eternal fame, unfortunately, as tragic heroines and martyrs: the Duchess of Malfi, Berenice, Lucretia, Masinissa's wife Sofonisba, Irene, and so many others recalled in this volume. Nor should we fail to recall Camilla Sarampa (Bandello, I,13) who, on hearing of her husband's beheading, killed herself. Many of these were transferred to the stage, but other equally loving heroines were noble in their insignificant way. One remembers the young wife in *Conde Lucanor* (44) whose husband loses an eye. Lest he ever feel mocked she puts out her own eye. What an irony to discover that Bandello, who recorded for posterity the tragedy of the

Duchess of Malfi, dedicated one of his tales (I,32) to the very
Cardinal Lodovico di Ragona who had his sister and her children
murdered!

Along with tales of young girls forced into convents, those
"caged birds" discussed earlier, married to Christ rather than to a
sweetheart, we find their counterparts who are victims of a forced
or arranged marriage. That the French called these *mariages de
raison* or *de convenance* was small consolation to the girl involved.
Most of them were not princesses able, as was Painter's princess
(I,34), to obtain intercession by a pope. Tirso devotes two tales to
these unfortunates denied thus the opportunity of true marital
love. In these tales Doña Victoria fights against an arranged
marriage with Don Ascanio and Dionisa flees with young Dalmao
to elude the wealthier husband her family intends for her. The
forced marriage continued unabated among the wealthier families
during the life cycle of the novella.

Fenton's *Tragical Discourses* on two occasions attack marriages
without parental consent. He condemns Livio and Camilla (II),
warning that young couples must not commit "the wrong to the
obedience of their parents in concluding privy contracts unpunished." He later (XIII) restates the need of obeying one's
parents in this matter, avoiding "secret contracts and marriages
made by stealth, where the honour of both contractors loses its
vertue and the commaundment of God is broken." Whereas the
Reformational spirit would lay heavy responsibility on Friar
Lawrence for conspiring in the confessional with Romeo and
Juliet, all novellists sensed the offense to the families in clandestine
marriages.

Divorce and annulment as alternatives to the marriage that was
not working out were only cautiously mentioned. Most audacious
was the further solution, polygamy, the biblical custom defended
by Chaucer's Wife of Bath. In her Prologue she argues:

> God no mention made he
> Of bigamye or of octogamye.
> Why sholde men speke of it vileinye?

Divorce is mentioned more openly in the novellas, of course. Yet

Boccaccio in the Trecento is prudent in his wording. When Gualtieri is preparing to dismiss his wife Griselda, Boccaccio makes it clear that letters from the Pope to the Marquis of Saluzzo "dispensing him to be able to take another wife and release (*lasciare*) Griselda" are counterfeit missives. Chaucer's version as "The Clerk's Tale" is less cautious. First of all, Chaucer tells us that "Rome" was long "cunningly apprised" of Gualtieri's scheme and had no objection to it. In addition, Rome went so far as to prepare a papal bull, in 'effect permitting the Marquis to move ahead with the dispensation if he chose. The message of the novellists is clear. The poor cannot obtain divorce, but the rich may.

In the cornice discussion of Nouvelle 60 of the *Heptaméron*, Marguerite de Navarre, victim of one unsuccessful marriage, has her characters voice two criticisms of the Church's divorce policy. Ennasuite observes that "those who tie other people into marriage, know how to tie the knot so well that it would take death to separate them." Yet Simontault observes cynically that even this deadlock would be broken by the Churchmen ere they would permit a priest to be separated from his chambermaid. Apparently sexual incompatibility was a cause for divorce or annulment in fifteenth-century France, for in tale 86 of the *Cent Nouvelles nouvelles*, a woman (wrongly) charges her daughter's new husband with such incompatibility, reassuring the bride, "So then, my daughter, we shall get you un-married (*desmarrier*). I'll be able to do so without fail. Be assured that it will be accomplished in forty-eight hours from now. Leave it to me."

It is surprising to find a Spanish novellist, one involved with the Church, taking a stand for justifiable divorce. In Tirso's novella "Los tres maridos burlados," María-Pérez, the painter's wife, is angry over her husband's neglect during her illness. She will go to the vicar and ask for a divorce.

Abortion, with its risks to women and its Church condemnation, was understandably a theme absent from the novellas. It was Bishop Bandello (III,52) who broke the silence. Having heard of a tragic abortion from a countess in Milan, Bandello was reluctant to include it among his tales until Lady Ippolita Sanseverino bade him to do so. Bandello's language is temperate as he relates the abortion undergone by one Pandora, whose character reminds him of Medea, maddened killer of her children from Jason. Fenton's version (IV), as to be expected, contains much purple prose. The young Milanese woman becomes "an unnaturall mordorer of the frute of her wombe." The clergyman-abortionist is a devil's agent: "a graye friar, a greate ghostly father in that citye, whom she affirmed to have wroughte marvelous effectes by the helpe of certeine distilled waters, tempered wythe the jewce of strong hearbes, growyng secretly within the intrailles of the earthe, the nature of hidden stoanes and mettals, pouder and seedes not knowen to manye, etc. etc." The long clinical description of the primitive abortion, ending up in sadism and savagery, seems the product of a sick mentality, even granted Fenton's antifeminism, anti-Italianism, and his hidebound moral code.

We have mentioned above the various Messalinas and Romildas and Pasiphaes with their egregious carnal appetites. However, we have not discussed prostitution, an occasional topic in the novellas. They wander around the periphery of these tales, starting as early as Don Juan Manuel's exemplum 46, "The Wise Man and the Prostitutes." The moral of this tale, like that of Heinrich Mann's narrative of Professor Unrat, is that association with whores can destroy in a moment a reputation built up over a lifetime. In the *Cento novelle antiche* a bishop is similarly embarrassed, having upbraided a curate for consorting with a woman and then being trapped in his bedchamber with a whore. Victims of society as much as of their own weakness, as were Gananciosa and Ceriharta in the penumbra of "Rinconete and Cortadillo," they were deprecated as a class. Bandello's novella IV,16 describes without sympathy the financial and legal problems of the headstrong Spanish whore in Rome, Isabella della Luna, whose effrontery caused her to be flogged publicly. Victims of men, they can be degraded by men, as Bandello (I,19) observes, even by men who may eventually be killed in bordellos. He notes that an enterprising prostitute may keep eleven assignations in one night once she gets inside a monastery (II,48). Finally, Bandello (III,31) scoffs that in Venice, Rome, and elsewhere whores are referred to by the "honest" word, courtesan. It is in this tale that the bishop-novellist, after recounting the vicissitudes of a young nobleman with a prostitute, advises men to sleep with whores, but never romanticize them. Houses of assignation were so common that Tirso alludes to their number among the *cigarrales* encroaching even on the Convent of Saint Augustín. Finally, the realistic *Cent Nouvelles nouvelles* informs male readers that the current gratuity to the prostitutes of Paris was ten crowns.

III. Special Plots Concerning Women

Many novellists were drawn to a plot involving bed-partners based on a curious, indeed dubious, premise. We shall call it the lover-in-the-dark theme, also known as the *fausse assignation*. This situation, which occurs in the very first scene of Tirso's play, *El Burlador de Sevilla*, was accepted by a general suspension of disbelief by several generations of novellists and their readers. In the darkness the villainous lecher inserts himself into a woman's bed and makes love to her unrecognized. Indeed, Siegfried had already proved such a feat possible in the mediaeval *Nibelungenlied* when he overcame Brünnhild's defiance. Curiously, the imposture is not discovered by the lady until after the sexual act is consummated, in some cases not until the following morning. Sometimes the ingenuous lover is however the male himself who believes in the darkness that he is embracing his own wife or mistress. In the *Decameron* (VIII:4) the rector of Fiesole thinks he is taking pleasure with his wife Piccarda, but makes love instead to a serving wench. He is thus caught *in flagrante* by the bishop. In the *Cent Nouvelles nouvelles* (35) another husband sleeps with his wife's maid, unaware that his spouse is off in bed with an old lover, a knight.

In the *Heptaméron* (30) a young gentleman believing to sleep with one of his mother's court ladies, impregnates instead his own mother, fathering a baby girl he will marry a dozen years later. This theme of the *fausse assignation* embodies as well Marguerite's Nouvelle 8, where husband and lover both sleep with the wife, thinking it is the *chambrière*. After exploiting the theme as well in tales 18, 35, 43, and 48, Marguerite through her *porte-parole* Parlemente, asks skeptically, "Who is the *sotte* who cannot tell the difference between her husband and another man, no matter what the disguise?"

Even the sophisticated Bandello (II,57) relates how a husband makes love twice to his own wife without recognizing her. He, like the Queen of Navarre, is compelled to admit that this old plot strains credulity. Yet he has recourse to it once again in his tale of the draper of Lyon (IV, 28).

By the time of the *Hundred Merry Tales* (68) the characters themselves in the novella question the credibility of the false assignation. A parish priest wagers forty pence with a parishioner that he could sleep unrecognized with the latter's wife in the dark. The curate is admitted to the lady's unlighted bedchamber and begins sexual intercourse. "She, feeling his crown, cried, 'By God, thou art not John Daw.' " The priest has obtained *coitus interruptus* for forty pennies. The question remains unanswered: Would the deception have been consummated had the wife's fingers not discovered the priest's tonsure (crown)?

Another curious plot in which woman plays an unflattering role is at least as ancient as the *Satyricon* of Petronius. It is known as "the inconsolable widow," although in its various mediaeval versions it bore the less flattering title of "The Woman Who Played the Whore on Her Husband's Grave." The widow of Ephesus does not have the strength of character of the novellists' popular Lucretia. The former spends days weeping prostrate on the tomb of her husband, only to be slowly comforted and finally seduced by a centurion guarding a crucified body in the vicinity. When the crucified body is stolen during their dalliance, the couple replace it with that of her husband. Bandello, Marguerite de Navarre, and Painter, on the other hand, pay fulsome praise to widows faithful to their husbands' memory.

The theme of the eaten heart is a savage and ancient one, with mediaeval sources Celtic *(Guirun)*, Provençal *(Linaura/Ignaure)*, and High German (Herzmaere).[16] All the versions have in common a lady, or group of ladies, involved in an extramarital affair, a jealous husband (husbands) or father, and a lover who is killed and dismembered for his adultery. In the *Cento novelle antiche* (62) Count Robert of Burgundy perceives that the countess and a maidservant were sleeping with a retainer named Baligante. He has a meat pie served up for the ladies. The dénouement is a dialogue in primitive thirteenth-century Italian:

"Was the meatpie warm enough?"
"Good."
"It isn't surprising that Baligante pleased you alive, if you like him dead."

As suggested above, Isolde in the *Tristan* of Thomas sings the "Lai Guirun" on this tragic theme, and the first Provençal version was that of Guilhom de Cabestaing. The latter tale inspired Boccaccio's novella, in which the distracted wife of Guillaume de Roussillon leaps to her death after the event (IV:9). However, the indignant wife gives the count a scolding for his unknightly conduct, and adds the insult: "God forfend that ever other victual should follow upon such noble meat!" During the same fourth day of the *Decameron* (IV:1) Tancred's daughter Ghismonda drinks a goblet of poisoned water containing her lover's heart. The Tancred version remained popular as late as *The Palace of Pleasure* (I,39) and was dramatically adapted two years later by Robert Wilmot (1568). A variant tale is found in the moralistic *Gesta Romanorum* (56). Here a prince forces his adulterous wife to eat every day food served from a human skull, that of her former lover with whom she had been discovered *in flagrante*. "The adulterer is the devil," the reader is told, "to cut off his head is to destroy our vices."

IV. Growing Importance of Women in the Novella

Surveying the entire tradition, it is intriguing to note the growing importance of women as the novella develops. Boccaccio and some of his disciples, like Straparola, claimed to write their tales solely for the pleasure and profit of the gentler sex. Given the lack of literacy among so many mediaeval women, as well as the paucity of women with the financial means to purchase copies of the *Decameron*, Boccaccio's claim need not be taken seriously, but should instead be more correctly seen as an example of the narrative device described above: the "protective screen." Indeed, a professional impatience with Boccaccio's protective screen is expressed by Des Périers' mocking suggestion that ladies should have their brothers and cousins read the tales first and then cross out those that are improper. Des Périers scoffs: "Ah, my little ladies, don't you trust them! They will make you read a quid for a quod!" He exhorts ladies to read all the tales.

Boccaccio's association of the novella with women is confirmed by the number of women (seven out of the ten storytellers in his *Decameron*) participating in relation of tales and cornice discussions, culminating in their exclusive role as narrators in the *Piacevoli notti* and the *Pentamerone*. With Marguerite de Navarre proving that she could beat her country*men* at their own game and María de Zayas reaffirming the Boccaccesque structure of the novella collection after Cervantes had challenged it, women eventually moved in totally, metamorphosing the once predominantly misogynistic genre into a vehicle for propounding their own strongly feminist ideas. Even those elements of society unready to accept these ideas could no longer stifle them.

And yet even during those misogynistic days of the Duecento and the Trecento an occasional novellist showed a moment of compassion for the essentially tragic destiny lying in wait for women, especially young women. The passage which we choose now as *envoi* to this chapter dates from 1350, a date which certifies it as anachronistic and which reveals at the same time the identity of its author.

Within their delicate breasts, fearful or shameful, young ladies hold their amorous flames hidden, more searing than flames open or apparent. This is only too well known to those who have felt or experienced it. Moreover, restricted from pleasures by the command of fathers, mothers, brothers, and husbands, they remain most of the time enclosed in the little circuit of their chambers, sitting in enforced idleness, longing for one thing, then for others within a single hour, turning over so many thoughts—thoughts which cannot possibly be happy ones.

Sitting and waiting, like little maidens without their unicorn to caress.

Notes

1. *Decameron*, p. 1081.
2. *Orígenes de la novela*, I, 145.
3. Chaucer, pp. 65 and 106.
4. Jourda, pp. 621 and 630.
5. *Life in Elizabethan Days*, p. 90.
6. Pettie, I, 196; Fenton, I, 169.
7. Fenton, II, 2-3.
8. Basile, pp. 131-33 and 337.
9. Pettie, II, 104.
10. *Decameron*, pp. 734-35.
11. Karl Vossler, *Lecciones sobre Tirso de Molina* (Madrid: Taurus, 1965), p. 111.
12. *The Early French Novella*, p. 44.
13. Jourda, pp. 869, 992, and 913.
14. Edwin Place, "María de Zayas: An Outstanding Woman Short-Story Writer of Seventeenth-Century Spain," *University of Colorado Studies*, 13, (1923-24), 23 and 40.
15. *Novelas amorosas y ejemplares*, ed. Agustín G. de Amezúa (Madrid: Aldus, 1948-50), I, 21-22 (omitted from Portal edition), and Lena E. V. Sylvania, *Doña María de Zayas y Sotomayor* (1922; rpt. New York: AMS, 1966), p. 7.
16. For two developments of this tragic theme, see John E. Matzke, "The Legend of the Eaten Heart," *Modern Language Notes*, 26 (1911), 1-8; and Henri Hauvette, "La 39ᵉ Nouvelle du *Décaméron* et la Légende du 'Coeur Mangé,'" *Romania*, 41 (1912), 187-93.

CHAPTER 8

Images of Society:
Church and Churchmen,
Sacraments, Reformation,
Counter-Reformation

I. Anticlericalism, Inquisition, Saints, Churchmen, Indulgences

A literary genre without status, often alleged to be written for women and thus not to be taken seriously, could more easily speak of churchmen, and, on occasion, even of church dogma. Boccaccio's claim that the *Decameron* need not be seriously considered by the clerics was, however, long in vindicating itself. The three offenses for which a book could be placed on the *Index Librorum Prohibitorum* were challenges to the doctrines of the Church, to Church authority, and finally to the morality preached by the Church. It becomes clear to one who studies the listings on the *Index* from 1559 to its final year, 1964, that the immorality of the volume in question bothered the Curia least. Preserved Smith makes the supportive observation: "It is noteworthy that the *Decameron* was expurgated not chiefly for its indecency, but for its satire of ecclesiastics. Thus, a tale of seduction of an abbess is rendered acceptable by changing the abbess into a countess; the

183

story of how a priest led a woman astray by impersonating the
angel Gabriel is merely altered by making the priest a layman
masquerading as a fairy king."[1] Although the *Decameron,*
bowdlerized or not, was not listed in the 1964 edition of the *Index*
and although in the Vatican Library the card file on Boccaccio is
today one of the most abundant on any author, nonetheless a
reading of the *Decameron* and other novellas is a rewarding exercise
in determining the issues which were to break Christendom in two
during the Cinquecento.

Since the novella prospered through various "stages" of the
Renaissance—the late Middle Ages, the Humanistic Renaissance,
the Reformation, and the Counter-Reformation—the attitudes
toward the traditional religion reflect to some extent the local
impact of these movements, as well, of course, as the religiosity of
the individual writer himself. Interestingly, in the Middle Ages,
with a more secure Church and its dismissal of the novella as no
more serious than a *fabliau,* farce, or *facetia,* the novellist had more
freedom than he did during the Counter-Reformation. Hence,
Giraldi Cinzio had little of the licentiousness of his predecessors,
and Bandello, eventually Bishop of Agen, did not avail himself, as
Griffith has shown,[2] of all the anticlerical material in his sources, or
all the ribaldry of the tales he surely heard in his sophisticated
salons. Tirso de Molina, holding high office in the Mercedarian
Order, also tempered his anticlericalism, taking churchmen to task
for bad judgment rather than evil intent. An evil friar in "Los tres
maridos burlados" is defined as prudent and well intentioned.
Rebuked by the Council of Castile for the obscenity of his plays,
including the *Burlador of Sevilla,* Tirso could obviously sense the
omnipresence of the Inquisition.

Criticism of churchmen and church dogma got off to a slow start
with Don Juan Manuel. As Andrés Giménez Soler writes, "If we
take into account that our rigid moralist did not admit a single
libidinous tale, even systematically reduced tales of love, . . . he did
not open the door either to the antimonastic and anticlerical
element so prominent in Boccaccio."[3] The fact that thirteen of the
tales in *Conde Lucanor* took their plots from Dominican sermon
collections illustrates the cautious beginnings of Juan Manuel's
attitude toward the Church.[4] However, Don Juan, as a powerful,

autonomous nobleman, had no hesitation in criticizing churchmen on occasion, as he roundly did in Cuento 31, scoring both the Friars Minor and the cathedral priests in Paris.

Novella 12 of the *Gesta Romanorum* allegorizes the widespread concern over the way Church doctrine is being preached and interpreted. A parishioner, scandalized by the wicked lies of his priest to the point of boycotting his sermons, wanders along a brook. In his thirst he drinks of its water which, unnoticed by him, gushes through the jaws of a decaying dog. He is horrified on learning this source and fears disease. An old passerby reassures him, drawing an analogy between the good water flowing through the rotting jaws and the valid doctrines and sacraments of the Church unspoiled by the jaws of stupid or ignorant prelates who serve as their intermediaries and interpreters.

The strong anti-Church and anticlerical sentiments in the early novella originate outside of Spain and Germany, notably with Boccaccio and Chaucer. We shall also see below that Marguerite de Navarre represents perhaps the strongest Catholic critic of the Roman Church among the novellists. Sister of François I, whom she persuaded to found the Ecole Trilingue in direct opposition to the book-burning Catholic Sorbonne, she protected several crypto-Protestants, notably Clément Marot, co-worker on the *Huguenot Psalter*. Until the death of her royal younger brother in 1547, Marguerite enjoyed an unusual freedom of expression which she gladly exercised in her novellas. The ritualistic nature of Catholicism she decried at the conclusion of Tale 34: "Blessed are they whom faith has so humbled that they have no need of outward acts to make them conscious of the weakness and corruption of their natures." [5] Her favorite target among churchmen, as we shall see, were the Cordeliers.

The active Spanish Inquisition and the role assumed by Spanish kings as protectors of the Church throughout Europe obviously led Cervantes to be cautious. During his life he experienced war, slavery, and jail, and he admitted in the Prologue to the *Novelas ejemplares* that he was not of an age to start gambling with the other life. Cervantes panicked rightly when he learned that pirated editions of his works were appearing in Spain and Portugal.[6] At one point the Spanish Inquisition forced him to delete from Book

II, Chapter 36, of the *Quijote* a sentence concerning works of charity, reminding him how easily he could be hauled before an *auto-da-fé*.[7] The caution of both Cervantes and the frocked Tirso de Molina was shared by their contemporary María de Zayas, whose tales so often drew the Christian moral that virtue is rewarded and vice punished, and of whom it has been written, "In all her literary work, Doña María reveals herself as an ardent Christian, to whom a religious life represents a perfect state." [8] Yet, as will be observed, even the Spanish novellists occasionally took an objective, critical look at the Church and churchmen.

The English novellists Painter, Fenton, and others were drawn toward the Reformation by a sense of nationalism as well as religion. Fenton rejoices after a trip to France that England "is happely purged of suche filth. . . . Neyther will I troble my historie with the sondry enormities and practises of hell whyche I noted in some religious houses in Fraunce, duryng my being there . . . for that yf I should but abridge their disorders into a tenthe parte, the volume wold excede the bignes of the bible." Again he berates the Roman Church as Babylonian (Luther's famous charge) and diabolical, whose abandonment of sincere and true doctrine is apparent even to the "dymmest eyes." [9] Not much, however, is made by Painter of the anti-Catholic feeling in England. Retaining a mildly negative attitude toward Catholicism, he was outvoiced by such fellow-countrymen as not only Fenton but also John Rastell, brother-in-law of Thomas More, a Catholic, and the printer of the *Hundred Merry Tales,* published in 1526, less than a decade before Henry VIII's break with Rome.

In viewing the various categories of religious commentary and criticism in the novella tradition, one notices at once that to the satire and skepticism of the novellist the concept of God was of course inviolate. Even though his ways are admitted to be beyond human understanding, God remains the only force for order in a disordered world. Boccaccio's Pamfilo begins thus the very first tale of the *Decameron:*

It is proper, dearest ladies, that man begin everything he does with the wondrous and holy name of Him that was the maker of all. Therefore, since in our storytelling I am chosen first, I

intend to begin with one of His miraculous deeds, so that
when it is heard, our faith in Him may rest immutable and
His name be ever praised among us.[10]

Interestingly, in Straparola's collection of the 1550s, Novella VIII:3
was condemned as irreverent to God. Straparola repudiated it,
substituting for it two other novellas, which explains why his
eighth night contains six tales instead of five.

Christ and the Virgin Mary also remained untouchable. Like
God the Father, the Savior is often referred to in the novellas, but,
except for such rare instances as those in the *Gesta Romanorum* (110)
and the *Cento novelle antiche* mentioned above, he hardly ever makes
an appearance in them. Despite her replacement by the Holy
Ghost in the Trinity during the Middle Ages, the Virgin Mary
remained, as Michelangelo called her, an available symbol of
mansuetude. For the novellists, particularly in Spain, the Virgin
retained her traditional function as guardian of maidens, as
Cervantes makes clear in his "Illustre fregona," the heroine of
which, Constanza, is "first and foremost devoted to Our Lady." [11]
In the "Perseguida triunfante" of María de Zayas, the heroine
Beatriz is also protected by the Virgin, who saves her from a
hangman's scaffold and restores life to a child. The youthful
martyr of Chaucer's "Prioress's Tale," we recall, sings in praise of
"Cristes mooder sweete." [12] A humorous story featuring the Virgin
is Tale 89 from the *Hundred Merry Tales*, in which Our Lady is
giving out portions of holy ointment to several parishioners. When
she arrives at Master Whittinton, who has built a college, she
refrains from anointing him since he cannot answer the key
question of what he has suffered for her sake.

Usually saints, too, as noted in Chapter Three above, were
mentioned or treated with respect, though not necessarily in
Protestant countries. St. Joan, for example, did not fare especially
well in England. On Belleforest's statement of fact, "The Duke of
Somerset had burned the maiden Joan ('la pucelle Jeanne'),"
Fenton's Discourse XI elaborates thus: "Wherein not longe afore
the Duke of Somerset had burned the counterfait prophet of
Fraunce, called La Pucelle Jeane; whome some pratinge Frenchmen doe affirme to have wrought merveils in armes during those

warrs; but chiefly, that under the conduite of her, our countrymen lost Orleance, with diverse other holdes in those partes." [13] Anticipating the rejection of the entire calendar of saints by the Reformation, Boccaccio courageously questioned the validity of that calendar by recording how a total scamp and liar like Messer Ciappelletto could be canonized. So seriously did he take this step that he prominently placed his novella as the very first of his collection.

In contrast to God (Father and Son) and the saints, men of the church crowd the pages of the novellas, their frequency being in reverse order of their hierarchical rank. Popes are rarely presented, whereas priests and friars are seen everywhere. When introduced, the pope is usually an abstraction, unidentified, as in Rabelais' fifth book. When the law student of Cervantes makes his pilgrimage to Rome, we are not told of which pope he kisses the foot. One exception is the surprisingly genial portrait of Boniface VIII, condemned by Dante to hell, in the *Trecentonovelle* (35). Sacchetti (203) pictures Gregory XI, on the other hand, as hoarding Church lands illegally acquired. A comic novella of Cimarosto's visit to Pope Leo is included in the *Piacevoli notti* (VII:3). Straparola depicts Pope Sixtus IV as possessing great severity, coupled with great magnanimity (XII:5). As might be expected, the Anglican novellists held the popes in less reverence. William Painter singles out Julius II as "more martiall than Christian" and as one who "loued better to shed bloud than give blessing to the people." [14] The power of the mere mention of a pontiff is satirized in the *Cent Nouvelles nouvelles* (14), where a maiden agrees to sleep with a hermit who predicts that the fruit of their intercourse will beget a pope. (The offspring, of course, turns out to be a girl.) Finally, the curious tale (11) of the *Conde Lucanor* about the prelate of Santiago who believes himself elected pope even while fascinated with necromancy is a sad commentary on the ambitions of churchmen.

Cardinals and archbishops are often subject to criticism. Surely the most villainous cardinal of the novellas was the relentless brother of the wretched Duchess of Malfi. This cruel man, Cardinal of Naples, conspires with the Cardinal of Mantua and the Cardinal of Siena to hound Antonio da Bologna to his death. Of his behavior Painter asked rhetorically, "Is thys the sweete observation of the Apostles, of whom they vaunt themselves to be the Successours and followers? And yet we cannot finde or reade that the Apostles ... hyred Ruffians and Murderers to cut the Throates of them which did them hurt." [15] The *Decameron* (II:5) records that the greedy Archbishop Filippo Minutolo of Naples was buried with rich vestments and with a ruby ring on his finger worth more than 500 gold florins.

The wealth of bishops, leading to their corruption, is illustrated in Boccaccio's tale of Antonio d'Orso, Bishop of Florence, who paid a man 500 alloyed gold coins to spend one night with the man's wife (VI:3). It is a case of the trickster tricked, and the cardinal is mortified when another girl he covets announces in a crowd that she might sleep with him, but "in any case I should want good [i.e., unalloyed] money." [16] The concupiscence of bishops is further demonstrated in Novella 54 of the *Cento novelle antiche*, wherein a priest who has been condemned by a bishop for fornication, surprises his superior in bed with a whore and thus wins exoneration. Marguerite de Navarre sets her sights on the clergy in her very first tale, showing how Jacques de Silly, Bishop of Sées, courted the wife of a proctor named Saint Aignan. Straparola and Bandello show, as we shall later see, that when bishops attempt to oversee the administration of nunneries, they are beyond their depth and look foolish indeed.

Another frequent target of attack in the novella was the institution of indulgences, a major factor, of course, leading to Luther's break with Julius II and Leo X. Novellists even in the most steadfastly Catholic countries demonstrated scorn of indulgences. Basile and many others before him scoffed at these "sellers of paternosters." In view of the claim that indulgences, alms, and gifts could elevate a man to heaven for a price, one recalls Sacchetti's tale (22) of two friars assigned to preach over the body of a rich and sinful man. The holy men, unlike many of their brethren, refuse to "lie through their throat" and proceed to paint the deceased in all the blackness of his character, despite his wealth. Cervantes makes his oblique criticism of indulgences by having his ruffian Rinconete initiate his career as a picaro by stealing the money which he and his father had earned selling papal bulls and indulgences.

Although the Holy Father set the quota of indulgences to be sold, the selling was done at lower echelons. The *Conde Lucanor* debunks indulgences (40) when someone who has bought salvation from both Dominicans and Franciscans is revealed to have gone not to heaven but to hell. One remembers Chaucer's Pardoner with his wallet brimful of pardons come from Rome all hot. Boccaccio leveled his attacks at friars: "They have placed and are placing all their zeal in frightening with rumors and pictures the minds of stupid people and in showing that with alms and masses sins can be purged, for they became friars through baseness, not through devotion." Having gone so far, Boccaccio adds with caution (III:7): "Certainly it is true that alms and prayers purge sins. But if those who proffer them could see or know to whom they offer them, they would keep them to themselves or just as well cast them to swine." In the following tale Boccaccio portrays a simpleton who believes that he has been brought back to life through his wife's payment to an abbot for special prayers: "Father, your prayers, as it has been revealed to me, with those of Saint Benedict and my wife, have brought me back from the pains of purgatory." [17]

II. Clerical Misbehavior, Nuns, Abuses of Power

Not only friars and abbots but priests and monks as well were the butt of hundreds of tales in the Middle Ages and the Renaissance. Even though his brother was a priest, Masuccio Salernitano admitted devoting the first ten stories of his *Novellino* to "shaming the clergy." Firenzuola, himself a priest, and the Bishop Bandello also indicted ecclesiastics roundly. There were of course many honest, courageous, unselfish, and devout clergymen—like Chaucer's Parson—but these, like upright lawyers, did not make good copy for humor and satire.

The great variety among the weaknesses satirized by the novellists is vividly documented by the records of a single religious order during the Middle Ages, as reported by G. G. Coulton. Examining the records of the Order of Cluny, the historian catalogued the misdeeds of the inmates between 1248 and 1334 as follows:

152 unchaste inmates, mostly priors of monasteries; forty murderers who together had been concerned in the death of sixteen victims and had slain eight of them within the walls of the church; twenty-four forgers, sixteen convicted of openly embezzling public moneys, besides countless other dishonesties; sixteen monks imprisoned by the town authorities for other offences; eight who had mutilated monastic servants; eight outlawed ruffians lying in wait on the highways to slay their religious superiors.

Coulton concludes, "The evidence of monastic decay, long before the Reformation, is simply embarrassing in its mass and variety." [18] One understands more easily why Patronio could tell Count Lucanor (Exemplo 3) not to become a monk, lest he be judged badly by everyone. In Tale 13 of the *Cent Nouvelles nouvelles* a young clerk is similarly discouraged by his master from becoming a monk.

Among other things, monks and priests are constantly accused of greed and avarice. One recalls Chaucer's Summoner demanding money from an old widow on pain of excommunication: twelve pence would secure an acquittal. Bandello's avaricious priest (III,25) mentioned briefly in Chapter Four above, is an even more despicable example. This man of the cloth forces an old widow to keep a corpse in her house which he refuses to have buried until the prepayment for internment is forthcoming. Upon learning of this a duke forces the priest to bury the corpse and then has the priest buried alive with the deceased. Some priests, as the novellists attest, apparently made a great effort to become the executors of their parishioners' wills, hoping eventually to come into the money themselves. The *Heptaméron* (56) tells of a Cordelier priest who serves as a matchmaker for a young girl and manages to get her dowry for himself, at least temporarily. Des Périers has a tale (3) accusing dishonest canons of holding back benefices owed their flock.

Endless are the charges against the clergy. Tedaldo's lengthy condemnation of churchmen delivered to Ermellina in *Decameron* III:7 is reducible to this theme: "Whereas the friars of old desired the spiritual health of mankind, our contemporaries want nothing so much as women and wealth." [19] The *Hundred Merry Tales* stresses their ignorance, as does Sacchetti (205) their hypocrisy, Straparola their tricking and cheating, Don Juan Manuel their contentiousness, and so on. One of the most amusing foibles of priests indicted in the many various stories is their gluttony. Granted that St. Augustine himself admitted in his *Confessions* that he had formerly eaten and drunk to excess, the meager fare of the poor parishioners clearly led them to resent those priests who ate high on the hog. According to the novellists, many churchmen forgot that gluttony was one of the seven deadly sins—a fact which probably explains the curious prominence given it in the novellas.

It is a common theme of the *Cent Nouvelles nouvelles:* 83 describes a religious mendicant eating "like a wolf let loose among sheep." [20] In 100, a Spanish bishop eats two partridges on a Friday, explaining that by uttering arcane words he could change meat into fish, just as he could convert the host, made of wheat and water, into the body of Jesus Christ. In Straparola's *Piacevoli notti* (Xi:3) Don Pomporio, a gluttonous monk, avoids punishment from his abbot by explaining that since the rough foods served to monks are so easily digested, he is simply constrained to overeat. Were he able to partake of the delicacies allotted to the abbot, on the other hand, he would surely eat far less. In Tale 47 of Des Périers, Jacques Colin, Abbot of Saint-Ambroise, has a problem with his monks since he holds the decidedly minority position that "sobriety is the source of all good, as gluttony is the source of all evil." [21] Tale 73 presents the clergyman Jehan Melaine, who at a single meal ate as much as did nine or even ten people. After giving one sermon in an abbey, he proceeded to eat all the food and wine there, so that nothing remained for others. Des Périers's final glutton is an anonymous monk (58) who guzzled food continually at table and who, between bites and gasps for air, tended to answer questions from his confreres, in rhymed monosyllables only: *bis/ gris, beuf/neuf, bon/non,* and so on. (This tale, without the rhyming, reappears in the *Mirrour of Mirth* of 1583.) Their gourmandizing did not, of course, stop such priests from warning their congregations against indulging in this deadly sin, like Chaucer's Pardoner or the gluttonous friar in the *Hundred Merry Tales* (70) who would steal puddings on a Sunday morning and subsequently preach against those who broke their fast that day before the high mass.

To chronicle the carnal sins of the clergy as recorded by the novellists would require a volume as thick as the book of the damned held by the recording angel in Michelangelo's *Last Judgment.* Curiously, Chaucer's epitome of priestly deceivers of women he called Don John. Historians, whether discussing the Middle Ages or Renaissance, merely confirm the wantonness of the clergy as depicted in the novellas. For example, Otto Cartellieri writes of the Burgundian clergy:

> The inferior clergy participated only too willingly in the dissolute pleasures of the masses. Wild orgies took place in the immediate neighborhood of the altar. . . . The priests often set a bad example by cursing and dice-playing. A canon of Notre Dame turned his house into a gambling hell. Sodomites burned at Arras included a priest among them . . . Priests regarded it as their prescriptive right to keep concubines. If they were deprived of them, they threatened to take vengeance upon the women and girls among their congregation.[22]

Cartellieri asserts, moreover, that the most scandalous tales of lascivious monks and wanton nuns in the *Cent Nouvelles nouvelles* acquired "through everyday life fresh justification and further development." Indeed, the anonymous author of that collection precedes Tale 44 with the observation that "Priests and curates nowadays are such gay blades that none of the follies committed by laymen is difficult or impossible for them." At least eighteen of the tales treat of such clergymen. Translator-editor Rossell Hope Robbins concludes logically, "If all the other situations and characters were drawn from real life, it would be surprising indeed were the clerics alone fictitious."[23]

The point need not be labored. The tolerant acceptance of priestly misbehavior on the part of higher churchmen is illustrated virtually everywhere in the tradition. In Boccaccio's second novella it is made clear to Abraam that churchmen high and low, popes included, were both natural and sodomitic lechers. The Friar in Chaucer knows many women; including all the barmaids. Sacchetti's priest Juccio (116), who refuses to wear breeches (thus stimulating his *pascipeco* to carnal activity), cannot be reformed, even by the Inquisition. Bandello's Fra Filippo (III,61) is driven to self-castration before he can reform. Hilariously concupiscent is Bandello's bishop (II,45), who baptizes all parts of an abbess' body and prefaces his coitus by the announcement: *"Orsù,* now I'm going to climb up Mount Gelboè and ring both of heaven's bells, then slither down to the middle of Jehosaphat's valley and do marvelous things."* Finally, Rastell's tale 87 concerns a priest who fears his bishop will learn of his three illegitimate children, only to discover that the bishop had fathered ten bastards. Churchmen in the novella, in short, seem anxious to seduce every female in sight: wives, daughters, widows, nuns, old maids, servants, girls, adolescents, or, as in *Heptaméron* 33, their own sisters.

Friars of all orders are equally prone to lechery. Marguerite de Navarre—noting that some priests who would not touch money are ready enough to handle a woman's thighs, which are much more dangerous—was particularly harsh on the Cordeliers. The *Hemptaméron* is a veritable catalogue of Cordeliers' sins: rape, incest, replacing husbands on the marital bed, seducing nuns, seizing girls' dowries, even causing a married couple's death. Oisille observes that such "admininstrators of the sacraments ought to be burned alive." 24

Carnal sinners among the clergy included in the tradition not just men—such as Masuccio Salernitano's notorious Fra Niccolò (I:3), who left his pants in Madonna Agata's bedroom (later proclaiming them to be the breeches of a saint and hence a holy relic) and Boccaccio's Frate Alberto, impersonating the angel Gabriel to seduce Lisetta—but abbesses and nuns as well. Here, too, we must let just a few examples stand for the myriad which could be culled from the tradition.

Three tales devoted to the sexual proclivities of nuns, by Boccaccio, Bandello, and Straparola, have received wide and lasting circulation. Young Masetto da Lamporecchio in the

Decameron (III:1) obtains the position of gardener at a convent whose inmates are famous for their piety. To win their sympathy and to get the job he pretends to be a deaf-mute. But his job becomes much more demanding than he could ever have anticipated, for, with an enforced discretion protecting them, the nuns enthusiastically satisfy their sexual appetites with Masetto, whose garden becomes a paradise on earth as he repeatedly "put the horns on Christ."

Although the Dominican novellist Bandello was probably more content to record the amatory recidivisms of the Friars Minor, one of his most amusing tales (III,56) concerns a nunnery on Lake Como as scandalous as Manzoni's nunnery of Monza turned out to be after twentieth-century historians exposed it. Bandello recalls that Cardinal Landriano of Milan campaigned to reform the many nunneries under his jurisdiction, "reducing them to the observance of religion." He delegated a priest as overseer and some progress was made. Five nuns, however, proved indefatigable, each one seducing the overseer, who within a few months had impregnated all five. Scandalized, Cardinal Landriano ordered the priest imprisoned, but the latter, prostrating himself before the prelate, cried, "Lord, you gave me five talents. Behold, I have produced from them another five talents!" This unique variant quotation of the parable of the talents saved his life and career.[25]

It was Straparola who thought up the extravagant tale of the cloistered nun Filomena, who, as it was discovered, was hermaphroditic. The nuns, delighted, hoped to enjoy her male characteristic. When her true physiological nature was revealed and it was necessary to remove her from the convent, the nuns were most unhappy. One imagines them (XIII:9) weeping in unison at the expulsion of their young sister. Less well known but not without interest is Straparola's bizarre tale (VI:4) of three nuns who vie for the position of abbess by demonstrating the unusual versatilities of their private parts. Sister Venerando urinates through the eye of a needle. Sister Modestie places five grains of millet atop a die; her flatulation selectively leaves the center grain intact. Sister Pacifique tosses a peach in the air, catching and crushing it with her hips. All of this in front of an astonished vicar, who understandably postpones any decision.

Foibles of abbesses and nuns are also recorded in the earlier *Cent Nouvelles nouvelles*, including adventures in a nunnery contiguous to an abbey, "where there was always a barn for the threshers" and where every single sister was familiar with the virile member of Brother Conrard (Tale 15). In Tale 21 an abbess who is ill is told that to be cured she must sleep with a man. Unwilling at first, she is convinced by her nuns, who assure her, "We will do the same as you," which is all the encouragement she needs. In Tale 46 the very first sentence reads, "It is not an unusual thing for monks willingly to chase after nuns," prefixing a tale of the misadventures of a Jacobin monk and a nun interrupted *in flagrantia*.

Many other, perhaps more serious, types of church corruption are similarly exposed in the tradition. An abuse of clerical power that particularly troubled the novellists was that stemming from the canonical court, and, especially during the Counter-Reformation, the Inquisitional courts and *autos-da-fé*. In the sixth tale of the

Decameron Boccaccio attacks an unnamed inquisitor of heretical depravity ever on the watch for victims with well-filled purses. Having heard of a wealthy man who boasts of owning a wine so good that Christ himself might drink of it, the inquisitor accuses him of blaspheming Christ as a drunkard. The victim, to be let off with a light penance, was thus obliged to "grease his palm with a goodly amount of Sir John Goldenmouth's ointment, which greatly allays that infirmity of avarice which afflicts the clergy." [26]

In Sacchetti's Novella 11 a certain Alberto da Siena, accused of being a heretic *(paterino)*, is summoned before an inquisition. He is so confused by the subtleties of the interrogation that the bishop inquisitor settles by having him recite the paternoster, which he misquotes while stuttering. His companion Buccio manages to intercede with the bishop and extricates Alberto from peril, but an addendum by the author makes it clear that if Alberto had been a rich man, the inquisitor would have demanded a financial redemption, lest he be burned and tortured.

III. Rites and Sacraments, Relics, Confession, Excommunication, Miracles, Pilgrimages

The many rites and sacraments which had been developed in the Roman Church received a mixed reception among the novellists, as indeed among the thinkers of the Reformation. Only two of the seven sacraments were retained by the Reformed Churches, prompting the Council of Trent to reaffirm the need and validity of rituals, sacraments, and relics. Decree XXV of the Council specified, "The faithful must venerate the holy bodies of Christ, the Virgin Mother, Saints, and Martyrs, honor relics and other sacred monuments."

A general skepticism about basic church dogma and practices can be found throughout the novellas, from the period of Boccaccio to that of Cervantes. Ritualistic or rote mouthings of catechisms, prayers, and formulas are dismissed by Boccaccio (VII:1) as being as meaningless as "the paternoster in the Vulgate, the song of Saint Alexis, the lament of Saint Bernard, the laud of Saint Matilda, and other such idiocies *(ciancioni)*." [27] A sym-

pathizer with the new Evangelical movement, Marguerite de
Navarre could not refrain, for her part, from scoffing at the formal
pageantry of the Roman Church, with its paintings, gilded
decorations, and rich ornaments needed for its rituals (Nouvelle
55). All this décor, she wrote, merely distracted one from true
piety. In "Rinconete y Cortadillo" Cervantes reports the skepticism of the humble people of Seville on Church observances: "We
pray with our rosaries throughout the entire week, and many of us
don't steal on Fridays, or hold a conversation with any woman
named Maria on Saturdays." [28]

Long before Martin Luther, Boccaccio and Chaucer attacked
the validity of relics with a vigor and humor which unleashed
several generations of critics among the novellists. Readers who
have laughed at the satire of relics in Mark Twain's *Innocents Abroad*
will find many more laughs in the novellas. No one could ever
forget Fra Cipolla's discomfiture on finding that the parrot's
feathers he had planned to exhibit as the wings of the Archangel
Gabriel had been mischievously stolen from his reliquary and
replaced by pieces of charcoal (VI:10). That he could assure his
parishioners that these coals were among those used to burn St.
Lorenzo is, of course, mere religious quackery. Even more
ridiculous and injurious to the very concept of relics is the list of
sacred objects which Fra Cipolla claims in his sermon to have seen:
the finger of the Holy Spirit, some rays of the star seen by the
Magi, the phial of St. Michael's sweat when he battled the devil,
the jaw of Death which struck Lazarus, and so on.

Chaucer was no less relentless on relics. His Pardoner's relics are
evocative of Fra Cipolla's absurdities: "Our Lady veil" (in reality a
pillow case) and a piece of sail from St. Peter's boat, not to
mention the "pigges bones" he kept in a jar for all occasions. "With
thise reliks," as Chaucer says, the Pardoner made a fool out of
many a parson and his flock:

And thus, with feyned flaterye and japes,
He made the person and the peple his apes.

He has no luck, however, with the forthright Harry Baily, whom he invites to purchase a pardon and kiss a relic. Baily was shockingly explicit:

"Nay, nay," quod he, "thanne have I Cristes curs!
Lat be," quod he, "it shal nat be, so theech!
Thou woldest make me kisse thyn olde breech
And swere it were a relik of a saint,
Though it were with thy fundament depeint.
But, by the cois which that Sainte Elaine foond,
I wolde I hadde thy coilons in myn hond,
Lat cutte hem of: I wol thee helpe hem carve.
They shal be shrined in an hogges tord." [29]

It is Sacchetti who explains to us how an honest priest felt at having to exhibit dubious relics to his flock. In Tale 60 Taddeo Dini, a respected Dominican preacher, was obliged during a fund campaign for a convent to carry to his pulpit "the true arm of Saint Catherine." Seized by a moment of candor, he announced to his flock, "Ladies and gentlemen, this arm you see before you is said by the sisters of the convent to be the arm of Saint Catherine. I have been to Mount Sinai and seen the body of Saint Catherine quite whole, specifically with two arms. If she had three, this is the third." In a commentary Sacchetti blames the sin of avarice for many deceitful relics. There is not, he alleges, a chapel which does not contain some milk of the Virgin Mary or nails from the True Cross. Such frauds, he predicts, will be punished in the next world.[30]

Later on, when Henry VIII decided to do away with monasteries and convents, he chose as a pretext their collections of relics. From the abbey of Bury St. Edwards his investigator John ap Rice reported: "Amongst the relics we find much vanitie superstition, as the coals that St. Lawrence was toasted withal, the paring of St. Edmund's nails, St. Thomas of Canterbury's pen-knife and his boots, and divers skulls for the headache, pieces of the Holy Cross, etc." One wonders whether John ap Rice borrowed two items from his list from Boccaccio's Fra Cipolla. Obviously the Anglican condemnation of relics elicited a strong amen from Fenton, especially when it came to French relics.

And for a memory of that forged ydoll [St. Joan] they kepe yet, amongest other relikes, in the abbay of S. Denys—which I sawe in May last—a greate roostie sword; wherwith they are not ashamed to advowche that shee performed diverse expedicions and victories against th'Inglische nacion.[31]

Among the many other observances of the Church mocked by Boccaccio's tale of Ciappelletto (I:1) are the doctrines of penance, Eucharist, and extreme unction. With her Reformist tendencies, Marguerite of Navarre adds her own satire of the sacrament of extreme unction in Tale 72, with its explicit title: "In Exercising the Last Rite of Mercy and Burying a Dead Body, a Monk Exercises the Rites of the Flesh with a Nun and Creates a Life." Another sacrament which Boccaccio satirizes is baptism by holy water, which will wipe away sin (III:4 and 8). This is directly ridiculed when Abraam the Jew (I:2), after contemplating the *dolce vita* of Christians in Rome, tells his friend Giannotto, "Let us off to a church, and there I shall be baptized according to the due custom of your holy faith." [32]

So many are the rites and trappings of the Roman Church under attack by the novellists that we single out one single minor element of ritual—one paid very little heed by the Reformation—and show the widespread ridicule it elicited. This element is the votive candle. Boccaccio's first novella makes it clear that right after the burial of Ciappelletto a superstitious populace starts to light candles to him, and prays to him as to a saint. Boccaccio's scamp Fra Alberto burns so many candles to the image of the Virgin that his inamorata Lisetta fears that he will leave her for Our Lady (IV:2). Lisetta herself, we are told, never fails to light a taper before the image of Gabriel. Boccaccio's simple Ferondo (III:8), believing himself dead and in purgatory, complains that his wife sent him the wrong wine and no candles for him to drink the wine with. His captor, the conniving abbot, reassures him that his wife had sent plenty of candles, "but they were all burnt for the masses."

Tale 121 of the *Trecentonovelle* mentions in two contexts the importance of votive candles. First, a court poet in Ravenna's Church of San Francesco notes that an old Crucifixion is half-burned and smudged by the cataract of candles before it. He removes all the candles and sets them on the sepulcher of Dante, a scandalous action which he defends successfully before the Archbishop of Ravenna. In fact, Sacchetti writes that when Pope Urban V lay in state illumined by a candle weighing over two pounds, a nearby Crucifixion could scarcely be noticed over its penny-candle. The irrepressible poet, Antonio da Ferrara, moved the heavy candle before the Saviour's effigy.

In the *Cent Nouvelles nouvelles* (11) the observance of lighting candles is ridiculed. In this variant of the Hans Carvel story, a jealous husband makes offerings to various saints in a church, and, just in case, lights a candle to the statue of a devil. Indeed, it is the devil who comes to his bedroom and gives him in a dream the notorious "Hans Carvel's ring" (see Chapter 7). Rastell's *Hundred Merry Tales* (4), however, makes the point that lighted candles and holy water will ward off devils.

In Marguerite de Navarre's popular tale, "The Miracle at Lyons" (65), plagiarized by several succeeding novellists, the candle plays a leading role. A simple woman in the Church of St. Jean at Lyon tries, after her devotions, to fasten a candle on a soldier lying asleep on a tomb. She is surprised when it will not cling to his forehead. Let Painter tell the consequence (I,65): "The old woman, which thought the cause that her candle would not cleave was the coldnesse of the Image, she warmed the souldiour's forehead with the flame of the candle, to stick it faste." When the startled soldier awoke and fled, she started crying, "Miracle! Miracle!" The tomb was thereafter "to get money" as the scene of a miracle.[33]

Cervantes shows us that candles themselves become in ignorant minds endowed with supernatural power. In "Rinconete and Cortadillo" the prostitute Gananciosa lends the thieves' spy Pipota a few pennies to buy some candles as church offerings which will absolve her of a lifetime's sins. If such a minor feature of church ritual as candles can so stir the satiric urge among the novellists, one can understand that major rituals and sacraments elicit far too many critical comments to be reproduced herein.

Confession, the prime means of attaining penance, makes frequent appearances as a theme of the novella. By the time of the

Council of Trent, when the *Decameron* was being expurgated, the Council reaffirmed the necessity of "open and modest" confession. The *scopatori*, a school of extreme mediaeval penitents, are mentioned in both the *Decameron* (III:4) and the *Trecentonovelle* (113). To the mediaeval and Renaissance satirists the misuses of the confessional were many and varied, and their fictions constitute a long catalogue of these. The indictments start with the false confession of Ciappelletto in Boccaccio's first tale, as though the author were eager to launch the trend. Thus we learn that a false confession may elevate one to the calendar of saints. His tale of Frate Alberto (IV:2) chastises not only concupiscent confessors, but also women who spend time in confessionals prattling about their own beauty. Confessors, it is true, betray husbands, but, as Boccaccio also shows (VII:5), occasionally allow jealous men to borrow cowled gowns and listen to the confessions of their wives. In a variant tale by Bandello (I,9) a husband pays a confessor to overhear his wife's confiteor, after which he kills her.

Other mediaeval novellists were happy to join the chorus of criticism. Chaucer's Friar was a wanton hypocrite who used his power of confession for illicit gain, for "pleasaunt was his absolucion" if he received a "good pitaunce." [34] Holding up staunchly the rite of confession, the *Gesta Romanorum* assumes its necessity. Even the widowed mother of Tale 13, who murdered her baby sired by her son, is forgiven by her confessor as a true penitent. In Tale 59 the Emperor Jovinian is deprived of his crown, throne, wife, and kingdom until his confessor is convinced of his repentance and rejection of pride. In the *Gesta's* parables, by the way, the confessor is not always a priest, but could be a shepherd (110), a neighbor or host (109), a seneschal (81), a serpent (119), or other agent.

The *Cent Nouvelles nouvelles* naturally adopted this anticlerical theme. In Tale 32 a group of monks in Catalonia invent a way to make the women whose confessions they hear sleep with them. They instruct the women of their village that, just as tithes are given to the Lord, "you must render to us the tenth of the number of times you sleep with your husbands." [35] The lady parishioners, simple and gullible, do their best to pay the *disme* in order to receive absolution for their sins. Tale 78 borrows from Boccaccio in depicting a husband disguised as priest who hears from his wife that he has been amply cuckolded during a long absence in the Near East. More than half a dozen tales in this corpus concern priest-confessors who are seducers.

The anticlericalism in the *Hundred Merry Tales,* including its treatment of confession, could only have delighted Cromwell and the group in power who would soon support Henry VIII's break with Rome. Thus, there would have been laughter over Tale 64, in which a priest is to shrive two nuns for lechery, but uncharitably balks at forgiving the older of the pair. "An old whore to lie with an old friar in the time of Lent—By Cock's body! If God forgive thee, yet will I never forgive thee." [36] Another all too fallible confessor from the same collection falls asleep in the middle of a confession and confuses two sinners (88). One gathers from the frequency of the tale about confession in the *Hundred Merry Tales* (see also 16, 25, 30, and 54) that it must have been a sacrament missed by many of the faithful when King Henry reorganized the Roman Church in England.

According to the *Heptaméron,* the Cordeliers not only exploited the secrecy of the confessional, but used it as a milieu to satisfy their lust. Tale 29 tells of a priest who seduces a young wife instead of shriving her; 41 describes how a monk refuses to absolve a young girl without her first permitting him to place his *corde* on her naked body. Lechery reaches new heights in the thirty-first *nouvelle*, in which a confessor murders a wife's servants and kidnaps her off to his monastery, only to be burned alive in the monastery itself along with his other conniving confreres. In the discussion following Tale 60 Hircan explains what he saw to be the chief weakness of the system of confession: attribution of the power of absolution to priests instead of to God leads to exploitation of their flock. "Believe me, it is a great boon for these fearful and secretive women to sin with those who have the power to absolve them, for there are some women who are more ashamed of confessing a thing than of committting it." Hircan adds bluntly, "It is very hard to confess things so pleasant. I have often confessed, but never repented." [37]

It was difficult enough to admit to a confessor heterosexual adultery, but it appears that sodomy, the sin against nature, was even more difficult and almost impossible to expiate, if one investigates its rare appearances in the novellas. It appeared at an allegorical level as early as the *Cento novelle antiche* (46) in the middle of the thirteenth century. Narcissus is pictured staring at his beautiful reflection in the pool of water. "He began to love and cherish him so much that he wanted to take *(pigliare)* him." That homosexuality should have been shunned by the mediaeval novellists is not surprising, considering the specific punishments of sodomites at the time and the mixture of contempt and Christian ridicule they incited, illustrated in the *Commedia* by Dante's encounter with Brunetto Latini, where pathos combines with ridicule. Yet Dante's biographer Boccaccio was emboldened to introduce sodomy in his tale of Pietro di Vinciolo (V:10). Pietro surprises his wife with a young stripling, and, instead of punishing him, forced him into a sexual *partie triangulaire*. Boccaccio concludes his tale: "After supper, what Pietro devised for the satisfaction of all three has escaped my mind. Yet I know that the following morning the youth was escorted back to the public square, not altogether certain which he had the more been that night, wife or husband."

References to homophilia were understandably indirect, and Vittore Branca has noted the suggestion of homosexuality in Boccaccio's references to males: "as fond of women as a dog is of a stick *(bastone, mazza)"* in I:1, V:10, and V:55; or the alternative formula: "as a child is of a palm's slap," used by Sacchetti (112). Cautious indirection seems present in Chaucer's description of the Pardoner, his long flaxen hair falling over his shoulders, his voice effeminate, his chin beardless. Then Chaucer enigmatically concludes; "I trowe he were a geldyng or a mare."

Similar suggestiveness coupled with caution is found in Boccaccio and Painter. Both titillate the reader with what seems to be a scene of two males enjoying intimacies in bed. However, in the *Decameron* (II:3) young Alessandro, bedded with "an English abbot," "put his hand to the abbot's bosom and found there two little breasts, round and firm and delicate." Painter's version of the same incident is consciously more salacious. Despite an occasional heavily veiled conjecture about the comportment of priests in their monasteries and nuns within their convents, Lesbianism is avoided in the novellas. Sappho is occasionally mentioned (six times in Bandello), but usually as one of antiquity's distinguished women with Penthesilea, Camilla, Zenobia, Themistoclea, and others.

It was however Bishop Bandello who based a lengthy and hilarious novella (I,7) on homosexuality and on its nature as the most vicious sin to have to reveal to one's confessor. He relates that the poet and historian Niccolò Porcellio refused at seventy to admit on his deathbed to any sin "against nature." At his wife's insistence, two confessors ask him over and over to confess this sin to save his soul. Finally, he bursts out, "You don't know how to interrogate me. Playing around with young boys is more natural to me than eating or drinking." Unfortunately the news spreads all over Milan, and after his recovery he dares not appear in public. The usually broad-minded prelate Bandello makes it clear throughout that committing sodomy is the equivalent to placing Christ in a blazing furnace.

The most famous fictional misuse of the confessional is in the tale of Romeo and Giulietta related by Da Porto, Bandello, Painter, and others before reaching its dramatic climax in Shakespeare. Friar Lorenzo in the tale would be guilty of two abuses in the eyes of his contemporaries: that in connivance with adolescents he used the confessional for planning a marriage and that he abetted a wedding of minors without parental consent, a practice to which even the broad-minded Rabelais objected. In the 1476 edition of Masuccio Salernitano (33), Giannozza the monk is no sympathetic Friar Lawrence, but a callow type who demands bribes not only to marry the young couple but to provide the potion which will adduce sleep. It is certainly possible that Painter and Shakespeare borrowed this plot partly from a desire to point out yet another reprehensible feature of the Roman Church.

Although a decree of the Council of Trent stipulated that the "sword of excommunication" should not be used inconsiderately, excommunication was a potent, often abused weapon which proved yet another issue that hastened the Reformation. Since to a true heretic excommunication carried no real threat, punishments usually accompanied an excommunicating ban. Boccaccio's and Sacchetti's tales made it clear that a threat of excommunication could be a means of extortion, while Solórzano illustrates how it can be a mechanism for private vengeance. From the Middle Ages to the Counter-Reformation the novellists were aware that, to their dismay, they were not writing in some safe area like that created by Boccaccio's Ghino di Taccio (X:2), whose men boasted to the Abbot of Cluny, "There is nothing for us to fear here where excommunications and interdicts are themselves excommunicated." [38] Threats of trials or excommunication were in fact known to the novellists. We have mentioned Cervantes' brush with the ecclesiastical authorities. Even the cautious Tirso de Molina found himself threatened by the Inquisition and subject to an *excomunión mayor latae sententiae*. Nor did Rastell in Anglican England avoid being called before the Archbishop's Court. Basing his contentions on the laws of God, nature, and man, he denied—as we derive from the tales which he printed—that curates might claim their living by tithes and oblations. He died in confinement.

Miracles were an integral part of Roman Church doctrine and had to be accepted as such. As usual, the novellas are better known for their spoof than for their acceptance of such divine interventions. As early as the second day of the *Decameron* (II:1) Martellino feigns a miracle, pretending to be a cripple cured, joint by joint and limb by limb, by having viewed the body of Saint Arrigo. Or again (III:1), young Masetto, the "mute" gardener, is declared by the abbess and nuns of the convent to have recovered the power of speech through their prayers and the intervention of the convent's patronymic saint. Centuries later, in Tirso's collection of the *Cigarrales* (3), miracles are satirized when Don Juan's servant Carillo mocks the resurrection of Lazarus by thrice commanding a dead weaver to rise from his grave. But it is Marguerite de Navarre, a sympathizer with the Reformation, and the Anglican Painter who provide the strongest satire of this fixture of Roman religious belief. Two of the tales of Marguerite de Navarre seem to question the very existence of miracles. Tale 33 of the *Heptaméron* ridicules the devout who believe in the miraculous pregnancy of a pious young girl only to find that her condition stems from her incestuous affair with her priestly brother. The other tale, concerning the lady of Lyon who confused a fleeing soldier in a church with a fleeing statue, has been related just above. Perhaps the most charming of miracle-tales in the Middle Ages, "Le jongleur de Notre-Dame," known to many in this century through its retelling by Anatole France, seems to have eluded the major tale-collectors of the Trecento and Quattrocento.

A final church custom treated in the novellas is a fascinating one, the pilgrimage. The validity of pilgrimages was very great in the Middle Ages—to Jerusalem if one were rich and powerful like Louis IX, to Rome especially during a jubilee year, to Saint James of Compostela, or to some nearby shrine like Chartres, Loreto, or Canterbury. The timing (Eastertide) and the benefits (principally the intercession of a saint) of a pilgrimage not required by a confessor as a specific penance are carefully mentioned in Chaucer's Prologue:

> Whan that Aprill with his shoures soote
> The drought of March hath perced to the roote . . .
> Thanne logen folk to goon on pilgrimages,
> And palmeres for the seken straunge strondes,

To ferne halwes, kowthe in sondry londes;
And specially from every shires ende
Of Engelond to Caunterbury they wende,
The hooly blisful martir for to seke.
That hem hath holpen whan that they were seeke.[39]

Although conspicuously absent in Boccaccio, other pilgrimages were mentioned in the novellas. The audacious author of the *Cent Nouvelles nouvelles,* for whom nothing appears to have been sacred, had to have his say about pilgrimages. To believe him, pilgrimages were viewed by women as an opportunity to escape marital surveillance and go off to cuckold their husbands. Tale 93 describes such a case: "In a large village . . . a gracious married woman loved the cleric or caretaker of her parish church much more than she did her own husband. In order to find a way to be with her caretaker, she pretended to her husband that she had to make a pilgrimage to some saint that was not far away." [40] Small wonder that, in the *Pentameron,* a husband threatened his wife, *"Affè,* I'm surely not going to send you up to Rome for your penance." One assumes that in certain families it would be the restless husbands who would be chafing to go off on this pretext. Tale 30 of the *Cent Nouvelles nouvelles* further denies that pilgrimages were the religious experiences they were made out to be. In this tale three merchants who go off to some shrine are soon replaced in their marital beds by the three monks who had preached all day long on the spiritual benefits of becoming a pilgrim and abstaining from pleasures of the flesh.

One novella, however, is very fruitful reading for one who would like to learn the details of a penitential sojourn in one of the world's greatest shrines. Bandello's novella IV,5 recounts meticulously the nine-day penance *(novendiale)* experienced by Duke William of Aquitaine, persecutor of Christian bishops, as a pilgrim in the Apostolic Church of Saint James of Compostela in the year 1137.

With the schism of the Church pilgrims were deprecated along with other rituals and sacraments. By the time Painter and Fenton were having their say, the Reformational view of pilgrimages as a form of papist idolatry held sway in England. Writing of Cornelio's desire to enjoy Plaudina in Discourse V, Fenton states sardonically that the anxious lover awaited "the approche of his hower of appointement, wyth no lesse devocion then the papistes in Fraunce performe their ydolatrous pilgrimage to theyr ydoll Sainct Tronyon, uppon the Mont Auyon besides Roan, or our supersticious catholikes of England of late dayes to the holye roode of Chester, or ymage of our Ladye at Walsingham." [41] Obviously the pilgrims of Geoffrey Chaucer and much of what they believed in would have been hopelessly out of place in the England of Geoffrey Fenton.

IV. Conclusion: The Novella and Reform

The influence of literature—or any form of art—upon society is a question still warmly debated by literary scholars, not to mention sociologists and even politicians. It is alleged by some that there is "precious little conclusive evidence that literary phenomena have any influence upon society." [42] But René Wellek, reviving the Platonic-Aristotelian tradition, states, "The writer is not only influenced by society: he influences it. Art not merely reproduces life, but also shapes it." [43]

Satire, which consciously aims to transform society, dominates the novella tradition. "The true end of Satyre," as John Dryden wrote in the Preface to Part I of *Absalom and Achitophel*, "is the amendment of vices by correction." [44] An even stronger proponent of satire's power to influence society was Gilbert Cannan, who added, "No tyrant, no tyrannous idea ever came crashing to earth but it was first wounded with the shafts of satire . . ." [45] When considering satire as an aid to effecting social, political, or economic change, one thinks at once of the novels of Dickens *(Hard Times,* among many others) and the Reform Bills of 1867 and 1882, or of George Bernard Shaw's Fabian Socialism and the economic system of modern-day England. The question that arises, then, is whether the novella tradition had the same kind of effect on the Renaissance and post-Renaissance periods as Dickens and Shaw apparently had on their times.

If one considers the ample documentation provided by these last few chapters alone, an hypothesis maintaining an affinity between the novella and the social, economic, political, and ecclesiastical reforms which followed in its wake would certainly seem tenable. To concentrate briefly on but one crucial change in the late Renaissance, one can indeed argue for something of a causal relationship between the considerable satire in the novellas aimed at the Church and the religious foment of the fifteenth and sixteenth centuries that culminated in the Protestant Reformation.

In fact, many of the satiric attacks on such sacred institutions of the Church as confession, the canonization of saints, the sale of indulgences, relics, and clerical sexuality found in the tales of Boccaccio, Chaucer, and their fellow novellists, were echoed, though in far more serious tones, in the sixteenth century by Martin Luther himself. Boccaccio, we recall, poked probably blasphemous fun at confession and the canonization of saints in his opening tale of Ciappelletto, the scamp who gained through a false confession not only extreme unction but sainthood as well. Luther also saw the weaknesses of the penitential system. Hence in *Table Talk* he stresses, as Marguerite's Hircan was later to do, that God, not the priest, is the confessor: "Christ sits there, Christ listens, Christ answers, not a man."[46] Luther goes further in *To the Christian Nobility of the German Nation* and demands that mendicants be relieved of hearing confession. In *The Babylonian Captivity* (we have seen above that the novellists, too, called Rome a Babylon) Luther includes penance among the sacraments to be eliminated altogether.[47] As for canonization and the worship of saints, Luther thought to minimize if not obliterate both. Arguing that only money and reputation are sought through canonization, he tells the German nobles, "My advice is to let the saints canonize themselves. Indeed, it is God alone who should canonize them."[48] For Luther it is God who is in fact to be worshipped, not the saints themselves; therefore in *The Judgment of Martin Luther on Monastic Vows* he writes, "The true way to salvation is to be subject to God. ... For we see in the followers of the saints nothing but a tumultuous confusion of works which they have seen in the saints."[49]

Many novellists, as we have seen, leveled assaults on the practice of selling relics. Luther is quoted in *Table Talk* as having said:

It is claimed that the head of Saint John the Baptist is in Rome, although all histories show that the Saracens opened John's grave and burned everything to powder. Yet the pope is not ashamed of his lies. So with reference to other relics like the nails and wood of the Cross—they are the greatest lies.[50]

Like Chaucer, Luther also inveighed against the enervating restrictions of monastic life. In his description of the Monk, Chaucer noted how this holy man chose to ignore the rules of his order so that he could pursue the pleasures of the hunt, and, in a rare example of satiric invective in the novella tradition the poet drops his mask of objective narrator and heartily seconds the monk's view:

> The reule of seint Maure or of seint Beneit,
> By cause that it was old and somdel streit
> This ilke Monk leet olde thynges pace,
> And heeld after the newe world the space.
> He yaf nat of that text a pulled hen,
> That seith that hunters ben nat hooly men,
> Ne that a monk, what he is reccheless,
> Is likned til a fissh that is waterlees,—
> This is to seyn, a monk out of his cloystre.
> But thilke text heeld he nat worth an oystre;
> And I sayde his opinion was good.
> What sholde he studie and make hymselven wood,
> Upon a book in cloystre alwey to poure,
> Or swynken with his handes, and laboure,
> As Austyn bit? How shal the world be served?
> Lat Austin have his swynk to hym reserved! [51]

Throughout *Table Talk* are registered caustic remarks against monks and the sterility of monastic life. Luther at one point cries out, "Away with monks and hermits! These are the inventions of Satan because they exist apart from all the godly ordinances and arrangements of God." [52] In *To the Christian Nobility of the German Nation* he writes of the monasteries, "Would to God they were dissolved!" [53] Elsewhere he asserts that the "civil works of the godly" are superior to "all the fasting and praying of the best and most pious monks." [54] Above all, Luther believed that the cloistered, inactive life of the monks actually encouraged vices of all sorts. His *On Monastic Vows* offers this conclusion: "Thus you see that the monastic life, with all its confusion of errors, lies, ignorance, laziness, deception, and illusion, represents the true Babylon." [55]

As for the libidinous activities of the clergy, which novellists never tired of relating, Luther noted the same clerical pursuits, albeit humorlessly. To him, of course, the root of the problem of priestly lechery lay in the vow of celibacy itself. Demanding sexual abstinence and yet permitting social contact with the other sex, he tells the German nobles, is "just like putting fire and straw together and forbidding them to smoke or burn." [56] In *Table Talk* Luther maintains that sexuality is a natural component of man—even the purest of soul are subject to its strivings; for him, then, the only way to prevent these sinful practices within the clergy is to permit clerical marriage:

> When he was quite old, Augustine still complained about nocturnal pollutions. When he was goaded by desire Jerome beat his breast with stones but was unable to drive out of his heart the girl he had seen dancing. Francis made snowballs and Benedict macerated his harassed body until it stank horribly. I believe that virgins also have temptations and enticements, but if there are fluxes and pollutions the gift of virginity is no longer there; then the remedy of marriage which God has given should be taken hold of. [57]

Gilbert Highet has written that all satirists are at heart idealists. [58] If he is correct, then surely Boccaccio and his disciples must be counted among history's most demanding idealists, for they refused to accept with complacency the clerical abuses surrounding them, choosing instead to attack them with a satirical pen. Moreover, in their criticism of, among other things, church corruption, confession, canonization, and worship of saints, the sale of indulgences and relics, monasticism, and the vow of celibacy, they clearly anticipated the later pronouncements of Luther and other Reformers. Indeed, the revolutionary nature of many of the novellas of Boccaccio and Chaucer, to name but two in the long tradition, was evidently observed by later generations, and their works were consequently feared or admired by many. The *Decameron*, as indicated above, was among those books immediately placed on the very first *Index Librorum Prohibitorum* of 1559. On the other hand, Caroline F. E. Spurgeon writes of Chaucer, "He was annexed by the Reformers, not without reason, as a kind of forerunner and sharer of their opinions with regard to Rome, as evidenced by his keen satirical exposure of the religious orders of his time." [59]

Yet one might well ask, to what extent does anticipation constitute influence? What actual effect did the novella tradition have on contemporary and future historical events—judicial and ecclesiastical reform, the undermining of feudal privileges and power, the rise and dominance of middle-class and mercantile values, the discrediting of the pseudo-sciences, the decline of the feudal marriage, the liberation of the role of women, and so on? The novella tradition did not of course single-handedly bring about either the Reformation—early Reformers like Marsilius of Padua, William of Ockham, and John Wycliffe (with their more limited public, of course), surely had their influence as well on later religious upheavals—or, for that matter, other socio-political changes. Nevertheless, because the novellists felt these matters deeply (we have seen that all but the Anglicans stayed within the Church) and because they employed in their corrective criticism the vehicle of satire—the sugar-coated pill, perhaps "the best appeal to reason that exists" [60]—they doubtless reached their wider audience more persuasively than most of the self-proclaimed reformers of their day. In so doing, they lowered their readers' tolerance of the injustices and sufferings they unnecessarily endured and hence made the idea of both social criticism and social change more acceptable, participating in the creation of an intellectual climate that hastened significant historical reforms, and, with them, for better or for worse, the modern age.

Notes

1. Preserved Smith, *Age of the Reformation* (New York: Holt, 1920), p. 442.

2. *Bandello's Fiction*, p. 117.

3. Andrés Giménez Soler, *Don Juan Manuel: Biografía y estudio crítico* (Zaragoza: Académia española, 1932), p. 198.

4. See Samuel A. Zimmerman, "Arabic Influences in the Tales of *El Conde Lucanor*," *DAI*, 31 (1970), 774A (Univ. of Florida).

5. Jourda, p. 946.

6. Clements and Levant, p. 85-86.

7. Henry Kamen, *The Spanish Inquisition* (London: Weidenfeld and Nicolson, 1965), p. 97.

8. Lena Sylvania, *Doña María de Zayas*, p. 15.

9. Fenton, I, 265-66 and 248.

10. *Decameron*, p. 46.

11. Cervantes, p, 942.

12. Chaucer, p. 163.

13. *French Bandello*, p. 75; and Fenton, II, 200-01.

14. Jacobs, III, 42.

15. Ibid.

16. *Decameron*, p. 715.

17. Ibid., pp. 388-89 and 416.

18. G. G. Coulton, *Ten Mediaeval Studies* (Cambridge: Cambridge Univ. Press, 1930), p. 97.

19. *Decameron*, pp. 387-88.

20. Jourda, p. 302.

21. Ibid., p. 473.

22. Otto Cartellieri, *The Court of Burgundy* (London: Paul, Trench, and Trubner, 1929), p. 182.

23. Rossell Hope Robbins, Introduction, *The Hundred Tales* (New York: Bonanza, 1960), p. xviii.

24. Jourda, p. 887.

25. Bandello, II, 534-35.

26. *Decameron*, p. 93.

27. Ibid., pp. 1107-08.

28. Cervantes, p. 839

29. Chaucer, pp. 23-24 and 154.

30. Sacchetti, p. 219.

31. Fenton, II, 201. For John ap Rice, see Clements and Levant, pp. 222-23.

32. *Decameron*, p. 72.

33. Jacobs, II, 141.

34. Chaucer, p. 19.

35. Jourda, p. 140.

36. Zall, p. 122.

37. Jourda, p. 1057.

38. *Decameron*, pp. 776-77.

39. Chaucer, p. 17.

40. Jourda, p. 324.

41. Fenton, I, 231-32.
42. See, for example, Priscilla Clark, *YCGL* p, 6.
43. Wellek and Warren, *Theory of Literature*, p. 162.
44. Dryden, *Works,* ed. H. T. Swedenberg (Berkeley: Univ. of California Press, 1956-), II,5.
45. Gilbert Cannan, *Satire* (London: M. Secker, 1914), p. 13.
46. *Luther's Works,* ed. Jaroslav Pelikan and Helmut T. Lehmann (Philadelphia: Fortress, 1958-), LIV, 394.
47. Ibid., XLIV, 17, and XXXVI, 81-90.
48. Ibid., XLIV, 187.
49. Ibid., XLIV, 271.
50. Ibid., LIV, 131.
51. Chaucer, p. 19.
52. *Luther's Works,* LIV, 268.
53. Ibid., LIV, 304.
54. Ibid., XLIV, 172.
55. Ibid., XLIV, 266.
56. Ibid., XLIV, 178.
57. Ibid., LIV, 270.
58. Gilbert Highet, *Anatomy of Satire* (Princeton: Princeton Univ. Press, 1962), p. 243.
59. Caroline F. B. Spurgeon, *500 Years of Chaucer Criticism and Allusion, 1357-1900* (1908-17; rpt. New York: Russell and Russell, 1960), I, xix.
60. David Worcester, *The Art of Satire* (1940; rpt. New York: Russell and Russell, 1960), p. 46.

CHAPTER 9

The Fate of a Genre:
From Novella to
Modern Short Story

I *Brevitas* and the Claim of Historicity

The earliest novellists, ever mindful of the rhetorico-literary nature of the narrative form to which they turned their hands, seem one and all to have dutifully conformed to the novellistic ideal of brevity of expression. The average length of a tale from the *Cento novelle antiche* is under 270 words: its shortest novella runs to fewer than forty words (17), its longest no more than 1,250 words (64). The stories in Manuel's *Conde Lucanor* range approximately from a hundred (Cuento 8) to 3,355 words (Cuento 27), the mean being little more than a thousand words.

If, embarking upon a little experiment, we estimate that a storyteller would recite something like 120 words a minute—a rather leisurely pace which would allow adequate time for one to pause for dramatic effect or for laughter, for drink or for breath—we can only conclude from the approximate recitation-times of the tales in these two pre-Boccaccesque collections that their respective authors probably had in mind for their novellas not only a reading audience but a listening audience as well. The very longest tale of the *Cento novelle antiche,* for example would take just over ten minutes to recite, the shortest less than half a minute, the average about two minutes. The typical tale of the *Conde Lucanor,* though admittedly longer than its counterpart in the Italian work, would still roughly average only eight and a half minutes to recite.

From Boccaccio onward the tendency toward the amplification of form grows stronger, but the approximate word-lengths and recitation-times of most of the later novellas continue to support the common claim of a Boccaccio, a Chaucer, or a Bandello that he is merely transcribing stories actually recited in his presence (see the table below).

Collection	Approximate Length of Average Tale	Recitation Time
Decameron	2,500 words	20.8 minutes
Canterbury Tales	7,100 words	59.2 minutes
Cent Nouvelles nouvelles	1,350 words	11.3 minutes
Heptaméron	2,200 words	18.3 minutes
Bandello's *Novelle*	2,900 words	24.2 minutes
Pentamerone	2,400 words	20.0 minutes

The ample length of some of Chaucer's tales obviously raises some problems. Since the *Canterbury Tales* is incomplete, one wonders if the longer stories were meant to stand as they now do, or if at some later stage they might have been condensed. To be sure several of Chaucer's narratives—those of the Reeve, Friar, Physician, Shipman, Prioress, and Manciple for example—would require less than a half-hour to recite. But, on the other hand, such tales as the Knight's and the Parson's would claim over two hours of a listening audience's time. One suspects that Chaucer's inordinately verbose "Tale of Melibee" is, just like the "Tale of Sir Thopas," that other story recited by Chaucer the Pilgrim, nothing more than a literary joke. It is also interesting to note that most of the longer tales in this early English collection (such as those of the Knight, Man of Law, Clerk, and Parson) are divided into smaller units of narration, perhaps signifying a number of intermissions consciously interspersed throughout the telling. For example, each of the four parts of the "Knight's Tale" would take about half an hour to narrate, a reasonable period of time to believe that the attention of the pilgrims was effectively held. Finally, with no other diversions or distractions for Chaucer's pilgrims—Boccaccio's frame-characters, we recall, take long walks in the woods, bathe in convenient lakes and streams, pet docile animals, weave garlands, dance, sing, and so on—and with little else to do during their journey to Canterbury, it is indeed quite plausible that they would both be tempted, on the one hand, to amplify their own tales, and, on the other, to be receptive to stories that average almost an hour in length.

Computation of approximate recitation-times for the novellas similarly offers support for the claims of historicity made by those novellists who rely upon a rigid unity of time in their frame-narratives. In the *Decameron*, *Heptaméron*, and *Pentamerone* the daily storytelling allegedly begins after Nones (around 3 P.M.). On the average day of the *Decameron* approximately 25,000 words of narration would be expended, covering about three and a half hours in time and hence ending roughly at 6:30 P.M., just in time for supper. The entertainments of the *Heptaméron* and *Pentamerone* would probably conclude even earlier, perhaps at 6:00.

We find this unique marriage of the novellistic ideals of brevity and verisimilitude in the Italian and French novella throughout the tradition and in the Spanish and English novellas in their earliest manifestations. At the end of the sixteenth and the beginning of the seventeenth centuries, however, novellists in both England and Spain—especially in works like Fenton's *Certain Tragical Discourses* and Cervantes' *Novelas ejemplares*—began to expand their tales in such a manner that this honored, long-standing marriage of ideals was rent asunder.

II *Amplificatio* and the Novella

The movement in the later novella toward the expansion of the genre is, of course, to some extent reflective of the traditional conflict in rhetoric between the concepts of *brevitas* and *amplificatio*. In both Cicero and Quintilian, for example, we find not only praise for the orator's use of brevity, but also acknowledgment of the virtues of *amplificatio* in speech.[1] The Middle Ages and the Renaissance inherited from classical rhetoric two general notions of amplification. Aristotle and others, on the one hand, in the main conceived of amplification as *auxesis (augere)*, which was designed primarily to increase the audience's opinion of an idea by elevating its significance beyond its actual importance and real dimensions. For the Sophists, on the other hand, amplification meant *peribola (ornare)*, the chief goal of which was magnification through ornamentation.[2]

Undoubtedly the most obvious example of the purely rhetorical expansion of the novella can be found in Fenton's *Certain Tragical Discourses*, an amplified translation of Belleforest's *Histoires tragiques*, which in turn is itself an amplified translation of some of Bandello's *Novelle*. By the time Belleforest and Fenton are finished with the Italian's brief narratives, the tales are almost unrecognizable. With apologies for the inclusion of yet another table, we present the list of comparisons shown below to offer a striking notion of the quantitative disparity between Fenton's novellas and their Bandellian sources.

Fenton's *Discourses*	Approximate Word-length	Bandellian Original	Approximate Word-length
I	25,290	I,49	8,460
II	15,340	I,33	1,540
III	12,800	III,52	3,710
IV	10,870	I,51	2,250
V	20,470	I,28	6,490
VI	9,900	II,7	3,370
VII	11,250	I,4	3,020
VIII	13,000	I,8	1,520
IX	13,480	II,33	2,470
X	13,340	II,26	1,510
XI	18,060	III,17	4,040
XII	8,600	I,14	1,410
XIII	29,520	I,27	12,320
Average	15,532	Average	4,008

Fenton's "Discourse," then, is on the average nearly four times the size of its Bandellian source—Discourse II is almost ten times longer than its source. Whereas the typical novella of Bandello would require about a half-hour to recite, it would take over two hours orally to narrate the *average* Fenton tale—indeed, Discourse XIII would probably stretch to more than four hours if one had the stamina and perseverance necessary to recite it.

To illustrate the nature of Belleforest's and Fenton's amplification, one must turn to the texts themselves. Let us observe, first, Fenton's treatment of a passage interpolated by Belleforest into a Bandello novella (I,49): the description of Angelica's grief at her unjustly imprisoned brother's desire for death.

Belleforest:

Ce complot prins, estant du tout resolu Charles en son propos de mort, c'estoit grand' pitié de veoir la belle Angelique se deschirer la face, & arracher les cheveux, voyant qu'il estoit impossible d'oster ceste cruelle deliberation de la teste de son frere. . . .[3]

Fenton (after taking a deep breath):

[Her brother's] resolution of death was furthwith imparted to the faire Angeliqua; who, besides whole rivers of tears distilling from her watery eyes with dollorous cryes in dolefull voyce, redoubled with an eccho of treble dule, entred into a mortal war wyth her garmentes and attyre on her head, neither forbearing to deschevel her crispy lockes and heare exceding the collor of amber, nor commit cruel execution upon the tender partes of her body. And giving free skope to the humor of her fury, she spared not to imprint with her nayles, upon the precious complexion of her oriente face, a pityfull remembrance of the tragicall troble of her desolate brother, whome she could not in any way perswade to a chaunge or alteracion of purpose. . . .[4]

The first type of expansion that we discover in Belleforest's translation of Bandello and in Fenton's translation of Belleforest as well reflects quantitative rather than qualitative, formal rather than substantive mutations. If Belleforest writes, "Ainsi durant ce matin contempla il. . . ,"[5] Fenton will translate, "But duringe the time of the sermon, and all the matutinall prayer, our unhappie Phillyberto wavered in contrarietye of thoughts . . . "; [6] "le païs de Piedmont" in the *Histoires tragiques*[7] becomes "the lymytrophall townes, confynyge the borders of Pyemount" in the *Certain Tragical Discourses*.[8] As René Pruvost has pointed out, Fenton's translation "consists in rendering the same idea as his original in a great many more words";[9] or as Frank S. Hook has put it, "Fenton apparently believed that if one word were good two would be better." [10]

A second type of amplification found in both Belleforest and Fenton results from the insistent moralizations each feels compelled to tack on to the work he is translating. For instance, Bandello concludes his witty story of Zilia and Filiberto with the young man's exacting his proper revenge on the uppity widow and then living the rest of his life in the good graces of his king.[11] Belleforest and Fenton, however, must append to the original ending these moralistic conclusions:

Belleforest:

. . . la force de l'homme est moins que rien, où Dieu ne opere par sa grace: laquelle nous defaillant, nos oeuvres ne peuvent sentir que la punaise & corruption de nostre naturel en laquelle il s'agrée & entretient, comme le pourceau se veautrant dans quelque bourbier fangeux, & plein de souïlleure.[12]

Fenton:

. . . the force of man is nothinge where God doth not worke by his grace; without whose assistance we can neyther learne that which is good, nor defende ourselves from the daunger of any evil. Like as, also, if we want that guide in our doing, our workes (smellynge of nothinge but corrupcion of our own nature) make us seame not muche unlike the loathsom swine, wallowinge in a dortye or moddie poodle, to encrease her filthynes.[13]

One can safely concur with C. S. Lewis that Fenton (faithfully following Belleforest) whenever possible "loads, or stuffs, every rift

with rhetorical, proverbial, and moral ore." [14] Indeed, the Elizabethan writer learned so well from Belleforest that he defeated the
Frenchman at his own game. René Pruvost correctly concludes,
"Rather than actual translations, his 'Discourses' are rhetorical
amplifications of Belleforest's 'Histoires.' He goes one better over
him, and submits his text to a treatment not unlike that which
Bandello had been made to undergo at his hands." [15]

Pruvost's connection of these amplified translations with rhetoric
seems most helpful, for the kind of amplification employed by both
Belleforest and Fenton are indeed the ancient ones: *auxesis* and
peribola. The constant moral digressions of Belleforest and Fenton
seem meant principally to enhance the reader's opinion of the
significance of the author's stories, while the inordinately effusive
style of each is doubtless intended solely for decorative purposes.

III Cervantes and the Modern Short Story

Like Fenton's *Certain Tragical Discourses*, the tales in Cervantes'
Novelas ejemplares average well over 15,000 words apiece—requiring,
that is, more than two hours to recite. Yet the Spanish author's
concern in his *novelas* for such matters as scene setting (including
costumbrismo), character development, and plot complication represents the use of amplification neither to make things appear more
important than they are nor merely to decorate, but instead to
develop more fully the purely narrative (rather than rhetorical and
moralistic) elements inherent in one's fictive material.

Interest in the depiction of *costumbrismo* is especially apparent in
Cervantes' "La gitanilla," a story rich—if not altogether accurate—
in detail of gypsy life. The *novela* commences with an account of the
gypsy upbringing of the heroine Preciosa: "Preciosa grew up rich
in carols *(villancicos)*, folksongs *(coplas)*, *seguidillas*, sarabands, and
other verses, especially ballads, which she sang with special
gracefulness. . . ." [16] Shortly thereafter, colorfully described for us is
a gypsy dance:

Preciosa made her first entry into Madrid on the day of St.
Anne, patroness and protectress of the city, with a dance in

which eight gypsy women took part, four old and four young, and one gypsy man, a great dancer, who led them. And although all were neat and well dressed, the neatness of Preciosa was such that little by little she cast a spell over the eyes of all who gazed upon her. From amid the sound of the tambourine and the castanets and the encircling steps of the dance there arose from the crowd a murmur of approval for the beauty and grace of the little gypsy.[17]

The story, moreover, contains two long ballads—one of twenty-five lines, the other 128 lines—sung by Preciosa accompanying herself on a tambourine. The "little gypsy girl" also tells the fortune of the Lieutenant's wife in some sixty-four lines of verse. When her beloved Andrés seeks to join the gypsy ranks he must undergo the appropriate rite of initiation:

... the ceremonies of the admission of Andrés into the gypsy life were performed as follows: They presently cleared out one of the best huts in the camp *(aduar)* and adorned it with branches and sweet roots, and, seating Andrés on the stump of a cork tree, they placed in his hands a hammer and tongs and made him cut a couple of capers to the sound of two guitars, which two gypsies played. Then they bared one of his arms and gently gave it two turns with a ribbon of new silk and a stick.[18]

Finally, after these ceremonies, the "ways" of gypsy life are enumerated for us by one of their elders. According to the old man, the gypsies faithfully observe the law of friendship. No one covets the goods of another; there is no jealousy. Although incest may not be infrequent, adultery is almost unknown. If wives or mistresses are unfaithful, their men are allowed to kill them and bury them as if the wayward females were nothing but malevolent animals. Except for the women, everything is supposedly held in common. For the gypsies, the elder continues, life at one with nature is the ideal:

"We are the lords of the plains, of the cultivated lands, of the forests, of the mountains, of the springs, and of the rivers. The forests give us wood free of cost, the trees fruit, the vines grapes, the gardens vegetables, the springs water, the rivers fish, the hunting preserves game, the rocks shade, the fissures fresh air, and the caves houses. For us the inclemencies of weather are breezes, the snow a refreshment, the rain baths, the thunder music, and lightning torches. For us the hard clods of earth are beds of soft feathers." [19]

Among Cervantes' fascinating gallery of character portraits surely one of the most psychologically complex, curious, and compelling is the almost Kafkaesque Tomás Rodaja, the titular antihero of the *novela* "El licenciado Vidriera." When Tomás recovered from a serious illness caused by a dose of poison inadvertently administered to him as a love-potion, he believed, to the amazement of all his doctors, that he was entirely made of glass; and "under this delusion, when anyone came near him, he would utter terrible cries, begging and entreating them with words and arguments that they should not approach him or else they would shatter him, since he was truly not like other men, but was all glass from head to foot." [20] Tomás also made it a point to wear loose-fitting clothes. When he passed through the streets, he walked in the very middle, afraid something might fall from a window and break him into pieces. For safety he slept in straw up to his throat, and whenever it thundered, he rushed out into the fields until the storm has passed.

Like Don Quijote and the Fool in *King Lear,* Tomás inevitably becomes the archetypal "wise madman," and he travels everywhere followed by a huge throng, spouting *bons mots,* many of which we have previously cited, on judges, physicians, poets, and so forth. The *novela* itself, which began almost like a travelogue—with descriptions of the many places that the young man had visited, like Salamanca, Málaga, Florence, Rome, Naples, Sicily, Venice, and Milan (e.g., "Florence pleased him very greatly as much by its pleasant setting as by its cleanliness, its sumptuous buildings, its refreshing river and agreeable streets . . ." [21])—thus concludes as a kind of compendium of *sententiae.*

"La ilustre fregona" presents a good example of the rather

complex plot structure that Cervantes was wont to fashion for many of his *novelas*. The complicated story owes much to the genre often referred to as the "Greek romance." Ruth El Saffar writes that both the "Ilustre fregona" and the "Gitanilla" reflect Cervantes' tendency "to adapt to Spanish prose fiction characteristics of the Greek novel." [22] It begins with the departure of a young man of quality from his father's house in search of adventure. After spending three "picaresque" years involved with tuna fisheries, the young man returns home, but within a very short time wanderlust wells up within him once more. He persuades his closest friend to join him, and the two depart for further adventures with the tuna fishermen. (Some readers may find the plot hard to follow because of the fondness of the young men for using aliases. The original adventurer, Don Diego de Carriazo, son of another Don Diego de Carriazo, calls himself Urdiales at first and then switches to Lope the Asturian; his friend, Don Tomás de Avendaño, prefers the name Tomás Pedro.) Certainly the highlight of the adventures of the two youths occurs when Avendaño (or Tomás Pedro) falls in love with the beautiful kitchen maid Costanza. Near the story's close, the innkeeper in a fairly lengthy flashback explains to an investigating corregidor that Costanza is not really his daughter. Many years ago, it seems, a well-born lady came to his inn, gave birth to the girl, and left her (conveniently with certain unmistakable tokens) to the innkeeper to raise. Immediately after the completion of this narrative, the fathers of the two young adventurers arrive at the same inn. One of them, Don Diego de Carriazo (the elder, that is), admits (upon seeing the aforesaid tokens) that he is the true father of Costanza. He then tells, in yet another flashback, of how as a younger man he forced his attentions upon the beautiful widow of a great nobleman. The widow, now deceased, turns out, of course, to be the mother of the lovely kitchen maid. A triple wedding concludes the story: Avendaño (or Tomás Pedro) marries Costanza, Carriazo (or Urdiales, or Lope the Asturian) marries the daughter of the corregidor, and Don Pedro (the corregidor's son) marries no one but the daughter of Don Juan de Avendaño.

If "La ilustre fregona" owes much to the romance tradition, then the influence of the picaresque novel can be detected in not only

"Rinconete y Cortadillo"—which A. A. Parker (mistakenly we believe) calls "Cervantes's only venture" in the picaresque[23]—but also in the "Coloquio des los perros." Although cast in what appears to be a Lucianic dialogue, the "Coloquio" may perhaps best be viewed as an account of a canine Lazarillo de Tormes. Like a true picaro, Berganza survives only by relying on his wits, taking up with and discarding masters as circumstances dictate. We have already discussed many of his experiences, including those with a butcher, a merchant, a police officer, a group of gypsies, and a Moor.

The *Novelas ejemplares* seems dramatically to mark an end as well as a beginning in the history of short fiction. With their roots firmly in the Renaissance novella tradition (as shown by their adherence to the concepts of recreational function, variety, verisimilitude, unity, harmony, and decorum in language and style), Cervantes' *novelas,* embodying as they do a radically different notion not only of invention but of amplification as well, constitute a significant movement toward the literary future, for it is in them that we perceive what appears to be the very moment of the metamorphosis of the novella into what for want of a better term we call "the modern short story." [24]

Specifically, Cervantes' type of amplification differs profoundly from that employed by Belleforest and Fenton primarily because the Spaniard's short fiction seems to indicate a permanent shift in the conception of the novella from a rhetorico-literary medium to a more strictly literary medium (it is significant that Fenton, despite their excessive length, is still calling his stories "discourses.") The very basis of Cervantes' more "modern" approach to the expansion of the novella therefore stems from his propensity to absorb into his *novelas* characteristics common to the more extended narrative forms of literature of his day, such as the Greek romance, the travelogue, the Lucianic dialogue, and, indeed, the picaresque novel.

Such "generic inclusionism," as the late Rosalie Colie has shown, was commonplace in the Renaissance.[25] Whereas Aristotelian-Horatian theorists of the age carefully defined and separated genres, one discovers in the actual practice of many Renaissance artists the veritable melting of "kinds" into one another, as evidenced by such literary products of the age as Rabelais' *Gargantua et Pantagruel,* Burton's *Anatomy of Melancholy,* and the *Don Quijote,* and by such new artistic genres as the emblem, the opera, the romance-epic, the tragicomedy, and the novella itself.

This communion of genres in the *Novelas ejemplares* also seems reflective of that "new synthesis" which Robert Scholes and Robert Kellogg have found in the narrative literature of the late Renaissance. According to Scholes and Kellogg, from the epic synthesis of classical antiquity there arose in the Middle Ages two antithetical types of literature: the *empirical* (subdivided into the *historical* and the *mimetic*) and the *fictional* (subdivided into the *romantic* and the *didactic*). However, through a gradual process— "beginning at least as early as Boccaccio"—a new synthesis in narrative appears to have emerged in post-Renaissance literature, and it was this new fusion of the mimetic, the historical, the romantic, and the didactic—"seen clearly in a writer like Cervantes"—that generated the "great and synthetic literary form," the modern novel.[26]

Notes

1. See Cicero, *De Oratore,* III, liii; and Quintilian, *Institutiones Oratoriae,* VIII, iv.

2. For helpful discussions of *amplificatio,* see Ernst Robert Curtius' thirteenth *discursus,* "Brevity as an Ideal of Style," in *European Literature and the Latin Middle Ages,* pp. 487-94 as well as the valuable study by Verne R. Kennedy, "Concepts of Amplification in Rhetorical Theory," Diss. Louisiana State University 1968.

3. *French Bandello,* p. 165.

4. *Certain Tragical Discourses,* I, 37. This illustration was first pointed out by Hook in his Introduction to *The French Bandello,* p. 23.

5. *French Bandello,* p. 57.

6. Fenton, II, 172.

7. *French Bandello,* p. 55.

8. Fenton, II, 167.

9. René Pruvost, *Matteo Bandello and Elizabethan Fiction* (Paris: Champion, 1937), p. 180.

10. *French Bandello,* p. 23.

11. Flora, II, 346.

12. *French Bandello,* p. 82.

13. Fenton, II, 212.

14. C. S. Lewis, *English Literature in the Sixteenth Century Excluding Drama* (Oxford: Clarendon, 1954,) p. 311.

15. *Matteo Bandello and Elizabethan Fiction,* p. 55.

16. *Obras completas,* p. 775. Boccaccio and his more faithful disciples understandably had little more than passing interest in scene setting. A typical Boccaccesque tale begins, "There was in Lunigiana, a country not very far from here . . ." *Decameron,* p. 64, which is in general the entire extent to which the Italian novellist and his followers went in their depiction of environment.

17. Ibid.

18. Ibid., p. 789.

19. Ibid.

20. Ibid., p. 880.

21. Ibid., p. 878.

22. *Novel to Romance,* p. 86.

23. A. A. Parker, *Literature and the Delinquent* (Edinburgh: Edinburgh Univ. Press, 1967), p. 30.

24. For a discussion of Cervantes' possible influence on the likes of Charles Sorel, Goethe, Tieck, Hoffmann, and Gogol, see Agustín G. de Amezúa y Mayo, *Cervantes: Creador de la novela corta española* (Madrid: Consejo Superior de investigaciones científicas, 1956), esp. the chapter "Influencias de las *Novelas ejemplares,*" I, 565-607. In a previously cited lecture (see Chapter One, n. 127), Mirollo independently suggested that Cervantes' *novelas* "simultaneously sum up and tear apart" the novella tradition and point to "its successor in the modern short story."

25. See Colie's above-cited study *The Resources of Kind.*

26. Robert Scholes and Robert Kellogg, *The Nature of the Narrative* (New York: Oxford Univ. Press, 1966), esp. pp. 3-16. Janet M. Ferrier, although viewing the phenomenon in a more "linear" fashion, seems essentially to have been on a similar course in her *Forerunners of the French Novel* (p. 5) when she spoke of the novella as "the vital link" between the romance and the novel.

APPENDIX A

Principal Novella Collections

Since virtually no novellist writing after Boccaccio escaped the influence of the *maestro*, we have chosen in this compilation to isolate those relevant collections of tales antecedent to the composition of the *Decameron*. We have, moreover, for obvious reasons, omitted such novellas as Machiavelli's "Belfagor" (c. 1515) and Luigi Da Porto's "Romeo e Giulietta" (c. 1530), which were atypically written as individual stories and not as part of a collection of such tales. On the other hand, we have chosen to include several Spanish works of the seventeenth century which differ markedly in form and content from the Boccaccesque model. As Thomas F. Crane has pointed out, in the later Spanish imitations of the *Decameron* (those of Tirso de Molina and Castillo Solórzano, for example), "the entertainments are most elaborate, and, in addition to the telling of stories and music and dancing, plays, sacred and profane, are performed, together with masques" *(Italian Social Customs of the Sixteenth Century*, p. 593). Such works, however, do represent one of the last manifestations of the novella tradition.

Pre-Boccaccesque Collections

Anonymous, *Gesta Romanorum* (thirteenth century?)
Anonymous, *Cento novelle antiche*, or *Il Novellino* (late thirteenth century)
Don Juan Manuel, *El conde Lucanor* (c. 1335)

Boccaccio and the Italian Tradition

Giovanni Boccaccio, *Decameron* (c. 1350)
Giovanni Sercambi, *Novelle* (1374)
Ser Giovanni Fiorentino, *Pecorone* (c. 1390)
Franco Sacchetti, *Trecentonovelle* (c. 1395)
Masuccio Salernitano, *Novellino* (1476)
Sabadino degli Arienti, *Porrettane* (1483)
Anton Francesco Grazzini, *Cene* (c. 1545)
Agnolo Firenzuola, *Ragionamenti* (1548)
Girolamo Parabosco, *Diporti* (1550)
Gian Francesco Straparola, *Piacevoli notti* (1550-53)
Matteo Bandello, *Novelle* (1554-73)
Pietro Fortini, *Novelle* (c. 1560)
Giambattista Giraldi Cinzio, *Ecatommiti* (1565)
Sebastiano Erizzo, *Sei giornate* (1567)
Ascanio de' Mori, *Giuoco piacevole* (1585)
Scipione Bargagli, *Trattenimenti* (1587)
Giambattista Basile, *Pentamerone* (posth. 1634-36)

France

Anonymous, *Cent Nouvelles nouvelles* (c. 1460)
Noël Du Faïl, *Propos rustiques* (1547)
Bonaventure Des Périers, *Nouvelles récréations et joyeux devis* (posth. 1558)
Marguerite de Navarre, *Heptaméron* (posth. 1558)
Pierre Boaistuau and François de Belleforest, *Histoires tragiques* (1559-82)
Jacques Yver, *Printemps* (1572)
Jean de la Fontaine, *Contes et nouvelles* (1664-74)

England

Geoffrey Chaucer, *Canterbury Tales* (c. 1390)
John Rastell (printer), *One Hundred Merry Tales* (1526)

William Painter, *Palace of Pleasure* (1566-67)
Geoffrey Fenton, *Certain Tragical Discourses* (1567)
George Pettie, *Petite Palace of Pleasure* (1576)
George Whetstone, *An Heptameron of Civil Discourses* (1582)
Robert Greene, *Penelope's Web* (1587)
———, *Farewell to Folly* (1591)

Spain

Juan de Timoneda, *Patrañuelo* (1567)
Antonio de Eslava, *Noches de invierno* (1609)
Miguel de Cervantes, *Novelas ejemplares* (1613)
Lope de Vega, *Novelas* (1621-24)
Francisco de Lugo y Dávila, *Teatro popular* (1622)
Tirso de Molina, *Cigarrales de Toledo* (1624)
Alonso del Castillo Solórzano, *Tardes entretenidas* (1625)
———, *Jornadas alegres* (1626)
———, *Tiempo de regocijo* (1627)
———, *Huerta de Valencia* (1629)
———, *Noches de placer* (1631)
Juan Pérez de Montalbán, *Para todos* (1633)
Castillo Solórzano, *Fiestas del jardín* (1634)
Tirso de Molina, *Deleitar aprovechando* (1635)
María de Zayas y Sotomayor, *Novelas amorosas y exemplares* (1637-49)
Matías de los Reyes, *Para algunos* (1640)
Castillo Solórzano, *Alivios de Casandra* (1640)
———, *Quinta de Laura* (1649)
———, *Sala de recreación* (1649)
Mariana de Carabajal y Saavedra, *Navidades de Madrid* (1663)

The Novella and
the Elizabethan Drama

The impact of the novella tradition on the literature of Renaissance Europe was immense, affecting the development not merely of short fiction but of drama as well, most especially in England. Curiously enough, however, complete translations of Italian collections came very late to English soil.

In France, on the other hand, Laurent Premierfait produced a translation of the *Decameron* around 1414, and Antoine Le Maçon, commissioned by Marguerite de Navarre, published his rendering of Boccaccio's stories in 1545. Straparola's *Piacevoli notti* was translated into French around 1560, and at about the same time Bandello through Boaistuau and Belleforest's *Histoires tragiques* became well known to Renaissance France. In Spain, in the meantime, the *Decameron* was translated in its entirety by the end of the fifteenth century, while Spanish versions of the tales of Straparola, Bandello, and Giraldi were in print by 1590. Lastly, thanks to the efforts of Dirck Cornhert and Gerrit Hendricx van Breugel, all one hundred tales of the *Decameron* were rendered into Dutch by 1605.

Yet English readers had to wait until 1620 for the publication of

the first complete translation of an Italian novella collection, that
being an anonymous rendering of the *Decameron.*[1] This, of course, is
not at all to say that the Elizabethans were unfamiliar with the
novella tradition—far from it. Before 1565, for example, one finds
at least two plays dealing with the Griselda theme as well as
scattered translations (mostly in verse) of individual tales from the
Decameron, including Sir Thomas Elyot's version of Boccaccio's
story of Titus and Gissipus that is contained in *The Governour*
(1531). Then, quite suddenly, in the last third or so of the sixteenth
century, England was simply inundated by a wave of what one
might call "novella-mania," which took the form not of complete
translations of novella collections, but of compilations or an-
thologies which drew their materials from a variety of sources,
conspicuously including the novella.

The first of these was William Painter's *Palace of Pleasure*
published in two volumes in 1566 and 1567. In addition to Livy,
Herodotus, Aulus Gellius, Plutarch, and other classical authors,
Painter included within his collection of some 101 stories selected
novellas by Boccaccio, Ser Giovanni Fiorentino, Bandello (through
Boaistuau and Belleforest), Straparola, Giraldi, and Marguerite de
Navarre. The *Palace of Pleasure* was such an immediate and
stunning success that it was quickly followed by Geoffrey Fenton's
Certain Tragical Discourses (1567), thirteen stories drawn from the
Histoires tragiques, and George Pettie's *A Petite Palace,* which ran
through six editions between 1576 and 1613. In fairly rapid
succession over the next decade or two came several other similar
collections, such as George Turberville's *Tragical Tales* (c. 1576),
George Whetstone's *Rock of Regard* (1576) and *Heptameron of Civil
Discourses* (1582) Robert Smythe's *Strange and Tragical Tales* (1577),
and Barnabe Rich's *Farewell to the Military Profession* (1581).[2]

In short, Italianate novellas were everywhere in Elizabethan
England, as Roger Ascham's famous puritanical diatribe against
such fiction strikingly attests. Among what he calls "the enchant-
ments of Circe brought out of Italy to mar men's manners in
England" the anti-Italian Ascham in his *Schoolmaster* (1570)
includes several of these very collections, or, as he describes them,
"fond books, of late translated out of Italian into English, sold in
every shop in London, commended by honest titles the sooner to

corrupt honest manners, dedicated overboldly to virtuous and honorable personages, the easier to beguile simple and innocent wits." [3]

It would seem only natural for these very popular tales to catch the attention of the acutely audience-conscious Elizabethan playwright and ultimately to make their way into the London playhouses. As early as 1582 we find another enflamed puritan, Stephen Gosson, including in his *Plays Confuted in Five Actions* Painter's *Palace of Pleasure* among those works which "have been thoroughly ransackt, to furnish the Playe houses in London." [4]

Ever since Gosson, English literary critics and scholars have pondered the immense debt of Elizabethan drama to the Renaissance novellists. In fact for some—especially those patently unfamiliar with the richness and scope of the novella tradition—the entire *raison d'être* for the study of the novella is centered in uncovering the plot materials which it provided for Shakespeare and his fellow dramatists. The surprisingly unsympathetic C. S. Lewis, for one, believed the principal function of the novella in England was "but to serve as a dung or compost for the popular drama." [5] Other critics, on the other hand, employing more congenial metaphors, have spoken of the tradition as "the obvious quarry of the English dramatists" (Felix E. Schelling) and as both a "treasury" (Sidney Lee) and even "the richest storehouse" (Wilhelm Creizenach) of dramatic plots for the Elizabethans. [6]

Since so many valuable analytical studies of the sources of Renaissance English drama continue to be undertaken, [7] it need only be necessary here briefly to make a few general remarks concerning, first, the suitability of the Italianate novella as plot material for the Elizabethan play, and, second, the manner in which this tradition of Renaissance short fiction helped determine the nature and perhaps even the form of drama in the age of Shakespeare.

Rapidity of composition, it is universally acknowledged, was an essential condition of the Elizabethan theater. As A. L. Attwater writes, "The repertory system and competition between the companies, as well as the limited number of theatre-goers, demanded a regular supply of fresh plays." [8] Hence during a time in which invention, as we have seen, did not necessarily mean originality of subject matter—the first use of *plagiary* in the *Oxford English Dictionary*, by the satirist Joseph Hall, is dated around 1598—it is no wonder that Elizabethan and Jacobean playwrights in plundering all likely sources for plot materials frequently offered their audiences, which had indeed already taken "deep draughts of Boccaccio and Painter," [9] novella stories in dramatized form.

As source material for drama the novella seems to have been particularly well suited. Some Renaissance theorists, we recall, like Giason Denores and Francesco Bonciani, even attempted to view the novella as a tragedy or comedy in narrative form, often discovering in certain tales such Aristotelian elements as recognition, reversal, perturbation, and the unities of time and action. In addition, the traditional brevity of the Italianate novella offered the Elizabethan dramatist a myriad of dramatic possibilities: the comic or tragic potential of a novella plot could be more fully developed; the stock figures so beloved by the novellist could be metamorphosed into characters of great psychological depth and complexity; a promising phrase or line could be transformed into a dazzling and moving dramatic monologue or soliloquy.

Since the Elizabethan audiences apparently demanded—and received—diversity in their dramatic fare, it is again only to be expected that the playwright of the age regularly turned for plot ideas to the novella tradition with its long-standing ideal of variety. Shakespeare's *All's Well that Ends Well* and *Cymbeline* show how readily Boccaccio could be adapted to serve the English taste for comedy. For tragedy there was Giraldi Cinzio (e.g., *Othello*) and especially Bandello, who served as the direct or indirect source of, among others, *Romeo and Juliet*, Marston's *The Insatiate Countess*, and Webster's *The Duchess of Malfi*. Bandello's tales—often filled, as Wilhelm Creizenach notes, with acts of "perverse depravity and obscene bestiality" as well as "appalling deeds of violence and crime" [10]—adequately filled the apparent passion of the Elizabethan and Jacobean for viewing sensationalist stories set in foreign lands.

It was, no doubt, its very foreignness, or more exactly its "Italianness," that to a large extent made the novella so particularly attractive to both the dramatists and the audience of Elizabeth's time. Peculiarly fascinated by the supposed strangeness

and horror of Italian life, the English, as John L. Lievsay writes in
his informative study *The Elizabethan Image of Italy,* envisioned
Renaissance Italy as "the very acme of beauty and culture, of
license and corruption," its charmed name making "an appeal
such as might be exercised upon the imagination of the modern
American by a combination of say, Paris, Hong Kong, and Rio de
Janeiro." [11]

The novella tradition not only served as a purveyor of plots for
the English stage, but was an important formative influence in the
development of Elizabethan drama as well. Joseph Jacobs was
among the first to remark that the "flood of Italian *novelle*
introduced into England by Painter and his school" during the
"seed-time of the Elizabethan Drama"—the quarter of a century
between 1565 and 1590—was a considerable factor in moving
English drama away from the classical direction it might well have
taken, as the example of *Gorboduc* (first performed in 1561) clearly
indicates. For Jacobs it was the novella tradition which principally
provided Elizabethan dramatists with "a sufficient stock of plots to
allow for that interweaving of many actions into one which is the
characteristic of the Romantic drama of Marlowe and his
compeers." [12]

More recently, Madeleine Doran has suggested that the Italianate novella may well have been a determining influence in the
adoption by Elizabethan dramatists "almost without exception" of
the "sequential method" of dramatic presentation. According to
Doran, whereas classical drama, following an "artificial order,"
always begins *in medias res,* the result of which being what the critic
calls "crisis drama," the Elizabethan play, just like the typical
Renaissance novella, follows a "natural" or historical order of
events, commencing at the beginning and proceeding straight
through in chronological order until the very end, gaining in
variety and abundance of action what it perhaps may lose in
concentration and intensity.[13]

Clearly then in both a qualitative and a quantitative sense, the
drama of the English Renaissance would have been of an entirely
different cast had it not been for its confrontation with and
absorption of the Italianate novella. Indeed, one strains to imagine

what the Elizabethan dramatic tradition would have been like without *Romeo and Juliet, Othello, Twelfth Night,* or *The Duchess of Malfi.*

It may perhaps be fitting to conclude with some notable examples of novellistic sources and analogues of Elizabethan plays:

Dramas	Possible Novella Sources/ Analogues
Ralph Radcliffe, *De patientia Griseldis* (1547-49	Boccaccio, *Decameron* (X:10); Chaucer, "Clerk's Tale"
John Phillip, *Patient Grissell* (c. 1566)	See first entry above.
Robert Wilmot et al., *Gismonde of Salerne* (1568)	Boccaccio, *Decameron* (IV:1); Painter, *Palace of Pleasure* (I, 39)
Anonymous, *Appius and Virginia* (1575)	Chaucer, "Physician's Tale"; Painter, *Palace of Pleasure* (I, 5)
Robert Greene, *James IV* (c. 1591)	Giraldi, *Ecatommiti* (III:1)
Anonymous, *Warres of Cyrus* (1594)	Bandello, *Novelle* (III,9); Painter, *Palace of Pleasure* (I,11)
William Shakespeare, *Romeo and Juliet* (c. 1595)	Masuccio Salernitano, *Novellino* (33); Luigi Da Porto, "Romeo e Giulietta"; Bandello, *Novelle* (II,9); Boaistuau, *Histoires tragiques* (1559 ed., 3); Painter, *Palace of Pleasure* (II,25)

Shakespeare, *Merchant of Venice* (c. 1596)

Anonymous, *Gesta Romanorum* (109); Masuccio, *Novellino* (14); Ser Giovanni Fiorentino, *Pecorone* (IV:1)

Shakespeare, *Merry Wives of Windsor*, (c. 1599)

Ser Giovanni Fiorentino, *Pecorone* (I:2); Barnabe Rich, *Farewell to the Military Profession* ("Of Two Brethren and Their Wives")

Thomas Dekker, Henry Chettle, and William Naughton, *Patient Grissil* (1599)

See first entry above.

Shakespeare, *Twelfth Night* (c. 1600)

Bandello, *Novella* (II, 36); Belleforest, *Histoires tragiques* (IV,7); Barnabe Rich, *Farewell to the Military Profession* ("Apolonius and Silla")

Shakespeare, *Hamlet* (c. 1601)

Belleforest, *Histoires tragiques* (V, 3)

Shakespeare, *All's Well That Ends Well* (c. 1602)

Boccaccio, *Decameron* (III:9); Painter, *Palace of Pleasure* (I,38)

Shakespeare, *Measure for Measure* (c. 1604)

George Whetstone, *Heptameron of Civil Discourses* ("Promos and Cassandra")

Shakespeare, *Othello* (c. 1604)

Giraldi, *Ecatommiti* (III:7)

John Marston, *Sophonisba* (c. 1606)

Bandello, *Novelle* (I,41); Painter, *Palace of Pleasure* (II,7)

Shakespeare, *Cymbeline* (c. 1609)	Boccaccio, *Decameron* (II:9)
John Webster, *Duchess of Malfi* (c. 1613)	Bandello, *Novelle* (I,26); Belleforest, *Histoires tragiques* (II,19)
Marston, *Insatiate Countess* (1613?)	Bandello, *Novelle* (I,4); Belleforest, *Histoires tragiques* (II,20); Painter, *Palace of Pleasure* (II,24); Fenton, *Certain Tragical Discourses* (7)
John Fletcher and William Rowley, *Maid in the Mill* (1623)	Bandello, *Novelle* (II,15); Painter, *Palace of Pleasure* (II,22)
Fletcher and Nathan Field, *Four Plays in One* (c. 1625): "Triumph of Honour"	Boccaccio, *Decameron* (X:3); Painter, *Palace of Pleasure* (II,18)
"Triumph of Love"	Boccaccio, *Decameron* (V:7)
"Triumph of Death"	Bandello, *Novelle* (I,42); Boaistuau, *Histoires tragiques* (1559 ed., 5); Painter, *Palace of Pleasure* (I,42)
Ben Jonson, Fletcher, and Thomas Middleton, *The Widow* (c. 1625)	Boccaccio, *Decameron* (II:2); Painter, *Palace of Pleasure* (I,33)
Philip Massinger, *The Picture* (1629)	Bandello, *Novelle* (I,21); Painter, *Palace of Pleasure* (II,28)
James Shirley, *Love's Cruelty* (1631)	Bandello, *Novelle* (I,35); Marguerite de Navarre,

Heptaméron (36); Painter,
Palace of Pleasure (I,58)

Shirley, *The Traitor* (1631)	Marguerite de Navarre, *Heptaméron* (12)
Shirley, *The Gamester* (1633)	Marguerite de Navarre, *Heptaméron* (8)
Shirley, *Royal Master* (1637)	Boccaccio, *Decameron* (X:7)

Notes

1.See Herbert G. Wright, *The First English Translation of the "Decameron"* (Cambridge, Mass.: Harvard Univ. Press. 1953).

2. See J. J. Jusserand, *The English Novel in the Time of Shakespeare,* trans. Elizabeth Lee, ed. Philip Brockbank (1890; rpt. London: E. Benn, 1966); Lewis Einstein, *The Italian Renaissance in England* (New York: Columbia Univ. Press. 1902); Henry S. Canby, *The Short Story in English* (New York: Holt, 1909); Mary A. Scott, *Elizabethan Translations from the Italians* (Boston: Houghton Mifflin, 1916); René Pruvost, *Matteo Bandello and Elizabethan Fiction* (1937); C. S. Lewis, *English Literature in the Sixteenth Century Excluding Drama* (1954); Herbert G. Wright, *Boccaccio in England from Chaucer to Tennyson* (London: Athlone, 1957); Margaret Schlauch, *Antecedents of the English Novel* (London: Oxford Univ. Press. 1963); and *Elizabethan Love Stories,* ed. T. J. B. Spencer (Baltimore: Penguin, 1968).

3. Roger Ascham, *The Schoolmaster,* ed. Lawrence V. Ryan (Charlottesville: Univ. of Virginia Press, 1974), p. 67.

4. Stephen Gosson, *Plays Confuted in Five Actions* (New York: Johnson Reprints, 1972), fol. D5ᵛ.

5. *English Literature in the Sixteenth Century Excluding Drama,* p. 309.

6. See Felix E. Schelling, *Foreign Influences in Elizabethan Plays* (New York: Harper, 1923), p. 51; Sidney Lee, *Shakespeare and the Italian Renaissance* (London: Annual Shakespeare Lecture, 1915), p. 19; and Wilhelm Creizenach, *The English Drama in the Age of Shakespeare,* trans. Cécile Hugon (Philadelphia: Lippincott, 1916), p. 193.

7. See especially J. Ross Murray, *The Influence of Italian upon English Literature during the Sixteenth and Seventeenth Centuries* (1886; rpt. New York: AMS, 1971); H.R. D. Anders, *Shakespeare's Books* (1904; rpt. New York: AMS, 1965); Sidney Lee, *Shakespeare and the Italian Renaissance* (1915); Wilhelm Creizenach, *The English Drama in the Age of Shakespeare* (trans. 1916); Felix E. Schelling, *Foreign Influences in Elizabethan Plays* (1923); Kenneth Muir, *Shakespeare's Sources, Volume I: Comedies and Tragedies* (London: Methuen, 1957); A. L. Attwater, "Shakespeare's Sources," in *A Companion to Shakespeare Studies,* ed. H. Granville-Barker and G. B. Harrison (New

York: Doubleday, 1960); Joseph Satin, *Shakespeare and His Sources* (Boston: Houghton Mifflin, 1966); and Geoffrey Bullough, *Narrative and Dramatic Sources of Shakespeare*, 8 vols. (London: Routledge and Kegan Paul, 1957-75).

8. *A Companion to Shakespeare*, p. 220.

9. William W. Appleton, *Beaumont and Fletcher: A Critical Study* (London: Allen and Unwin, 1956), p. 42.

10. *The English Drama in the Age of Shakespeare*, p. 194.

11. John L. Lievsay, *The Elizabethan Image of Italy* (Ithaca, New York: Cornell Univ. Press, 1964), p. 1.

12. *Palace of Pleasure*, I, xxix-xxx.

13. Madeleine Doran, *Endeavors of Art: A Study of Form in Elizabethan Drama* (Madison: Univ. of Wisconsin Press,1954), pp. 259-65.

Index Nominum

Adams, Nicholson B. 59
Addison, Joseph 93
Aesop 81, 82
Alciati, Andrea 145
Alessio, Giovanni 28
Alfonso X ("El Sabio") 40, 96
Alfonso XI 96
Alphonsi, Petrus 40
Alter, Jean 125
Amezúa y Mayo, Agustín G.
de 58, 182, 228
Anders, H. R. D. 240
Andersen, Hans Christian 84,
118
Appius and Virginia 237
Appleton, William W. 241
Apuleius 37
Arabian Nights 51
Arberry, A. J. 59
Aretino, Pietro 29, 84, 137

Arienti, Sabadino 11, 18, 31,
33, 48, 82, 86, 91, 230
Ariosto, Ludovico 15, 143
Aristophanes 123
Aristotle 6, 7, 8, 10, 17, 20, 21,
48, 171, 209, 226, 235
Ascham, Roger 233, 240
Attwater, A. L. 234, 240, 241
Auerbach, Erich 16, 33, 60,
92, 125
Averroes 135
Avicenna 135, 138

Bacon, Francis 133
Bainton, Roland 126
Bakhtiyar-nama 38, 51
Bandello, Matteo 9, 18, 24,
25, 28, 30, 55, 58, 72, 76, 88,
89, 90, 91, 96, 97, 99, 108,

243

109, 110, 111, 112, 113, 116, 120, 124, 126, 131, 133, 139, 153, 156, 162, 164, 169, 174, 176, 177, 179, 184, 189, 190, 191, 194, 195, 205, 206, 208, 214, 217, 219, 220, 221, 222, 227, 230, 232, 233, 235, 237, 238, 239

Bardi, Giovanni de' 15, 32

Bargagli, Girolamo 15, 17, 32, 33

Bargagli, Scipione 46, 48, 52, 230

Barlaam and Josaphat 39, 54

Basile, Giambattista 6, 24, 25, 28, 36, 46, 51, 52, 83, 84, 93, 97, 102, 118, 125, 126, 129, 131, 141, 142, 144, 152, 153, 158, 164, 168, 182, 189, 217, 218, 230

Battisti, Carlo 28

Beaumarchais, Pierre Augustin Caron de 95

Bédier, Joseph 60

Belleforest, François 72, 76, 111, 117, 119, 120, 126, 145, 187, 214, 219, 220, 221, 222, 226, 227, 230, 232, 233, 238, 239

Bembo, Pietro 15, 32

Bennett, E. K. 1, 34

Benvenuti, Giacomo 28

Bermúdez, Alonso Chirino 48, 52

Blackmur, Richard 27

Blecua, José Manuel 30

Boaistuau, Pierre 72, 108, 111, 230, 232, 233, 237, 239

Boccaccio, Giovanni x, xi, 2, 4, 5, 6, 7, 8, 10, 11, 12, 13, 14, 15, 16, 17, 18, 20, 21, 22, 24, 25, 26, 28, 29, 31, 32, 33, 34, 36, 38, 40, 41, 42, 43, 46, 49, 51, 52, 53, 54, 55, 59, 60, 62, 63, 65, 67, 68, 71, 72, 73, 74, 75, 76, 77, 79, 80, 81, 82, 85, 86, 90, 91, 95, 96, 98, 99, 100, 101, 102, 104, 105, 107, 108, 114, 118, 121, 125, 126, 130, 131, 134, 135, 143, 144, 148, 149, 150, 153, 155, 156, 159, 160, 161, 162, 164, 165, 166, 167, 169, 170, 176, 178, 180, 181, 182, 183, 184, 185, 186, 188, 189, 190, 192, 193, 194, 195, 197, 198, 199, 200, 202, 204, 205, 206, 207, 208, 210, 212, 213, 214, 216, 217, 218, 227, 228, 229, 230, 232, 233, 235, 237, 238, 239, 240

Boethius 92

Boissard 84

Bonciani, Francesco 7, 10, 15, 20, 21, 22, 29, 30, 31, 32, 33, 34, 59, 235

Bonvesin da la Riva 13

Book of Five Headings see *Panchatantra*

Booth, Wayne C. 42, 60, 62, 63, 90

Bouchet, Jean 88

Bourdeille, Pierre de see Brantôme

Bourland, Caroline F. B. 60, 63, 90

Bowden, Muriel 96, 125

Bowers, Robert Hood   30
Brant, Sebastian   93, 156
Branca, Vittore   28, 41, 60, 76, 91, 205
Brantôme   172
Breugel, Gerrit Hendricx van   232
Brihat Katha   37
Brognoligo, Gioacchino   89
Bryan, William F.   32
Bryskett, Lodowick   10, 30, 31
Buchanan, George   145
Bullough, Geoffrey   241
Burton, Robert   227

Caballero Zifar   141
Caburacci, Francesco   15, 32
Calila y Dimna   39
Calvin, John   132
Camargo, Joracy   131
Canby, Henry S.   240
Cannan, Gilbert   209, 215
Caravajal y Saavedra, Mariana de   46, 48, 52, 69, 231
Cartellieri, Otto   193, 214
Casalduero, Joaquín   59
Castelvetro, Ludovico   13, 18, 33, 49, 60
Castiglione, Baldassare   7, 20, 22, 23, 29, 33, 34, 47, 84, 88
Castillo Solórzano, Alonso de   45, 46, 48, 50, 52, 63, 69, 113, 206, 229, 231
Cavalca, Domenico   67
Cellini, Benvenuto   124
Cent Nouvelles nouvelles   25, 29, 51, 54, 61, 67, 68, 70, 71, 73, 80, 81, 82, 85, 87, 89, 94, 101, 106, 120, 126, 129, 136, 137, 144, 151, 164, 166, 167, 170, 176, 178, 188, 191, 192, 193, 196, 201, 202, 208, 214, 217, 230
Cento novelle antiche or *Il Novellino*   4, 25, 28, 110, 129, 131, 133, 135, 139, 140, 143, 177, 179, 187, 189, 204, 216, 217, 229
Cerf, Bennett A.   27
Cervantes Saavedra, Miguel de   12, 14, 16, 19, 21, 24, 26, 31, 32, 33, 34, 49, 58, 59, 63, 64, 72, 81, 103, 112, 113, 114, 117, 123, 126, 129, 130, 139, 144, 145, 149, 152, 154, 155, 158, 160, 161, 162, 163, 164, 166, 170, 177, 181, 185, 186, 187, 188, 189, 197, 198, 201, 206, 214, 218, 222, 223, 224, 225, 226, 227, 228, 231
Chaitanya, Krishna   59
Champion, Pierre   57, 61
Chandler, Richard   59
Chapuys   110
Charles V   110, 121
Chaucer, Geoffrey   xi, 11, 16, 18, 22, 25, 31, 32, 33, 34, 45, 53, 56, 63, 64, 66, 68, 70, 71, 73, 79, 80, 81, 82, 83, 86, 87, 90, 91, 92, 93, 96, 98, 99, 100, 101, 106, 107, 110, 111, 115, 122, 124, 125, 126, 127, 128, 129, 130, 131, 135, 136, 138, 140, 141, 143, 144, 146, 147, 149, 153, 155, 156, 157, 158, 159, 161, 163, 164, 166, 167,

175, 176, 182, 185, 187, 190, 191, 193, 194, 198, 199, 202, 205, 207, 208, 209, 210, 211, 213, 214, 215, 217, 218, 230, 237, 238

Chettle, Henry 238

Cholakian, Patricia and Rouben 27, 63, 90, 171, 182

Cicero 4, 9, 13, 14, 17, 20, 23, 25, 29, 30, 31, 32, 33, 34, 218, 227

Clark, Priscilla 215

Clemens, Samuel L. *see* Twain, Mark

Clements, Robert J. 28, 60, 61, 126, 214

Clopinel, Jean *see* Jean de Meung

Coghill, Neville 122, 126

Colie, Rosalie L. 50, 61, 226, 228

Columella 4

Conrad, Joseph 3

Cordié, Carlo 29

Corippus Johannis 4

Cornhert, Dirck 232

Cotarelo y Mori, Emilio 29

Cottino-Jones, Marga 28

Coulton, G. G. 190, 214

Crane, Thomas F. 60, 229

Creizenach, Wilhelm, 234, 235, 240, 241

Croce, Benedetto 89, 125

Cromwell, Thomas 203

Curtius, Ernst Robert 29, 227

Dahlberg, Charles 91

Dante Alighieri 4, 87, 121, 132, 143, 144, 188, 204

Da Porto, Luigi 19, 76, 123, 206, 229, 237

Davis, Robert Gorham 27

Davis, William S. 164, 167, 182

De Bèze, Théodore 84

Dekker, Thomas 238

Della Casa, Giovanni 7, 8, 17, 20, 22, 23, 25, 29, 30, 31, 33, 34

Denores, Giason 6, 29, 235

De rege et septem sapientibus 39

Des Périers, Bonaventure 11, 31, 32, 58, 93, 99, 123, 126, 134, 137, 142, 144, 153, 157, 181, 191, 192, 230

Dickens, Charles 209

Di Francia, Letterio 59, 60, 89, 102, 125

Dioscorides 135

Directorium humanae vitae 39

Donatus 21

Dolopathos 39

Donovan, Mortimer J. 91

Doran, Madeleine 236, 241

Douglass, Robert L. 30

Dryden, John 49, 60, 209, 215

Du Bellay, Joachim 97

Dubuis, Roger 28

Du Faïl, Noël 131, 137, 157, 167, 168, 182, 230

Dunlop, John 59

Edward III 96

Einstein, Lewis 240

El Saffar, Ruth S. 72, 91, 225, 228

Elyot, Thomas 233

Erasmus, Desiderius 84, 93, 124, 156
Erizzo, Sebastiano 30, 45, 53, 71, 73, 102, 123, 169, 230
Erné, Nino 2
Eslava, Antonio de 45, 73, 231
Este, Ercole I d' 11
Este, Isabella d' 88
Eustachio, Bartolommeo 137
Evanthius 21, 33

Fabri, Pierre 13, 32
Fallopio, Gabriele 137
Federico II 143
Fenton, Geoffrey 9, 26, 30, 56, 57, 92, 101, 108, 116, 117, 119, 120, 124, 125, 126, 129, 131, 138, 144, 154, 157, 164, 168, 175, 176, 182, 186, 187, 199, 200, 208, 209, 214, 218, 219, 220, 221, 222, 226, 227, 231, 233, 239
Fernández de Avellaneda, Alonso 16
Ferrier, Janet M. 60, 228
Field, Nathan 239
Firenzuola, Agnolo 49, 190, 230
Fletcher, John 239
Flora, Francesco 30, 33, 227
Florio, John 13, 32
Flower, Dean S. 35
Forster, E. M. 62, 90
Fortini, Pietro 49, 69, 230
Fracastoro, Girolamo 88
France, Anatole 207
François I 84, 95, 96, 97, 185
French, Robert Dudley 53, 61

Froissart, Jean 96
Frye, Northrop 6, 29, 73, 91

Galen 6, 135, 137, 138
Galway, Margaret 91
Gambara, Veronica 88
Gellius, Aulus 83, 233
Génin, François 97, 125
Gesta Romanorum 65, 67, 68, 70, 72, 73, 75, 79, 80, 81, 83, 85, 94, 103, 114, 125, 128, 132, 135, 137, 143, 149, 150, 162, 180, 185, 187, 202, 229, 238
Gibaldi, Joseph 60
Gide, André 2
Gigli, G. 30
Gillespie, Gerald 28
Giménez Soler, Andrés 123, 184, 214
Giovanni Fiorentino, Ser 46, 69, 70, 74, 86, 87, 115, 133, 155, 230, 233, 238
Giraldi Cinzio, Giambattista 5, 6, 8, 20, 29, 30, 44, 45, 51, 53, 55, 60, 76, 94, 97, 102, 109, 113, 118, 124, 148, 155, 160, 164, 184, 230, 232, 233, 235, 237, 238
Goethe, Johann Wolfgang von 2, 3, 50, 228
Gogol, Nicolai 228
Gollancz, I. 30
Gorboduc 236
Gosson, Stephen 234, 240
Gotthelf, Jeremias 50
Gottlieb, Stephen A. 120, 126
Gower, John 155
Gracián Dantisco, Lucas 8, 29
Granville-Barker, H. 240

Gratian of Bologna 146

Grazzini, Anton Francesco 9, 16, 30, 32, 46, 47, 48, 52, 60, 159, 230

Greene, Robert 45, 52, 56, 69, 231, 237

Griffith, T. Gwynfor 91, 184, 214

Grimm brothers 84

Guardati, Tommaso see Masuccio Salernitano

Guazzo, Stefano 14, 25, 30, 32, 34

Guidotto da Bologna 17, 20, 23, 33, 34

Guilhom de Cabestaing 180

Guiron 179

Hall, Joseph 235

Halliday, F. E. 164

Hamalian, Leo 35

Harding, Alan 146, 151, 152, 156, 157, 163, 164

Harrison, G. B. 240

Harvey, W. J. 28

Harvey, William 137

Hassell, Jr., James W. 32

Hauvette, Henri 182

Hazar Afsana 38

Hemingway, Ernest 2

Henel, Heinrich 26, 34

Henri III 123

Henry VIII 84, 110, 117, 186, 199, 203

Herodotus 37, 233

Herón, A. 32

Herrick, Marvin T. 29, 33

Herzmaere 179

Heyse, Paul 1

Hidalgo, Gaspar Lucas 48, 52

Highet, Gilbert 59, 212, 215

Hippocrates 135, 138

Historia septem sapientium 39

Hoffmann, E. T. A. 2, 50, 228

Hoffmann, Richard L. 59

Holbein, Hans 162

Homer 26, 36, 52

Hook, Frank S. 126, 221, 227

Horace 8, 9, 22, 25, 48, 93, 162, 226

Hösle, Johannes 29

Hotson, J. Leslie 91

Howe, Irving 35

Hubbell, H. M. 32

Huguenot Psalter 185

Hundred Merry Tales see Rastell, John

Index Librorum Prohibitorum 183, 184, 213

Jacobs, Joseph 30, 33, 61, 91, 125, 126, 164, 214, 236, 241

James, Henry 2, 3, 27

Jatakas 39

Jean de Meung 93

Jenks, Edward 163

John of Austria 121

John of Gatesden 136

John of Gaunt 96

Jonson, Ben 142, 239

Jourda, Pierre 31, 33, 34, 60, 125, 126, 144, 164, 182, 214

Julius II 189

Jusserand, J. J. 240

Justinian 4, 145, 146

Juvenal 93

Kafka, Franz 224
Kalila wa-Dimnah 39
Kamen, Henry 214
Keller, Gottfried 2, 51
Kellogg, Robert 227, 228
Kennedy, Verne R. 227
Kern, Edith 60
Kittredge, George Lyman 56, 61, 107, 125
Klein, Johannes 1
Knight, George Howard 102
Kunz, Josef 27

La Fontaine, Jean de 9, 31, 230
Lalita Vistara 39, 54
Lazarillo de Tormes 19, 226
Lee, A. C. 32
Lee, Sidney 234, 240
Lehmann, Helmut T. 215
Le Maçon, Antoine 232
Leo X xi, 189
Leopardi, Giacomo 26
Lessing, Gotthold Ephraim 73
Lewalski, Barbara K. 61
Lewis, C. S. 29, 221, 227, 234, 240
Lewis, C. T. 28
Levant, Lorna 126, 214
Levtow, Harry 28, 30, 60, 90
Libro de los engannos et los assayamientos de las mugeres 39
Lievsay, John L. 236, 241
Li Gotti, Ettore 31
Linaura Ignaure 179
Lionel, Duke of Clarence 96
Livy 4, 155, 233
Longfellow, Henry Wadsworth 51

Lo Nigro, Sebastiano 28
Lopez, Robert S. 126
Lorian, Alexandre 28
Louis IX 207
Lozano, Cristóbal de 63
Lucian 226
Lugo y Dávila, Francisco de 8, 16, 17, 20, 29, 30, 32, 33, 50, 231
Lukács, Georg 92, 125
Lupi, S. 30
Luther, Martin xi, 186, 189, 198, 210, 211, 212, 213, 215

Machiavelli, Niccolò 19, 68, 88, 125, 133, 229
Mackensen, Lutz 26, 34
Manginelli, Guido 89
Manley, J. M. 91
Mann, Heinrich 177
Mann, Thomas 2, 26
Manuel, Don Juan 8, 25, 30, 40, 66, 67, 79, 82, 85, 90, 95, 96, 99, 112, 118, 122, 123, 132, 141, 143, 166, 174, 177, 184, 188, 190, 191, 192, 214, 216, 217, 229
Manzoni, Alessandro 195
Marguerite de Navarre 2, 5, 18, 20, 24, 29, 33, 34, 43, 44, 51, 53, 55, 58, 60, 63, 78, 80, 87, 88, 89, 92, 95, 96, 97, 99, 104, 108, 118, 119, 125, 126, 139, 144, 158, 169, 171, 172, 173, 176, 178, 179, 181, 182, 185, 189, 191, 194, 198, 200, 201, 203, 204, 207, 210, 214, 217, 218, 230, 232, 233, 239, 240

Marlowe, Christopher 236
Marot, Clément 185
Marsilius of Padua 213
Marston, John 235, 238, 239
Marti, Mario 32, 33
Marie de France 81
Martines, Lauro 147, 163
Martínez del Portal, María 61, 182
Martini, Fritz 26, 34
Massinger, Philip 239
Masuccio Salernitano 18, 33, 55, 58, 86, 190, 194, 206, 230, 237, 238
Matzke, John E. 182
Mazzali, Ettore 32
Medici, Cosimo de' 46
Melville, Herman 3
Menéndez y Pelayo, Marcelino 59, 166, 182
Meyer, Conrad Ferdinand 51
Michelangelo Buonarroti 187, 193
Michele, Agostino 32
Michele Scotus 143
Middleton, Thomas 239
Minturno, Antonio Sebastiano 6
Mirollo, James V. 34, 228
Mirrour of Mirth 137, 192
Mishle Sendebar 39
Molière 137
Molza, Francesco Maria 88
Montaigne, Michel Eyquem de 145
Montalbán, Juan Pérez de 50, 52, 57, 63, 231
Monteverdi, Claudio 28
Morcuende, Federico Ruiz 31

More, Thomas 134, 186
Moreno Báez, Enrique 66
Mori, Ascanio de' 47, 48, 230
Morris, William 51
Muir, Kenneth 240
Murray, J. Ross 240
Murstein, Bernard I. 125

Naughton, William 238
Nelson, Benjamin 144
Nelson, William 33, 42, 60
Newstead, Helaine 60
Nibelungenlied 178
Nicolini, F. 30
Nietzsche, Friedrich 94
Northup, George Tyler 59
Nostradamus 141

Olsen, Glending 31
Orellana y Rincòn 58
Ovid 4, 37, 59, 69, 82

Pabst, Walter 2, 13, 32, 58, 60, 61
Pafford, J. H. P. 30
Painter, William 9, 19, 28, 30, 33, 58, 61, 69, 71, 74, 75, 76, 82, 83, 91, 92, 96, 101, 102, 108, 111, 116, 125, 126, 134, 145, 153, 155, 164, 175, 179, 180, 186, 188, 189, 201, 205, 206, 207, 208, 214, 231, 233, 234, 235, 236, 237, 238, 239, 240
Panchatantra 37, 38, 39, 54
Parabosco, Girolamo 8, 30, 45, 47, 53, 171, 230
Paré, Amboise 137

Parker, A. A. 226, 228
Parks, George B. 126
Paris, Gaston 59
Patrizi, Francesco 6
Paulson, Ronald 34
Peacham, Henry 84, 150, 151
Peele, George 72
Pelikan, Jaroslav 215
Pellicer, Juan Antonio 58
Perrault, Charles 84
Petrarch 74, 84, 107, 121, 135, 165
Petronius 37, 59, 179
Petrocchi, Giorgio 33
Pettie, George 9, 30, 32, 34, 37, 69, 71, 91, 97, 125, •152, 168, 169, 231, 233
Pfandl, Ludwig 59
Phaedrus 81
Phillip, John 237
Place, Edwin 173, 182
Plato 37, 59, 92, 209
Plautus 4
Pliny 4, 148
Plutarch 233
Poggio Bracciolini 167
Polheim, Karl Konrad 1, 2, 26, 27, 34
Pontano, Giovanni 10, 14, 17, 25, 30, 31, 32, 34
Pope, Alexander 134
Premierfait, Laurent 232
Pruvost, René 221, 222, 227, 240
Putnam, Samuel 97, 125

Quevedo y Villegas, Francisco Gómez de 93

Quintilian 17, 20, 23, 25, 29, 30, 33, 34, 218, 227
Quinze Joyes du Mariage 173

Rabelais, François 93, 134, 137, 152, 156, 157, 165, 188, 206, 227
Rackham, H. 29
Radcliffe, Ralph 237
Rastell, John 9, 51, 58, 69, 102, 121, 131, 134, 136, 138, 141, 152, 153, 157, 159, 164, 167, 179, 186, 187, 192, 193, 194, 201, 203, 206, 214, 230
Régnier, Henri 31
Remak, Henry H. H. 92, 125
Roman de Renard 81
Ronsard, Pierre de 97
Reyes, Matías de los 45, 231
Ricci, Pier Giorgio 29
Rice, John ap 199, 214
Rich, Barnabe 7, 233, 238
Richard II 122
Rickert, Edith 144
Rico, Francesco 31
Riley, E. C. 6, 12, 29, 32, 59, 61
Risicato, A. 30
Robbins, Rossell Hope 193, 214
Robinson, F. N. 31
Rodax, Yvonne xi, 27, 60
Rodríguez Marín, Francisco 58
Rogers, Katharine M. 91
Romains, Jules 136
Romei, Annibale 69
Rowley, William 239

Rua, Giuseppe 30
Ryan, Lawrence V. 240

St. Augustine 165, 192
St. John Damascene 39
Sacchetti, Franco 11, 15, 24, 25, 31, 32, 34, 73, 86, 98, 99, 113, 115, 116, 129, 133, 136, 138, 141, 163, 188, 192, 194, 197, 199, 200, 201, 202, 205, 206, 214, 230
Said Armesto, Victor 144
Salinari, Giambattista 30, 61, 164
Salviati, Lionardo 6, 7, 13, 29
Sánchez Reyes, Enrique 59
Sancho IV 96
Satin, Joseph 241
Scaligero, Giulio Cesare (Scaliger), 88
Schelling, Felix E. 234, 240
Schiller, Johann Christoph Friedrich von 112
Schlauch, Margaret 240
Schoeck, Richard 61
Scholes, Robert 227, 228
Schwartz, Kessel 59
Scott, Mary A. 240
Segni, Bernardo 6, 29
Segre, Cesare 33
Seneca 56
Sercambi, Giovanni 43, 53, 69, 70, 71, 86, 230
Seventy Tales of a Parrot 37
Sforza, Ippolita 88
Shakespeare, William 76, 77, 96, 109, 113, 115, 118, 133, 166, 206, 224, 234, 235, 237, 238, 239

Shaw, George Bernard 209
Sherman, Gilbert 157
Shirley, James 239, 240
Short, Charles 28
Sidney, Mary 102
Sindibad-nama 38
Sindban 39
Sir Gawain and the Green Knight 26
Sklare, Arnold 28
Smith, Preserved 183, 214
Smythe, Robert 233
Solomon 147, 149
Sophocles 93
Sorel, Charles 228
Speirs, John 91
Spencer, T. J. B. 240
Speroni, Sperone 13
Spingarn, Joel E. 41, 60
Springer, M. D. x, 26, 34
Spurgeon, Caroline F. B. 213, 215
Steinhauer, Harry 2, 27, 28,
Stevick, Philip 28
Steward, Desmond 125
Storm, Theodor 51
Straparola, Gian Francesco 9, 18, 24, 30, 33, 47, 48, 82, 83, 121, 129, 134, 137, 143, 144, 152, 160, 162, 164, 180, 181, 187, 188, 189, 192, 194, 196, 230, 232, 233
Straw, John 122
Striggio, Alessandro 28
Style, William 8, 29
Swedenberg, H. T. 215
Suka Saptati 37
Sullivan, Edward 30
Sutton, E. W. 29

Sylvania, Lena   173, 182, 214
Symonds, John Addington   60
Syntipas   39

Tales and Quick Answers   167
Tasso, Torquato   6, 13, 32
Taylor, Jerome   61
Téllez, Gabriel   *see*   Tirso de Molina
Terence   21, 31
Thousand and One Nights   38, 51
Thomas of Brittany   180
Tibullus   4
Tieck, Ludwig   1, 228
Timoneda, Juan de   11, 31, 231
Tirso de Molina   8, 30, 45, 48, 52, 69, 103, 116, 121, 138, 144, 156, 171, 175, 176, 178, 182, 184, 186, 206, 207, 229, 231
Toffanin, Giuseppe   89
Tolstoy, Leo   2
Turberville, George   233
Twain, Mark   198
Twenty-Five Tales of the Vampire   37

Ulster, Countess of   96
Utley, Francis   91

Valbuena Prat, Angel   31
Valency, Maurice   28, 30, 41, 60, 62, 90
Valerius Maximus   123
Varese, Claudio   31, 91
Varro   4
Vasari, Giorgio   89

Vega Carpio, Félix Lope de   9, 31, 49, 61, 231
Vergil   4, 36, 52, 68
Vesalius, Andreas   137
Vetala Panchavimsati   37
Villani, Giovanni   86
Volpe, Edmond   35
Voragine, Iacopo da   67, 68
Vossler, Karl   171, 182

Waidson, H. M.   34
Walzel, Oskar   1
Warren, Austin   62, 90, 125, 215
Warres of Cyprus   237
Watson, George   60
Watt, Ian   92, 125
Webster, John   235, 237, 239
Weinberg, Bernard   29, 32, 33, 60
Wellek, René   62, 90, 92, 125, 209, 215
Whetstone, George   48, 52, 77, 231, 233, 238
Wieland, Christoph Martin   50
Wiese, Benno von   2
William of Ockham   213
William the Conqueror   146
Wilmot, Robert,   180, 237
Wilson, Thomas   9, 17, 23, 30, 34
Wilson, Robert N.   125
Winterbottom, M.   30
Wood-Leigh, K. L.   91
Worcester, David   215
Wright, Herbert G.   240
Wyatt, Thomas   97

Wycliffe, John 213
Wykes, Henry 167

Yutang, Lin 37, 59
Yver, Jacques 12, 18, 31, 33, 45, 52, 230

Zall, P. M. 164, 214
Zayas y Sotomayor, María de 6, 46, 48, 52, 57, 61, 63, 78, 94, 113, 118, 120, 153, 164, 173, 181, 182, 186, 187, 214, 231
Zimmerman, Samuel A. 214